"Edwards has written a book that is at once playful and serious, idiosyncratic and traditional, provocative and edifying. I wish more theologians wrote such crisp and unguarded prose."

—**Adam Neder**, Whitworth University

"Edwards has a knack for translating sophisticated theology into ordinary language while elevating everyday popular music to mature theological heights. Edwards . . . reminds his reader—neophyte or specialist—that good theology delights even as it demands everything from us. This contribution will be a powerful aid to those just beginning their pilgrimage and to teachers who hope to chart that rugged terrain to others."

—**Lindsey Hankins**, George Fox University

"Edwards's book embodies the very claims made by Barth—that God's revelation is free and breaks into our world in surprising ways—and we would do well to listen. For those wondering, 'Who is Jesus?' 'What is revelation?' 'Was the world created or has it always existed?' Edwards provides a rocking theological journey to the tune of funk, grunge, and alt-pop."

—**Katherine M. Douglass**, Seattle Pacific University

"Edwards's lyrical storytelling, passion for the wilderness, and penchant for discerning parables of the kingdom among a panoply of rock-and-roll legends combine for a fresh, chili-pepper-infused un-taming of modern theology. This is a theology in service of the community accompanied by musical reconsiderations of divine and human natures, trinity and election, church as event, the sacramentality of food, and the meaning of time. Rock on!"

—**Matthew Puffer**, Valparaiso University

"The academic captivity of theology is a scandal that deprives the uninitiated of the best that has been said about God. By setting the most demanding (and true!) theology to the soundtrack of a generation, Mark Edwards has smashed the academy's decorative pumpkins and made from them a delectable and nourishing meal."

—**Matthew J. Milliner**, Wheaton College

"In my time in Dr. Edwards's class, I saw him cultivate ideas and allow students' minds to evolve and flourish. In his new book, Dr. Edwards explores the convoluted topic of time, using Karl Barth as a tool to unravel its complexities."

—**Michael Crockett**, The College of New Jersey, Class of '24

"This is something that, even knowing that it's written by someone I admire and appreciate, I would immaturely roll my eyes at before making a sarcastic comment concerning religion and politics in this country. That said, Dr. Edwards had me on board from the start with the Beastie Boys. . . . In the interest of meeting my grievance/criticism quota, here's what I have for Dr. Edwards: No David Bowie?"

—**Jina Park**, The College of New Jersey, Class of '20

"Well, it looks like our early debates over predestination turned into something productive. You've got me reading Barth these days too. As for listening to Red Hot Chili Peppers . . . Mom and I will take your word for it."

—**James R. Edwards**, Whitworth University, emeritus (and Mark's dad)

"Mark has managed to get one classically trained church musician to open his ears to The Smashing Pumpkins and Nirvana and open his heart to the impassioned theology of Barth. Being a part of his church small group on Barth has been transformative, and I hear echoes of Mark's voice throughout his excellent book. This short guidebook to the mountain ranges of Church Dogmatics could inspire anyone to begin the climb with fearlessness and joy."

—**Noel Werner**, Director of Music, Nassau Presbyterian Church

"This is the writing of a scholar who is equally at home teaching in a graduate-level classroom, a youth group, or a prison. His genius is not only in making Karl Barth more accessible but more fascinating. Throughout the book, Mark Edwards directs the reader's attention to the ways Barth's theology has pressing relevance for the contemporary yearnings of those 'who wonder about, and wander after, the truth.'"

—**M. Craig Barnes**, Princeton Theological Seminary

Christ Is Time

Christ Is Time

*The Gospel according to Karl Barth
(and the Red Hot Chili Peppers)*

Mark James Edwards

CASCADE *Books* · Eugene, Oregon

CHRIST IS TIME
The Gospel According to Karl Barth (and the Red Hot Chili Peppers)

Cascade Books
An Imprint of Wipf and Stock Publishers
199 W. 8th Ave., Suite 3
Eugene, OR 97401

www.wipfandstock.com

PAPERBACK ISBN: 978-1-5326-9124-9
HARDCOVER ISBN: 978-1-5326-9125-6
EBOOK ISBN: 978-1-5326-9126-3

Cataloguing-in-Publication data:

Names: Edwards, Mark James, author.

Title: Christ is time : the gospel according to Karl Barth (and the Red Hot Chili Peppers) / by Mark James Edwards.

Description: Eugene, OR : Cascade Books, 2022 | Includes bibliographical references and index.

Identifiers: ISBN 978-1-5326-9124-9 (paperback) | ISBN 978-1-5326-9125-6 (hardcover) | ISBN 978-1-5326-9126-3 (ebook)

Subjects: LCSH: Barth, Karl,—1886–1968. | Religion and culture. | Christianity and culture.

Classification: BR118.C8 E33 2022 (print) | BR118.C8 E33 (ebook)

02/08/22

To

Ed Kowalczyk, Chad Taylor, Chad Gracey, and Patrick Dalheimer,
who made up the band Līve
and whose 1991 *album,*
Mental Jewelry,
more than any others
made me think.

"And from the lungs of a child
will come the everlasting breath of God"
Līve, "Brothers Unaware"

Contents

Playlist

Acknowledgments

With gratitude for the many people who have informed my interest in Barth, I must acknowledge this work is most deeply indebted to Dan Migliore, whose guidance in faith seeking understanding first led me to read Barth in long-distance fashion; George Hunsinger, whose lectures, soliloquies, and texts helped me learn how to read Karl Barth; and Bruce McCormack, whose many years of Socratic patience eventually formed me into a critically realistic dialectical theologian. As is noted in the Introduction, Bruce played the definitive role in this volume since it mainly derives from our semester teaching together. Thank you.

I also will acknowledge this volume could and should be better. One problem with it is that Barth's work is simply too large to offer commentary upon, in the traditional sense of the term. Normally, a commentary takes a smaller work and enlarges upon it by giving background, contextualization, and further explanation. Barth's Himalayan work makes the task of "saying more" wholly impractical. Conversely, as an attempt at intellectual cartography, this work seeks to say less by mapping great stretches of text into a more portable format. By nature of the task then, there are many worthy ascents left out of this brief guidebook.

Much is owed to the Princeton Seminary students of Systematic Theology (Spring '13) who sat through these original lectures. Your encouragement throughout that semester has stayed with me, especially those who suggested I write a theology of rock 'n roll. This is not exactly that.

Further gratitude is owed to the many students I have been challenged by at Princeton Seminary, The College of New Jersey, Princeton University, and especially the theology students of Young Life's Winter Training (Jan '18), in Sandestin, Florida—all 174 of you! Forgive me for not listing each of you by name, but know your feedback, encouragement to put this in print, and devotion to truth, ministry, and even engineering has motivated me.

Darby, your "Thanks for introducing me to this madness . . . I hope I can read your books one day" note is still on my desk.

To the staff, youth, and families of Nassau Presbyterian Church, with a special shout-out to members of my "Adventures with Barth" reading group, thank you for encouraging this addiction and for gifting time and resources to enable us to live, think, and grow together in response to the challenge of the gospel.

To Noel Werner, Adam Neder, Tyler McQuilken, Matt Puffer, John Parker, and Katie Douglass: thank you for your comments and corrections on early drafts. Any remaining mistakes and errors are mine alone.

To the bands I have included. Thank you for making music.

Thank you, Charlie Collier, Blake Adams, Calvin Jaffarian and the entire Wipf and Stock team for accepting, revising, and publishing this odd text. It is an honor to have this work stamped with the Cascade logo, and not only because I have loved and suffered beyond description in those mountains. You are doing good work, and I am delighted to be counted among your crew.

More pertinent to individual chapters, credit is owed to the following:

"Creation": I am appreciative for comments from Paul Rorem on my section treating Meister Eckhart. Paul's intellectual rigor and respect for students' questions was a major reason for my not leaving Princeton during my first year in seminary.

"Justification": thanks to Bruce McCormack for his assistance in the preparation of this material. I have especially benefited from his unpublished lecture, "Justified by Grace" (Princeton Theological Seminary, Spring '10), and his personal correspondence of March 14, 2013, which is passed along in revised form in the section detailing the differences between Calvin and Barth.

"Christology + Humanity": my summarization of Barth's anthropology is greatly indebted to the January I spent with seminarians reading CD III/2 and working with Habitat for Humanity. Thank you, Annalise Hume and Brandon Watson, for your rigorous questioning regarding what a "being with God" is. The Afterword on Nietzsche had its genesis under Alexander Nehamas at Princeton University, Spring '06. Dr. Nehamas, Sigurd Bark, and Kevin Wolf are to be thanked for their comments and feedback.

"Prayer + Ethics": thanks is owed to Nancy Duff for her generous invitation to assist with a course on Bonhoeffer (Spring '16). I remain grateful for the opportunity to soak up Dietrich's life and thought from a learned guide.

"Sacrament": it is relevant to point out Rachel Khoo's cookbook was a gift from a Parisian housemate, whose presence quickly went from stranger to member of our family, largely because of meals prepared and shared. Thank you, Melody.

"Trinity and Election": this chapter is modified from a paper I originally presented in a Princeton Theological Seminary seminar on February 14, 2012. The seminar was on Barth's election and ethics of *Church Dogmatics* II/2 and was led by Bruce McCormack and John Bowlin. The paper was poorly received. I had to defend it with all my ability against my colleagues' objections that the debate had been resolved (obviously, the other side had lost) and that my wish for a solution, rather than a one-sided victory, was misplaced. Typical of my personality, I am grateful for the rigorous negative feedback, which further convinced me I was on the right track. Perhaps I have read too much Nietzsche's *Ecce Homo*: "I attack only causes against which I cannot expect to find allies, against which I shall stand alone."[1] That it has taken nearly a decade to release this to the public is because I hoped the problem would resolve itself. I was delayed as well by an obsession that led me to jail: I became consumed by reading and teaching great works of philosophy and theology written by "imprisoned minds." If this proposal on Trinity and election fails, I still hold out hope for a lasting reconciliation.

Finally, to my family, Janine, Adeline, and Elias: Now that it is in print, perhaps I will stop talking about my friend Karl? I hope not. But don't worry, others may be listening.

---

1. Nietzsche, *Portable*, 659.

Abbreviations

CD	Karl Barth, *The Church Dogmatics*
DBWE	Dietrich Bonhoeffer, *Dietrich Bonhoeffer Works English*
KD	Karl Barth, *Die kirchliche Dogmatik*
ST	Thomas Aquinas, *Summa Theologiae*

Introduction

The following comprises (mostly) a dozen lectures I gave as part of the course Systematic Theology at Princeton Theological Seminary in the spring of 2013. During my final year of my doctoral program in philosophy and theology, Bruce McCormack asked me if I would be willing to co-teach the required Systematic Theology course with him. I said yes. I was especially honored because I had for eight plus years felt out of place in Princeton. And while the systematics course had typically been team-taught, I had never heard of a doctoral student being offered the chance to be a lead teacher, rather than a preceptor (a small-group discussion leader). I was terrified.

Because the material for this course resides at the heart of the seminary's curriculum in biblical studies, history, and ministry preparation, and because the Department of Theology, not to mention the broader faculty, was at the time notoriously fractured in terms of outlooks, goals, and styles, the course had always been a bit of a battleground. Sadly, it had repeatedly been the case that rival professors were co-teaching the course together using their lecture on Wednesday, as might be the case, to argue against the lecture given by their colleague on Monday. Students were frequently confused about what was going on, since disagreements on starting points, fair assumptions, and unassigned material overshadowed coherent introductions to texts, authors, and traditions that had long been influential. Indeed, more than one professor in the rotation used the course to dismiss, accuse, and sideline the Protestant tradition and its older ancestors without giving students much of an opportunity to learn what it was that was being dumped in the trash bin. While I will not deny the importance of teaching from a standpoint of conviction, I also became deeply frustrated that much of our education was focused on inculturation that verged on indoctrination. Conclusions were assumed from unquestioned assumptions. Starting points and goals were enforced while not being open to analysis or defense. On top of being frustrating and alienating, this also had the tendency to leave students bored, since often their priorities, values, and hopes were left unattended. Many students had quit jobs, rented Penske trucks, uprooted families, and hauled themselves across the country to gain resources for work in churches, campus ministries, and theological education. Disgruntled by the education they were receiving (or weren't receiving), many abandoned plans for ministry and even their faith, a move often applauded by some faculty members who saw it as their duty to educate students out of the Christian faith.

I had come to seminary because I had had experiences with the divine, met people influential on my life, and was hooked on the big questions. I was also ready for a change and I wanted deep immersion in the great texts, materials, and traditions. I had been doing media relations and book publicity for a think tank in Seattle that was the institutional home for the theory of intelligent design. I had been around many academics working in matters of history and philosophy of science, the hard sciences, theology, and biblical studies. I wanted more. I knew many who had been through Princeton Seminary and it seemed the place to study deeply and widely. Friends, fellow students from the theology departments I was a part of at Jamestown College and Whitworth College (now both a "University"), family members, and indeed ex-girlfriends had all gone to Princeton Seminary. Admittedly, during my time after college, Princeton had been the last place I wanted to go and, perhaps a bit like Jonah, I had fled to Seattle to climb in the Cascade mountains and be vomited up by alpine storms. Visiting my sister, while her husband was a student at the seminary, I sensed that "Princeton was a disease I was going to catch." After getting married in Seattle (2001), my wife and I spent a year backpacking around Europe and SE Asia (Thailand, Laos, Cambodia, Vietnam, China, Tibet, and Nepal). We then packed up our Ford Econoline 350 (extended version, baby blue with large wheelchair symbols on the side as it had been an Oak Harbor, WA, city vehicle) and rolled to Princeton where everyone seemed to be clean shaven in khaki pants and blue blazers. I was in sandals, construction-grade work-pants, and after a year of travel had the longest beard of my life. Most of my other clothes bore granite abrasion holes as victims of my climbing addiction. After feeling like an outsider for three years of the MDiv program and five more years in the doctoral program, I was now given the chance to teach systematic theology with the professor I respected the most. Having virtually no institutional status (what were they going to do, not pay me? They were already doing that!), I wanted to do things differently and tried to risk it all on Jesus. I plugged in my iPhone. Still somewhat novel at the time, it was laced with favorite tunes from my earlier years. And it turns out the amphitheater style classroom on the second floor of Stuart Hall at Princeton Seminary had a pretty good sound system.

With regards to his offer to co-teach the systematics course, Professor McCormack generously offered to split the twenty-four lectures with me. Teaching with him, though intimidating at times, was a total delight. With the class meeting twice a week, we would normally each give a lecture every week. This saw some disruption when Bruce had to have foot surgery reminiscent of Stephen King's *Misery* and the lecture on justification is a result of that. I remain grateful for his assistance on that material. As for the class texts, we made Calvin's *Institutes of the Christian Religion* and James Cone's *A Black Theology of Liberation* required reading and augmented these with additional selections. As I was wrapping up a dissertation on Barth's treatment of time and eternity, I tended to lecture on how Karl Barth's theology builds on the tradition and/or seeks to answer questions left unresolved. Thus, while students were primarily reading Calvin and Cone, and Bruce was giving deeper doctrinal background and historical work, I was attempting to introduce them to the constructive theology of Barth. And it must be said that many students had a bad impression of Karl, largely through the (shallow, in my opinion) reasoning of, "I don't like Karl Barth because everyone talks about him here, he had an affair, his fans are obsessive, and even though he's right about election, he's wrong on natural theology."

My own introduction to Barth had happened just a few years earlier, really in my final half of the MDiv program, through a course with Dan Migliore on Barth and Charles Hodge as church theologians; through "majoring" in Bruce McCormack and taking as many courses from him as I could (notably a course with Bruce and Beverly Gaventa on Paul and Karl, which focused on Barth's commentary on *Der Römbrief*); through an impromptu reading group with George Hunsinger (focusing on five pages a week in the *Church Dogmatics*, George would "reply all" weekly to seminary-wide emails reminding *everyone* campus-wide of the meeting; a practice no longer allowed at PTS); and through the many doctoral students ahead of me who were studying Barth. As I went through my graduate education, taking history, biblical studies, and theology courses at the seminary, philosophy courses at Princeton University, and serving as a teaching assistant in the Princeton University Religion, Philosophy, and Sociology departments, I came to conclude that Barth was where the real action, and answers, resided. Though initially skeptical, especially because of what I also perceived as a misguided stubborn grumpiness concerning natural theology, I became something of a convert. Or maybe an über-fan-boy-Barth-zealot-head. After-all, I drive a

Fiat 500 *Abarth,* named my son Karl, my daughter Barthiane, nicknamed my wife Charlotte, and named our dog Nelly.[2]

I do not say terribly much in the following about who Barth is and what his life was like. This is well-traversed terrain and I recommend John Franke's *Barth for Armchair Theologians* for a basic biography. For those who want more, Bruce McCormack's epically named *Karl Barth's Critically Realistic Dialectical Theology* is a must-read whodunnit detailing how Karl became Barth. Likewise, George Hunsinger's *How to Read Karl Barth* (not word by word, it turns out!) is useful for clarifying the epistemological scrubbing that only Barth offers. Beyond this, while there are shelves and shelves of secondary literature on Barth's theology, and while much seeks to be helpful, I generally recommend them for fire-starter and suggest you simply read the *Church Dogmatics* (twenty to thirty pages at a time), think for yourself, and enjoy the warm blaze you will have built. Much of the secondary literature is limited in scope, technical in style, and often hesitant with regards to Barth's project. Moreover, I remain convinced that those who have encountered the *Church Dogmatics* and who continue to debate academically the merits of the *opus* do not, despite whatever credentials they may bear, understand the *Church Dogmatics.* On the contrary, those who do understand Barth and his voluminous work go out to set the captives free, giving praise for the wondrous things Jesus Christ hath done. Punk-funk-slap-metal, after all, is not intended to put you to sleep on the couch. In fact, as I hope to argue in my next work, the pulpit and the prison, more than the classroom or journal, are principally the proper locations for those who claim to think like Karl. A statement, no doubt, with which many academic skeptics or philistine critics would agree! Yes, this is hyperbole.

The following chapters are thus left largely in the style and feel of live lectures. I was often pulling material (frequently at 4 am the day of) from previously written papers, portions of my dissertation, or even youth group talks. That spontaneity and thrill-of-the-clock, I think, came through in the lectures, and I hope it is still present as I pass them along in finalized and formalized written form. Or maybe these are just tedious texts, technical in style, limited in scope, and with too many misunderstandings of

---

2. In the spirit of Kurt Vonnegut's *Book of Bokonon* maxim that "All the true things I'm about to tell you are shameless lies," these final admissions are wholly untrue, being blatant falsehoods designed to elicit a chuckle from those who know too much about Karl's biographical drama. See Vonnegut, *Cat's Cradle,* 5. For more on Karl's domestic situation, see Selinger, *Charlotte von Kirschbaum and Karl Barth,* 1–20. Like Selinger, I believe the complex, tragic, and yet also beautiful situation needs thick description rather than thin speculative judgment. It is also entirely rude and unfair to make light of their difficulties, as I have done.

Barth's project to make them of long-term value.[3] And while I too present these lectures from a vantage point of conviction, I hope you will feel free to interrupt me and raise your hand with a question. I have edited them for typos, cleaned them up in style, and in a few cases reconstructed them from notes, outlines, and memory. Chapters ten and twelve, which interact more with Bonhoeffer, include material from a series I led at Nassau Presbyterian Church in Princeton, where I now work.

As you will discover, I have included my playlist notes in the lectures. The dark grey in the song visualizations is intended to show what aspect of the song I hope you will splice in. This is based on how I myself used (or would use again) the songs in my lectures. Thus,

Red Hot Chili Peppers: *Higher Ground*

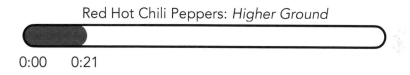

0:00   0:21

means you should play the first twenty one seconds of the song *Higher Ground,* while

Red Hot Chili Peppers: *Give it Away*

0:00   4:43

intends for you to play (and perhaps even enjoy) the whole song, *Give it Away.* While the instrumental sections are intended largely as sound effects to wake you up, in most cases the sections with lyrics are intended to illuminate some eternal truth. Listen closely. Or look up the lyrics on the net.

It has been ten years now since I have written some of this material. Following the completion of my "disastertation" (another story for a later time), and unable to secure a permanent teaching post, I fell into a rapid cycle of adjunct teaching, often six or seven courses a year, with The College of New Jersey, Princeton Seminary, Fuller Seminary, Young Life, and

---

3. In which case, per my earlier suggestion, enjoy the heat of *Fahrenheit* 451. This is assuming, of course, the political and cultural dystopias of Guy Montag, Adolf Hitler, or High Chancellor Adam Sutler are not being actualized by doing so.

Princeton University, all while trying to be married, raise two kids, undertake a major renovation (resurrection) of our first home, a foreclosed 1870s macro-project with vines growing inside, all while serving as the director for the youth ministry at Nassau Presbyterian Church. Extended thanks are owed to the many who have been patient with me. Apologies are owed to the many with whom I have been impatient. For those who are curious, the house stands completed (a standing seam metal roof this past summer was the last major undertaking), the marriage has lasted (twenty-plus years), the kids seem healthy enough, and the ministry has, I am sure, enriched my own life and faith more than anybody else's.

As Bonhoeffer wrote, "Ten years is a long time in the life of every human being."[4]

What a long, strange trip it has been.

Perhaps Jerry Garcia knew more about following Christ than he let on when he sang those words.

ME
Nassau Presbyterian Church
Princeton, NJ
July 2021

---

4. Bonhoeffer, *Reader*, 762.

— 1 —

Trinity: Give It Away

When I was young and immature, I listened to the psychedelic funk-punk band Red Hot Chili Peppers. At the time, the Chili Peppers were just breaking out of their original underground LA fan base and, largely through the help of MTV, were being broadcast to the far reaches of the universe. This is how I, growing up in the great plains of North Dakota and desperate for something more than country music or the skinny pop of Mariah Carey, came to think of myself as a pure die-hard Pepper head. I had never been to a punk show, and to this day still have not seen the Chili Peppers in concert. Still, at the time, no one's heart beat faster when the Chili Peppers played, and I repeatedly used them to amp me up for cross-country races. The possible exception was my mom. One day while cleaning up, she came across the album, read some of their many graphic and offensive lyrics, and furiously snapped my *Blood Sugar Sex Magik* compact disc in two. That disc was promptly replaced by a gift from a soon-to-be girlfriend, who not only gave me a copy of her album but also a hand-embroidered pillow case that matched the rose and tattoo tongues of the album's cover art. In a statement of adolescent defiance, I put the pillow center on my bed and hung the broken compact disc from my ceiling light as a shrine to the oppression the grunge generation must endure.

The hit song that kicked all this saga off was the rowdy, aggressive, and fairly absurd *Give it Away*:

Red Hot Chili Peppers: *Give it Away*

1:24   2:05

Thankfully I am no longer young, immature, and consumed by those self-proclaimed "Funky Monks." I went to college, read Augustine, Aquinas, and Nietzsche, fell in love with philosophy of religion, became a Christian, continued through seminary, got hooked on Barth in doctoral work and now am seeking higher ground.

Red Hot Chili Peppers: *Higher Ground*

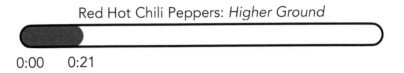

0:00   0:21

Even though they no longer dominate my identity and it is my preference to think to the rhythms of a critically realistic dialectical theology, it will be my thesis that Anthony Kiedis, Michael "Flea" Balzary, Chad Smith, and John Frusciante correctly identified, even if accidentally and a bit crudely, the key attribute of the being of God. The thesis driving this chapter, and indeed this very book, is that the God who is, is the God who "gives it away."[1]

Red Hot Chili Peppers: *Give it Away*

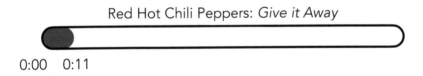

0:00   0:11

I. The God Who Gives It Away. Eternally.

Karl Barth (1886–1968) has often been described as a "christocentric" theologian, and indeed he is, especially in his epistemology. Yet, his future legacy may well focus more on his work as a "trinitarian" theologian. For the theology of Barth's *Church Dogmatics* is, at least in my eyes and those of some of my colleagues, the most lengthy, systematic, and coherent treatment of the triune God the Christian church has ever seen. You should read it. Perhaps these

---

1. Kiedis and Sloman, *Scar Tissue*, 273. Had I been less immature and more diligent about reading the lives of the saints, I might have also been equally impacted, as I am these days, by Dorothy Day who writes, "Going to confession is hard. Writing a book is hard, because you are 'giving yourself away.' But if you love, you want to give yourself." Such begins her story of her being "haunted by God." Day, *Long Loneliness*, 10, 11.

reflections will inspire you to do so. Yes, it is Himalayan in size. But disciple-ship is a long journey and long-haul times require long-haul texts.

Barth's diverse and extended discussions of the Trinity can be distilled by looking at what might be called the "Triune Moment." Think of the Tri-une Moment as one slice or snapshot of God's eternal life.[2] In this chapter, we will look at two ways in which Barth describes this so-called Triune Mo-ment and in the next we will look at a third way. In each of the three ways, Barth seeks to describe God's "triunity" using a fresh vocabulary that aligns with what he says elsewhere. What he offers are essentially three comple-mentary descriptions of the nature and character of the triune God, and though he was not exactly listening to the Chili Peppers while writing the *Church Dogmatics* (he dosed daily on Mozart), in all three Barth portrays a God who gives it away. Eternally.

The Triune Moment: The First Way

In an exposition in the first volume of *Church Dogmatics* on the Nicene Creed's clause that the Holy Spirit proceeds from the Father and the Son, Barth describes what I am calling the Triune Moment in a traditional creedal way:

> As God is in Himself Father from all eternity, He begets Himself as the Son from all eternity. As He is the Son from all eternity, He is begotten of Himself as the Father from all eternity. In this eternal begetting of Himself and being begotten of Himself, He posits Himself a third time as the Holy Spirit, i.e., as the love which unites Him in Himself.[3]

In this description, Barth articulates God's triunity using the traditional creedal language of "begetting" and "being begotten." For Barth, as indeed for all thinkers who have wanted to steer clear of Arianism, God is and always has been, *in* and *as* this eternal begetting of the Father, the being begotten of the Son, and their unification in and by the Holy Spirit.[4] Barth thus seeks

---

2. Though to my knowledge Barth does not use the phrase "Triune Moment," he comes quite close. This can be seen in his discussion of why God's triune modes of being are not "Modalistic": "The doctrine of the Trinity means on the other side, as the rejection of Modalism, the express declaration that the three moments are not alien to God's being as God (*CD* I/1, 382). "Die Trinitätslehre bedeutet aber andererseits, als Abweisung des Modalismus, die ausdrückliche Erklärung: jene drei Momente sind dem Gottsein Gottes nicht etwa fremd" (*KD* I/1, 402).

3. *CD* I/1, 483.

4. For ease of reading, this work will generally adopt Barth's convention of masculine

to affirm that God is triune, and eternally so, with no member of the Trinity pre-existing without the others. That is to say, God's eternal nature is a Trinity. As God is triune, God is God. As God is God, God is triune.

Though not without profound power, in some sense this creedal way is minimalistic. Its basic intent affirms the eternality of the "distinctive genetic relations"[5] and the eternality of each triune "mode of being" (*Seinsweise*).[6] Yet as we will see, Barth has much more to say regarding the Trinity than just how each mode of being genetically relates to the others. This is because Barth seeks to derive knowledge of the triune relations from revelation and not from speculation about the ideal qualities (i.e., to whom?) of a divine being. And so it is worth noting here that Barth's adage of his earlier commentary on Romans still holds true for the *Church Dogmatics*: "What men on this side of the resurrection name 'God' is most characteristically not God."[7] Apart from the revelation of God at Easter, from the God of the cross and the God of resurrection, any formulation of God will fall short and thus become idolatry. It is through the cross and resurrection that Barth believes we see the God who gives the divine life away for others. So it is from this standpoint that Barth seeks to work outwards to the eternal nature of God, all while trying to say, now again in a fresh new way, what it was the creeds were trying to confess in the first place. In this resurrection epistemology, Barth reads Easter's temporal events outwardly as indicative revelations of each mode of being's eternal mode of existence.

With these two elements in mind, the first being the eternality of God's triune modes of being and the second being the true disclosure of God's

---

references (such as *Mensch,* which means man or human) for God and humanity, and which were meant to be broadly inclusive in Barth's original German. For Barth's own disclaimer concerning the inadequacy, and yet the inescapability, of terms like Father and Son, see *CD* IV/1, 209–10, where Barth admits: "We have no better term, and this one forces itself necessarily upon us." It is my opinion that Barth's theology, in its deepest elements, is the most sustained critique of a natural theology of masculinity, or indeed any gender, the church has ever seen. Deifying any human trait, gender, stereotype, or anthropological norm is idolatrous for Barth, and in Jesus we see how even basic terms like "son" are "burst wide open." *CD* IV/1, 210.

5. *CD* I/1, 363.

6. Barth initially prefers "mode of being" to "Persons" (*CD* I/1 §9). In short, Barth feels "mode of being" is the clearest way of avoiding "three personalities in God" (*CD* I/1, 351), "tritheism" (*CD* I/1, 355), and "Modalism" (*CD* I/1, 382). In *CD* II/1, having thus set out the full groundwork for preferring "mode of being," Barth finally, and on his own grounds, applies the concept of "Person" to God: "This one God as the Triune is—let us say it then—the personal God" (*CD* II/1, 297). For Barth's broader defense of God's "personality," see *CD* II/1, 287–97.

7. Barth, *Epistle to the Romans,* 40. This explosive commentary and his Himalayan *Church Dogmatics* will be the two main resources of Barth that we encounter.

modes of being through the cross and resurrection, we can now set forth a second complementary way in which Barth discusses the Trinity.

The Triune Moment: An "Other" Way

A second way in which Barth restates the creedal position based on the events of Easter is by articulating how the loving of "others" is analytic to God's being. If God's self-revelation as Christ on the cross is a true *self-revelation* of God, then God's love for others—God's give-it-away-ness to others—must be basic to who and how God is. Barth reads God's give-it-away-ness to "others" then right into the immanent Trinity. In fact, God's give-it-away-ness to "Others" *is* the immanent Trinity. This is because God has Otherness even in God's self.

In the first part of the second volume of *Church Dogmatics*, Barth restates and extends the creedal position of the first part of the first volume by reasoning that the triune way of being is analytic to God's loving. Because the triune fellowship (κοινωνία) in its three modes of being is the way in which God has His being, Barth argues, "triunity" is the way in which "God is."[8] For Barth, to say "God is" is to say *God is real, God really is,* or even *God has objective reality.* Later in the volume, Barth expounds on the notion of God's being and the objectivity of this being in regard to the objectivity of God's existence, the objectivity of God's self-knowledge, and even the objectivity with which we can know God in His revelation.[9] Barth does so throughout by opting to use the German term *Gegenständlichkeit.* In the employment of *Gegenständlichkeit,* we can see Barth describe in a second way what I am calling the Triune Moment.

Barth's choice of the term *Gegenständlichkeit* is significant. *Gegenständlichkeit* is translated as "objectivity" but it literally means "the state of standing-over-and-against something or someone." In this thought-form, Barth argues that God's reality *is* as He "stands over and against" an "Other" (*Andere*). Yet this is not a process theology in which God's being evolves to a higher form through its relation with a created order. It is not a process theology because the "primären" form of God's *Gegenständlichkeit* is His "selbst Gegenständlichkeit."[10] In Barth's formulation of the divine *Gegenständlichkeit,* God's *standing-over-and-against-an-other* is seen primarily in His relational standing over and against *Himself.* How,

---

8. *CD* II/1, 257. This knowledge is always *analytic a posteriori* to God's revelation. Barth's critique of natural theology renders its being *analytic a priori* impossible.

9. *CD* II/1 §25. Most notably in §25.1, *God before Man,* and §25.2, *Man before God.*

10. *KD* II/1, 53.

might we ask, does God stand over and against Himself as an "Other" in a way granting Him *selbst Gegenständlichkeit*? Barth argues that this can be so because God knows Himself objectively, and thus has His being, in the *Gegenständlichkeit* of Father, Son, and Holy Spirit. God's being and God's knowledge of God's own being is thus inherently relational and trinitarian. In a key passage, Barth frames the matter this way:

> First of all, and in the heart of the truth in which He stands before us, God stands before Himself; the Father before the Son, the Son before the Father. And first of all and in the heart of the truth in which we know God, God knows Himself; the Father knows the Son and the Son the Father in the unity of the Holy Spirit. This occurrence in God Himself is the essence and strength of our knowledge of God.[11]

In Barth's formulation of *Gegenständlichkeit,* the Father and the Son stand "over and against" each "Other." The Son stands "over and against" the Father and the Father stands "over and against" the Son. The Father and Son stand over and against each "Other" as unique and self-differentiated modes of being. The Father and Son's self-differentiation as unique modes of being renders them distinct from each other. They are "Others" to each other.

    Gegenständlichkeit is further significant since *Objectivität* or *Sachlichkeit* would have been other options for describing God's objectivity. Barth's choice of *Gegenständlichkeit* arguably avoids the reification of the triune modes of being, since the primary sense of their *Gegenständlichkeit* is constituted by their relationality to each other, not a brute or impartial *thatness* in relation to an impartial or impersonal observer or thing. As Barth clarifies:

> The fact that the *alius–alius–alius* [another–another–another] which can be illustrated by these other ternaries does not signify an *aliud–aliud–aliud* [another thing–another thing–another thing]; that the One and the Same can be this and that in the truly opposing determinations of these original relations without ceasing to be the One and the same; and that each of these relations as such can also be the One in whom these relations occur—for this there are no analogies. This is the unique divine Trinity in the unique divine unity.[12]

"Otherness" is thus primarily relational in a personal, I-Thou sense; a point emphasized by Barth's consistent use of the verb of personal and relational knowing, *erkennen* ("to know in a personal/relational/familiar way").[13]

---

11. *CD* II/1, 49.
12. *CD* I/1, 364.
13. See for example, *KD* II/1 §25, §26, and §27.

This theme and language of "otherness" represents an immense, if subtle, tool throughout Barth's entire theology. Indeed, one need only investigate the influence and impact of the "Wholly Other" God of *Der Römerbrief*. Yet, the basis for "otherness" in the *Church Dogmatics* is the simple affirmation that "otherness" means a genuine distinction willed and maintained by God Himself. True "Otherness" has its basis, therefore, only in the willing and relational interacting of God with God. Such distinctions can exist, and apparently do, in the freely willed self-differentiation of the triune God. And so, in a rather simple move that nevertheless funds what is at times an immensely complex theology, Barth claims, "God Himself becomes Another in the person of His Son."[14] And yet, even as "Another," the Son is fully God eternal, for, "As the Son of God this Other is God Himself."[15] So it is, as Barth claims, "Before all worlds, in His Son He has otherness in Himself from eternity to eternity."[16] Boom. Like a simple, addictive, and explosive bass-line, this logic kicks off a radical rhythm that has the capacity to make stadiums erupt.

Despite this "otherness," this radical self-differentiation in which the Son is not the Father, and in which the Father is not the Son, for Barth, the Father and the Son do not "stand over and against" one another in a spirit of aggression, hostility, or alienation. Rather they stand before each other in a spirit of peace, service, and unity *with* and *for* each other.[17] They stand before each "Other" in the spirit of their love.[18] Their spirit of love for each other is real and, as such, it too is a distinct "Other." It too is divine. It is their Holy Spirit. This eternal self-differentiating distinction in God as the Father of the Son, and as the Son of the Father, in the presence of their *uniting* Spirit is, as Barth says in II/1, the primary form of God's being, God's *primären Gegenständlichkeit*, God's *selbst-Gegenständlichkeit*.[19] This is, in Barth's logic, God's inward being, His being *ad intra*. Father, Son, and Holy Spirit are thus the eternal modes of being in which God is. Father, Son, and Holy Spirit is how God is. Their unity in distinction is the triune κοινωνία, the internal and eternal fellowship of the trinitarian God.

---

14. *CD* II/1, 317.

15. *CD* II/1, 317.

16. *CD* II/1, 317.

17. See for instance, *CD* IV/2, 352–53.

18. For instance: "God is One. That He is Father, Son and Holy Spirit, and that in this Trinity He is the epitome and sum of all riches, does not mean that His being is inwardly divided. The older dogmatics spoke here of the *perichoresis* of God's three persons or modes of being. It meant by this that He is always the One, not without the Other, but in and through the Other" (*CD* III/4, 32).

19. *CD* II/1, 317.

For Barth, then, God's eternal being is thus *Otherly* oriented for fellowship even in and as Himself. Ontological predications about the divine must always be qualified in this way. For instance, "He can and will not only exist but co-exist."[20] Moreover, the theme of *Gegenständlichkeit* is not relegated to God alone. *Gegenständlichkeit*, in fact, becomes the premise for our knowledge of God. So, for Barth, God "is not only immanent in Himself but He moves over to others."[21] In the theology of II/1, God "repeats" Himself with an absolute and pure continuity in a "sekundären Gegenständlichkeit in seiner Offenbarung."[22] Barth thus maintains that the God who stands objectively before us can do so because He first and foremost has *Gegenständlichkeit* in Himself. In other words, already in His *ad intra*, God is oriented, as we have seen, towards the "Others" by which He is Himself as Father, Son, and Holy Spirit. In revelatory self-disclosure, God then offers Himself towards other "others" *ad extra*. This offering is nothing other than a free continuation of His love for Others into a "reality which is distinct from Himself."[23] In other words, for Barth, God's love for *Others* is extended as God's love for *others*.

---

20. *CD* II/1, 667. Against the charge of "social trinitarianism," this does not mean there are multiple autonomous wills in the Trinity in the way as there would be if three autonomous biological people got together to make a social contract or communal compact. As Barth has affirmed from I/1, and throughout the *CD*, in God there is "one will in three modes of being" with each mode of being uniquely "personifying" and "personalizing" this one will. For instance, see II/1's fine print on the "personality of God," pages 287–97, especially page 297: "What is meant here is the being of God in the three modes: Father, Son and Holy Spirit. In our treatment of the doctrine of the Trinity we took the view that the concept 'person' should be dropped in the description of this matter, because in all classical theology it has never in fact been understood and interpreted in the sense in which we are accustomed to think of the term to-day. The Christian Church has never taught that there are in God three persons and therefore three personalities in the sense of a threefold Ego, a threefold subject. This would be tritheism, which the concept *persona*, understood as *modus subsistentiae*, is in fact meant to avoid. . . . The one God is revealed to us absolutely in Jesus Christ. He is absolutely the same God in Himself. This one God as the triune is—let us say it then—the personal God." If this one will is seen as something akin to "the perpetual actualization of love for an other in freedom," or to modify Barth's own section title from §28, if God is "the One who loves Others in freedom," then this will is embodied and personified uniquely by each divine mode of being. In this will each mode of being is self-differentiated from each other and self-determining for each "Other." Regarding the Son, this means He uniquely personifies God's one will by actively and passively putting Himself in a dependent and serving relationship to the Father, in the power of the Holy Spirit. The Son thus exists *perichoretically*.

21. *CD* II/1, 667.

22. *KD* II/1, 53. Translated "secondary objectivity in His revelation" (*CD* II/1, 49).

23. *CD* II/2, 99.

Barth calls upon this theme of otherness repeatedly as a sort of basic and placeholder language, one which then needs to be filled in and finally defined in relation to biblical revelation.[24] The language and logic of otherness is itself a simple way to put God *ad intra* and God *ad extra* in continuity and correspondence, while at the same time always sustaining the priority of the former. For instance, "The One who rules by His Word and Spirit recognizes the creature which He rules as a true *other*, just as He Himself as a Ruler of this type remains a true *Other*."[25] Likewise, the "eternal co-existence of the Father and the Son by the Holy Spirit" means that "the Son in His relation to the Father is the eternal archetype and prototype of God's glory in His externalization, the archetype and prototype of God's co-existence with another."[26] That the Son's relation to the Father in the Spirit is the archetype and prototype for "Otherly" existence, means we too as "others" are united to God by the Holy Spirit:

> But the Holy Spirit is not only the unity of the Father and the Son in the eternal life of the Godhead. He is also, in God's activity in the world, the divine reality by which the creature has its heart opened to God and is made able and willing to receive Him. He is, then, the unity between the creature and God, *the bond between eternity and time.*[27]

Let us say a few more words about the simple logic of "otherness."

In God's "externalization"[28] toward us, Barth argues that God extends the triune Other-oriented love out into the "darkness,"[29] out into the

24. This is not to say language of otherness is itself non-biblical. One need only to recall Luke 6:31 ("Do to others as you would have them do to you") or Phil 2:4 ("Let each of you look not to your own interests, but to the interests of others") to see that "otherness" language is also basic to the New Testament.

25. *CD* III/3, 144.

26. *CD* II/1, 667.

27. *CD* II/1, 670; emphasis mine. The temporal role of the Holy Spirit is not to be underplayed, even if we cannot fully develop its role here. See for instance: "For this God does not let go the creature; He does not allow it to fall, *not for a single moment* or in any respect . . . This God has taken into His own Hands the relationship between Himself and the creature, and *He has no time* for representatives or vice-regents. This God is *directly present* to the creature always and in all places by the Holy Spirit" (*CD* III/3, 131; emphasis mine). Given that my doctoral dissertation focused on Barth's treatment of time and eternity, the reader will note the temporal element is a recurrent theme in this work. It is so, because it is also a major element of Barth's *Church Dogmatics*. This will be drawn out explicitly in chapter 11, especially section III: "Christ Is Time."

28. *CD* II/1, 670.

29. *CD* II/1, 278.

"nothingness,"[30] out into a realm *ex nihilo.* "Creation" is, therefore, "the establishment and maintenance" of a realm "distinct from Himself,"[31] a world brought and sustained out of the nothingness of non-existence in order to be a theater for Jesus Christ who is the "particular" in which "the general has its meaning and fulfillment."[32] Creation is thus not the realm of God *ad intra* or the realm of what is *homoousios* with God. Creation is a world *ad extra* and *ex nihilo.* It is not *homoousios* with God but is thus a realm of total and absolute ontological otherness, or as Barth repeatedly refers to it throughout the *CD,* it is "a reality distinct from God."[33] Addressing this ontological issue from the angle of creation, Barth writes, "Creation by God—even the creation of man—means the institution of an existence *really distinct* from the existence of God. Between God and man, as between God and the creature in general, there consists *an irrevocable otherness.*"[34] Simply put, and with logical equivalence, this is to say that creation is "not God" but is "a reality distinct from God."[35]

It is with this ontological otherness, this *not-God,* that God Himself seeks to have a relationship. So for Barth, in extending Himself towards the *nihilo,* God "seeks and creates"[36] many "others" with whom He can have fellowship (κοινωνία). This κοινωνία reduplicates the "fellowship of the One," the fellowship existing among the triune Others (*homoousios*). For Barth, all of this is in absolute continuity with God's own inner nature, for God's fellowship with this creation *ex nihilo* reduplicates the fellowship in and by which God is the triune God. In Barth's thinking, God chooses to continue this, His love for an Other *homoousios/ad intra,* in freely choosing to repeat the fellowship of this love for others *ex nihilo/ad extra.*[37] In this, His love for "others" *ex nihilo/ad extra,* we therefore can see the true nature and essence of God's love for "Others" *ad intra.* One can see God *ad extra* in a way wholly authentic and continuous with how

---

30. *CD* IV/1, 213.

31. *CD* II/1, 274.

32. *CD* II/2, 8.

33. *CD* II/1, 274.

34. *CD* II/1, 189; emphasis mine.

35. *CD* II/1, 182.

36. *CD* II/1, 278.

37. Trinity is essentially God's love in Himself, as His being. And in Him there is no alienation since He loves His own "substance." But the creation *ex nihilo* means that the world is not His substance, and so He is able to demonstrate His love for something ontologically "alien" and foreign even to Him—something completely and "wholly" other. Thus, contra Hegel, and arguably Aquinas, there is no necessity upon God requiring His love of the world.

God is *homoousios/ad intra*. As Barth declares concerning God's *opus ad extra* (God's so-called "outward work"),

> The love which meets us in reconciliation, and then retrospectively in creation, is real love, supreme law and ultimate reality, because God is antecedently love in Himself: not just a supreme principle of the relation of separateness and fellowship, *but love which even in fellowship wills and affirms and seeks and finds the other or Other in its distinction, and then in separateness wills and affirms and seeks and finds fellowship with it.* Because God is antecedently love in Himself, love is and holds good as the reality of God in the work of reconciliation and in the work of creation. But he is love antecedently in Himself as He posits Himself as the Father of the Son.[38]

The distinctions arising from "Otherness" are thus always love-funded. Indeed for Barth, it is "only because God loves that there is any *aliquid* or *aliquis* at all towards whom His will can be or is directed."[39] Using this language and logic, Barth seeks to ensure that in God's love for "others" we truly see how God is in Himself as His love for "Others." This allows us to truly know God in His works *ad extra* as God truly is in the triune loving *ad intra*.

Through the language of *primären* and *sekundären Gegenständlichkeit,* and its employment of the multivalent language of "otherness," Barth seeks to demonstrate that God's triune being *ad extra* is continuous with God's triune being *ad intra*. Indeed for Barth, God *ad extra* is simply God *ad intra* with us in a hidden and veiled manner. Yet this—God's being with "others" *ad extra*—need not be the case. As Barth says: "Indeed God does not need the creature as the other for whom and by whom to be glorious, because before all creation He is the other in Himself as the Father and the Son."[40] Still Barth goes on to affirm, "He is this One first of all in Himself, and on this basis He is it secondly . . . for us."[41] Indeed for Barth, the *ad extra* is "*the* natural expression"[42] of how God is *ad intra*. In God's love for "another" (*ad extra*), we see a fundamental repetition of God's true love for "Another" (*ad intra*). As Barth writes, "God repeats in this relationship *ad extra* a relationship proper to Himself in His inner divine essence."[43]

---

38. *CD* I/1, 484; emphasis mine.

39. *CD* II/1, 277.

40. *CD* II/1, 667.

41. *CD* II/1, 227.

42. *CD* II/1, 317.

43. *CD* III/2, 218.

And because there is "Otherness" in God, due to the self-differentiation between Father and Son, Barth concludes, our "world is, because and as the Son of God is."[44] We derive from the Son. Hence, the "whole point of creation," continues Barth, "is that God should have a reflection in which He reflects Himself."[45] Or again, God creates because, "God wills to find again in another the reflection and image which He finds in Himself from eternity to eternity in His Son."[46]

For the purposes of speaking about the primary and secondary forms of *Gegenständlichkeit* via a single referential phrase, we could say, summarizing Barth, that God's essence is His repeated willingness to love *Another* and *another*. We could also say the Triune Moment is the ontological manifestation of God's ongoing will to love Others (*homoousios*) and others (*ex nihilo*). We could go a small step further and unite the two ontologically distinct realms, while still maintaining the priority of the former *ad intra*. We could do this by referring to "O/others." In this case, the common term is something that has *Gegenständlichkeit* with God. In the first instance, God has *Gegenständlichkeit* with Himself through "Others" (*homoousios*) via God's triune pattern of self-relating, while in the second instance this same triune God puts His own *selbst-Gegenständlichkeit* into an additional *Gegenständlichkeit ad extra* with us who are "others" *ex nihilo*.

In this second way of describing the Triune Moment, we can see that in God's *Gegenständlichkeit* before us as others, God offers us the opportunity and invitation to join the κοινωνία of the Divine *Andere*; the κοινωνία in which the Father, the Son, and the Holy Spirit repeatedly have their being in their loving of each Other. Consequently, in this theme of *Gegenständlichkeit* (in its primary and secondary forms) we can see a second way in which Barth details the nature of the Triune Moment. This second way of describing the Triune Moment, it will be noted, entails significantly more than the first way. Barth's intent however is to retread, effectively in a new tone and rhythm, the same ground as was covered in the "begetting/being begotten" language.

II. Give It Away. Really.

I began this chapter with the borderline irresponsible declaration that with "Give it Away," the Chili Peppers had articulated the chief attribute of the eternally triune God. I imagine this may come as news to them since I

44. *CD* II/1, 317.
45. *CD* II/1, 673.
46. *CD* II/1, 673.

know a punk articulation of Barth's doctrine of God was not their chief motivation in 1991. For if Barth was not listening to the Chili Peppers when he wrote the *Dogmatics*, it is equally improbable that the Chili Peppers were reading Barth while drafting *Blood Sugar Sex Magik*. Yet as it turns out, Anthony Kiedis did in fact understand this life-altering mantra better than I ever assumed. Since many of their songs are about *Californication*, I had always generally assumed that "Give it Away" was an anthem for hedonistic promiscuity. Hence, my pleasant surprise eighteen years later, when I read the following—might we say *parable*?—about the song's origins from Kiedis' memoir, *Scar Tissue*:

> [W]e never turned our back on being a funk band, based in grooves and improvised jams. One of those jams would lead to the breakout song on the album. . . . On one of those latter days, Flea started playing this insane bass line, and Chad cracked up and played along. I was so struck by Flea's bass part, which covered the whole length of the instrument's neck, that I jumped up and marched over to the mike. . . . I took the mike and belted out, "Give it away, give it away, give it away now."
>
> That line had come from a series of conversations I'd had years earlier with Nina Hagen. Nina was a wise soul, and she realized how young and inexperienced I was then, so she was always passing on gems to me, not in a preachy way, just by seizing on opportunities. I was going through her closet one day, looking at all her crazy clothes, when I came upon a valuable exotic jacket. "This is really cool," I said.
>
> "Take it. You can have it," she said.
>
> "Whoa, I can't take this. This is the nicest jacket you have in there," I said.
>
> "That's why I gave it to you," she explained. "It's always important to give things away; it creates good energy. If you have a closet full of clothes, and you try to keep them all, your life will get very small. But if you have a full closet and someone sees something they like, if you give it to them, the world is a better place."
>
> I had come from such a school of hard knocks that my philosophy was you don't give things away, you take whatever you want. It was such an epiphany that someone would want to give me her favorite thing. That stuck with me forever. Every time I'd be thinking, "I have to keep," I'd remember, "No, you gotta give away instead." When I started going regularly to meetings, one of the principles I learned was that the way to maintain your own sobriety is to give it to another suffering alcoholic. Every

time you empty your vessel of that energy, fresh new energy comes flooding in.

I was busting out on that mike, going, "Give it away, give it away," and Flea was flying down the length of his bass, and Chad was laughing hysterically, and John was searching for his spot on the canvas to put his guitar part, and we just didn't stop. We all came away from the jam convinced we had the makings of a great song.[47]

A great song indeed. And not only to my ears, but apparently to millions of others as well. And maybe it is more than a song. Perhaps it is a parable or even an epiphany. For in its origins, lyrical content, and performative style, "Give it Away" exhorts us to clothe ourselves with the most valuable garment bestowed upon us by another in a generous act of love. And rather than keeping such gifts like a selfish Caesar, we ought give away with an ebullience that knows no limits. That is freaky style-ly. That is divine. That is biblical. That is, ultimately, totally Barthian too. For in Barth, we do not see three divine persons who may or may not decide to cooperate and love each other. Rather, in Barth's conception, we have the one will of God to love A/another manifested in the differentiated, but united, three eternal modes of being of Father, Son, and Holy Spirit. And it is in their perpetual and repeated threefold give-it-away-ness that they uniquely personify the will of God to love. Once this lens turns towards us, this means we will never know what it means to be a true person until we encounter the God who gives it away. And if it is true that this is the God of Gethsemane and Golgotha, this means we will never know the triune God until we bring ourselves to pray, "Not my will, but thine be done" (Luke 22:42). This means we must come to Simone Weil's realization that "God gave me being in order that I should give it back."[48] Only then will our personhood begin to be what it was meant to be. And that will not happen until we take our life and "give it away now."

Red Hot Chili Peppers: *Give it Away*

0:00   4:43

47. Kiedis, *Scar Tissue*, 272–73.

48. Weil, *Gravity and Grace*, 40.

— 2 —

Eternity: Stairway to Heaven

Led Zeppelin: *Stairway to Heaven*

0:00   0:52

I n Led Zeppelin's classic *Stairway to Heaven*, we meet a lady who seeks transcendence by means of accumulating the wealth and goods of this world. She is sure the glitter of the world's gold is of lasting infinite value. Her hope for salvation lies in her ability to accumulate riches enough for eternal security: she is *buying* a stairway to the celestial.

Even if you are not such a crass materialist as this, the question is worth asking, "How do I think I can get to heaven?" And one need not only ask this question regarding death and the afterlife, for many philosophers, poets, spiritual seekers, and even mathematicians have asked themselves, "How can I learn what is eternally true?" Do the truths of this world lead to some lasting *divine* truths? If a stairway to heaven cannot be bought, perhaps it can be thought? And yes, much of Western philosophy, even while denying the eternal value of worldly riches, has argued the rich wisdom of this world can lead one to lasting eternal truths about goodness, beauty, love, and the nature of God.

The issue is of crucial importance. Someday somebody is going to ask you about God. It might be in a class, it might be at a bar, it might be on a chairlift, or in an airplane. It might be in a hospital, a prison, or even a church. What will you say? What will you talk about? Will you talk about a church tradition? Will you talk about Led Zeppelin? The feelings you get when you look to the west? An idea that some poet, preacher, politician, or philosopher has had? Will you talk about a football game? And if you do talk about those things, how do you expect that these are really supposed to be talking about *God*? Do such things offer a stairway to heaven?

A matter immediately presents itself. When we talk about God, do we talk about things that we like, and then call that God? Do we talk of our experiences? Do we talk of our ideas? Or are we really going to let our talk about God be informed by how God speaks of God's own being? If it is the latter, then this means that we must get all our "thing talk" out of the way and let God speak to us. Whether we are very good at it or not, we are faced with a decision. Will we talk about ourselves and the stuff around us? Or will we talk of the living God?

I would like to select the issue of the eternity of God as a case study for two ways in which one might go about learning about and talking about an attribute or quality of God. First we are going to see how the greatest medieval theologian, St. Thomas Aquinas, gets to and unpacks a notion of God's eternity. I will argue that, in effect, Thomas thinks we can build an intellectual stairway to heaven based upon a philosophy of "being" or what is called more traditionally a natural theology founded upon an *analogia entis* (analogy of being). Upon doing so, we will then return where we left off on in the last chapter with Barth. I promised you a third way in which he discusses what I have called the Triune Moment, and I am sure you're anxious to hear it. Barth's third way is a real mind-blower and offers, I believe, a way to talk about God that is fundamentally informed by God's own self-disclosure. As such it offers, not a ground-up stairway to heaven, but a sort of Jacob's ladder that is lowered from above. Before we get to it, let us deal with a more traditional theological approach in which one of God's attributes, in this case God's eternity, is accessed through the tools of metaphysics.

I. The Immutable Thomas Aquinas

St. Thomas of Aquino, Italy (1225–1274), was, and remains, the greatest philosopher and theologian of the medieval era. Studying under Albert the Great, Aquinas was introduced to the works of Aristotle, works that represented an "intellectual invasion" into Europe in the years 1130–1280. The rediscovery of Aristotle from the Arabic world was among the medieval world's biggest headlines:

> [T]he entry into the Latin world of an enormous Aristotelian
> and Neoplatonic philosophical literature rapidly precipitated for

Christian thinkers a conflict which no preceding century had fully known or experienced, the conflict between Hellenism and Christianity. A sophisticated Greek reason, with sophisticated traditions and masters, is abroad in the thirteenth century, a reason which could not but be attractive because of its brilliance, dangerous and difficult because of its remarkable development, no less dangerous because of its errors.[1]

Aquinas' two great masterpieces, the *Summa Contra Gentiles* and *the Summa Theologiae* are designed, at least in part, to show that the truths professed by Christians are, to a large degree, reconcilable with many of the more basic truth claims advanced by Aristotle and other Greek philosophers. These two works are real masterpieces; the summit of scholastic rigor, Catholic theology, and medieval philosophy. Moreover, their influence is not over. On August 4, 1879, Pope Leo XIII stated that Thomas's theology was a definitive exposition of Catholic doctrine. Thus, Thomas is an official thinker of the Catholic church. So not only is the teaching of Thomas supremely intelligent, influential, and interesting; it is also authoritative.

In addressing eternity and our method for understanding it, we are raising the question of natural theology, and I think Thomas proves to be a prime example of one who does natural theology. In fact, I think he does it better than anybody else. Now for the past few hundred years, the claim that Aquinas does natural theology was about as controversial as that he was an Italian or a Catholic. Nowadays, however, largely because of Barth's critique against natural theology, a growing number of scholars have sought to deny that Thomas was ever doing any such thing. I read Thomas long before I read Karl. I learned natural theology from Thomas, natural theology meaning that knowledge about God "may be obtained by human reason alone without the aid of Revelation."[2] It was not until I came to Princeton Seminary and started wrestling with big Mac[3] over there and then with Karl himself that I came to see more clearly the problems with the very thing I was interested in sustaining. You can guess who won.

Now, Thomas begins his *Summa* with the famous five proofs for the existence of God. What these five proofs seek to establish is *that* there is a being at the front and head of all our being; that there is something that is effectively some primary being from which all other being derives. If you

---

1. Pegis, "Introduction," in Aquinas, *Basic Writings*, xxxvi.

2. *Oxford Dictionary of the Christian Church*, s.v. "Natural Theology."

3. Bruce McCormack is nearly 6'10" tall. I am 5' 9" and made all efforts as a graduate student to either speak to him while he was seated or to find a step, curb, or desk to stand on if he was not.

are not familiar with them, you need to be. In my opinion they should be in-cluded even on applications at Starbucks. What the five ways give us, in the eyes of Thomas, are reasonable evidence that there is (1) a first mover, (2) a first efficient cause, (3) a necessary being, (4) a single cause of all "being, goodness, and every other perfection," and (5) an intelligent being directing the governance of the world. In each case, these are five ways to the same thing, a being which Thomas concludes "everyone gives the name of God."[4] The rest of the questions in the *Summa's* opening section, *De Deo uno*, then treat what kind of being that being or thing is. These questions deal with God's attributes of perfection, simplicity, infinity, immutability, eternity, and unity. Only then does Thomas move on to discuss truths about God revealed in Scripture. I am not going to work through all of these, so now we will only look at three of the more significant attributes of the primal and pure divine being: simplicity, immutability, and eternity.

Aquinas on Divine Simplicity

Having, through the five ways, established *that* there is a being from which all other being flows, the first question Thomas poses concerning this "primary being" is whether this being is material or composite, that is, "whether it has a body." This is to ask if the primary being is made up of something. Thomas reasons it is not. This being is neither material nor composite for all material and composite things rely on something else, namely smaller, earlier, or more basic parts or units for their being. Because "God is uncaused," "God is in no way composite, but is altogether simple." Likewise, "There is neither composition nor quantitative parts in God."[5] As an example, take this Lego dune buggy my three-year-old made. Can't quite see it? Use your imagination. It obviously has parts. It is composite. The existence of this dune buggy is dependent upon the existence of its smaller blocks. But this is also true of each block itself, for each block is divisible and reducible to smaller units of sub-sections, plastic molecules, chemicals, atoms, and so on. But if God is the absolute first and most perfect uncaused being, Thomas reasons that God must exist in non-compositeness because God cannot be reduced to anything smaller, earlier, or more basic. This means God must be One in a way so as to entail that this Oneness is indivisible, mono, singular, solitary, atomic, and a monad, for any plurality in God would be a unity of more basic components. Aquinas is clear on this—simplicity is not just about a material composition, though certainly

4. Aquinas, *ST* I.2.3.
5. Aquinas, *ST* I.3.7, 34.

that is included. For Aquinas, that God's being is "absolute" being means "he can be in no way composite"[6] and that "The perfection of the divine goodness is found in one simple thing."[7] More could and really needs to be said about simplicity, for the logical force it produces is equivalent to the gravitational power of a black hole. It really does pull, for Aquinas, all other attributes under its domain. What I want to do now is to move forward and defend this last claim by showing how, for Aquinas, immutability and eternality are attributes that also are governed by simplicity.

Aquinas on Divine Immutability

Can God change? Thomas argues no, for God's non-compositeness, that is, God's simplicity, means that God is immutable; God cannot change. The reason for this is all change requires an interval from one state to another; a movement from a now to a then; an alteration from a *this* to a *that*; a succession from a here to a there; a procession from a one to an other. God's singular, uncaused, perfect, incorruptible being means, for the likes of Aquinas, that God cannot be in motion or in any kind of change in any way. A change would, among other things, introduce *at least* a duality, a *this and a that,* into the being of God. But as the *first* and only prime mover, as a singular indivisible *mono*, there can be no such duality in God. Following the Platonists, for Aquinas, simplicity denies any movement from a "potentiality" to an "actuality," or from a "this" to a "that" in God, because this would be an interval or movement from one thing to another, and this would render God as composite. For Aquinas, there cannot be anything multiple or composite in a non-composite being. "Perfection is perfected."[8] So for Aquinas, the fact that God is not composite also entails God's immutability, and necessarily so.[9]

6. Aquinas, *ST* I.3.7, 34.

7. Aquinas, *ST* I.3.8.

8. Dr. Dre, "Nuthin but a G'Thang."

9. Here is Aquinas on immutability from *ST* I.9.1: "First, because it was shown above that there is some first being, whom we call God; and that this first being must be pure act, without the admixture of any potentiality, for the reason that, absolutely, potentiality is posterior to act. Now everything which is in any way changed, is in some way in potentiality. Hence it is evident that it is impossible for God to be in any way changeable. Secondly, because everything which is moved, remains as it was in part, and passes away in part; as what is moved from whiteness to blackness, remains the same as to substance; thus in everything which is moved, there is some kind of composition to be found. But it has been shown above [*ST* I.3.7] that in God there is no composition, for He is altogether simple. Hence it is manifest that God cannot be moved. Thirdly, because everything which is moved acquires something by its movement, and

Aquinas on Eternity

We arrive at Aquinas's treatment of eternity where it is reasoned that "The notion of eternity follows immutability, as the notion of time follows movement."[10] Hence, as God is supremely immutable, it belongs to Him to be eternal. Adopting Aristotle's definition of time as "the measure of motion,"[11] Thomas thus equates change with time, and consequently unchangeability with timelessness. As time is the mutability and movement through past, present, and future, eternity is anti-time, timelessness, being without past, present or future. Just as simplicity denies any parts and just as immutability denies any motion, so too, eternality denies any temporality, for time is simply the movement of things through a divided and complex existence. For instance, we who live in time have part of our life in the past, part of it in the present, and part of it in the future. This means we are complex, divided, and mutable. Simplicity and immutability mean that God's being cannot be divided into such temporal parts or phases with movement from one to the other. For Aquinas, composition, motion, and time are all part of the same logical package. Thus God, who by definition is not such things, is singular, static, and atemporal. Such a God is purely, totally, and absolutely timeless. And such a conception of eternity is totally motionless and changeless—it is the pure static existence of a perfect and immutable being.

Now two quick implications/problems of what this might mean. These are two "problems" commonly diagnosed with an understanding of eternity as timelessness:

1. The denial of any change in God and of God's unchanging knowledge of changing realities essentially threatens us with the possibility that *there is no change*, even if the world gives appearances to the contrary. Because there is no succession or temporality in God's knowledge, and because God knows all there is to know both truly and unchangingly, the warranted conclusion is "in the actual world there is no motion or change relative to God."[12] Yet, since God's knowledge is "cognitively perfect"[13] and thus *true*, this must mean that change,

---

attains to what it had not attained previously. But since God is infinite, comprehending in Himself all the plenitude of perfection of all being, He cannot acquire anything new, nor extend Himself to anything whereto He was not extended previously. Hence movement in no way belongs to Him. So, some of the ancients, constrained, as it were, by the truth, decided that the first principle was immovable."

10. Aquinas, *ST* I.10.2.
11. Aristotle, *Physics* 4.11 (221a1).
12. Leftow, *Time and Eternity*, 227.
13. Leftow, *Time and Eternity*, 218.

motion, temporality, and even causality are not true realities of this world, for God does not know them as true. Perhaps they are illusory fabrications of our minds? The affirmation of God's immutable eternality, itself a mainstay of classical philosophical theology, thus seems to terminate in a denial of the time, motion, change and causality upon which it is predicated. To call it out more clearly, this is a refutation ("there is no change") of the argument's initial undeniably true first premise ("there is change in this world"). This is a troubling, if not fatal, double internal contradiction. Metaphysically speaking, it means there is no change at all anywhere ever, even though this is all we perceive. Epistemologically speaking, it means all perceptions of change and time are ultimately false, undercutting the main rational foundation for the proof of God's existence in the first place. This seems no good.

2. Though this methodology aims for a maximally perfect God, an *ens reallissimum*, it is especially interesting to find that God's maximal perfections can actually *rule out* omniscience. As Christian analytic philosopher Brian Leftow pops the cork: "That perfection precludes omniscience may sound paradoxical, but philosophy is full of surprises."[14]

Leftow argues against an absolute and exhaustive form of divine omniscience on the basis that there are some things it would be better for a perfect being not to know. As he argues:

> Suppose that I want to show you how failure feels. I rig a test for you before a jeering throng, you fail miserably, the crowd hoots, and you slink away. I then say, "being a failure oneself feels like *this*." . . . You and I can know that being a failure oneself feels like *this*, but if God cannot fail, God cannot. For if God cannot fail, God cannot have the kind of experience "this" picks out and so in a sense cannot even understand the proposition that "being a failure feels like *this*." If God logically cannot fail, He cannot even try to grasp this proposition, for if He tried, He would fail.[15]

In this example, we have the attribute of God's perfected immutability rendering God unable to undergo any kind of experience that requires imperfection or even change. Now given this, you may wonder how such a God could ever become incarnate. I am in agreement. This is a severe problem. Like Robert Plant, the lead singer of Led Zeppelin, "It makes me wonder."

14. Leftow, *Time and Eternity*, 324.
15. Leftow, *Time and Eternity*, 323, text and footnote 16.

Led Zeppelin: *Stairway to Heaven*

4:43   4:54

What we have then, in this Thomistic account of the eternality of God, is an attempt that starts with some element in this world: namely a composite, changing, temporal creaturely form of being. From this Aquinas works upwards, via negation in *De Deo uno,* through a logically rigorous and philosophically sophisticated method in an attempt to arrive at a non-composite, unchanging, atemporal, *divine* form of being. In a very real sense, then, it is an attempt to build a stairway to heaven. Not one that can be bought, but one that can be thought. It is an attempt that starts with the physics of motion, change, and time and then moves to philosophical considerations of first principles, causation, teleology, and necessary being. It is then one that seeks to define the being of God according to our understanding of how a perfect being must exist. Such is one way to attempt to speak of divine attributes according to a deification of the number one. If social trinitarianism begins with assumptions about three persons and then struggles to work upwards to show how they might be one God, this starts with a premeditated understanding of one being and then struggles to show how it can be triune. In my opinion, in that neither starts with God revealed as three-in-one and one-in-three, they are both forms of natural theology. And my own fear is that this boxes God in while also setting in place a logical inertia that has a consistent tendency to lock God out of time, as when Brian Leftow argues that "though God exists, there is no time at which He exists" and that God is "no way in time."[16]

Such is one way in which we might talk about eternity. Such talk typically terminates in a timeless, static, frozen, and indivisible instant. Sooner or later, however, this levee of reason will break, being overcome by the self-determination of the divine person. Let us then look at another route, for Christ's call to repentance suggests there is always another path open to those who wonder about, and wander after, the truth.

16. Leftow, *Time and Eternity,* 2–3.

Led Zeppelin: *Stairway to Heaven*

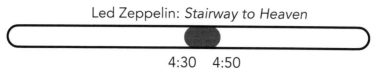

4:30   4:50

II. Back to Barth

If you recall, earlier we made it through two complementary examples of the Triune Moment: the first using the language of "begetting and being begotten," and the second using the language of God's "give-it-away-ness" to "Others." In a third treatment of God's triunity, Barth describes the Triune Moment in a third, less technical, non-creedal way.[17] He does so with an intentional theological pun, the brilliance of which is without end. See if you can catch it:

> A correct understanding of the positive side of the concept of eternity, free from all false conclusions, is gained only when we are clear that we are speaking about the eternity of the triune God. We are speaking about the God who is eternally the Father, who without origin or begetting is Himself the origin and begetter, and therefore undividedly the beginning, succession and end, all at once in His own essence. We are speaking about the God who is also eternally the Son, who is begotten of the Father and yet of the same essence with Him, who as begotten of the Father is also undividedly beginning, succession and end, all at once in His own essence. We are speaking about the God who is also eternally the Spirit, who proceeds from the Father and the Son but is of the same essence as both, who as the Spirit of the Father and the Son is also undividedly beginning, succession and end, all at once in His own essence. It is this "all," this God, who is the eternal God, really the eternal God. . . . God is once and again and a third time . . . If in this triune being and essence of God there is nothing of what we call time, this does not justify us in saying that time is simply excluded in God, or that His essence is simply a negation of time. On the contrary, the fact that God has and is Himself time, and the extent to which this is so,

---

17. Though to the sharp eye, one can see the seeds of this in the earlier excerpt from *CD* I/1, that God "posits Himself *a third time* as the Holy Spirit." *CD* I/1, 483; emphasis mine.

is necessarily made clear to us in His essence as the triune God. This is His time, the absolutely real time, the form of the divine being in its triunity, the beginning and ending which do not mean the limitation of Him who begins and ends, a juxtaposition which does not mean any exclusion, a movement which does not signify the passing away of anything, a succession which in itself is also beginning and end.[18]

In this crucial section, we see the links that Barth makes between the ongoing triune begetting, the ongoing triune self-knowing, and therefore the ongoing and uniquely *temporal* triune relating. This is all distilled in the elegant yet fully serious theological pun: "God is once and again and a third time," which when translated a bit more literally from the German is, "God is one time, and again one time, and again one time."[19] In this way, God is *one time* ("once") as the Father; God is God "again one time" as the begotten Son; God is self-posited *a third time* ("and again one time") as the Holy Spirit. This captures how God is "once and again and a third time"[20] in both a temporal/chronological way and also in an ontological one.[21] Barth's point is this: God is *repeatedly* this same *triune* God over and over again *ontologically* and *chronologically.* As Barth summarizes, "The name of Father, Son and Spirit means that God is the one God in threefold repetition."[22]

It is in and out of this "uninterrupted cycle"[23] as the triune God that God effectively generates a "supremely temporal"[24] life and has, in God's own and unique way, an "absolutely real time"[25] which is His eternity. God is God again and again and again. For Barth, this trinitarian unity-in-differentiation "settles the fact" that although God is singular, God is "not therefore solitary."[26] Rather, God has in Himself the freedom to be in fellowship: God is "One and yet another, but One again even as this other, without confusion

---

18. *CD* II/1, 615.

19. *KD* II/1, 693.

20. *CD* II/1, 615. "*Gott einmal und noch einmal und noch einmal*" (*KD* II/1, 693).

21. Barth can rephrase this yet another way. For instance: "God in Himself wills a first and therefore a second. And conversely He wills a first for the sake of a second. Again, He wills a second and therefore a first, and, again conversely, a second for the sake of the first" (*CD* II/1, 593).

22. *CD* I/1, 350. See also: *CD* I/1, 376: "The biblical witness to God's revelation sets us face to face with the possibility of interpreting the one statement that 'God reveals Himself as the Lord' *three times in different senses*"; emphasis mine.

23. *CD* I/1, 370.

24. *CD* II/1, 614.

25. *CD* II/1, 615.

26. *CD* II/1, 475.

or alteration, yet also without separation or division."[27] As Barth explicates, "God already negates in Himself, from eternity, in His absolute simplicity, all loneliness, self-containment, or self-isolation."[28] Rather, God's triune loving, in negating this singular isolationism, is inherently successive both ontologically and chronologically, but again, always perichoretically and simultaneously. Now the fun thing about this way of describing the Triune Moment as God "once and again, and a third time" is that it maps onto our notions of past, present, and future. Indeed for Barth, this is *why* time has a threefold form as past, present, and future, for God in His triune self is behind us, with us, and before us. This is the God who "hems" us in, as Psalm 139:5 says. This is the One who is for us again and again and again.

Barth parses eternity up into the unity of its three distinct phases: pre-temporal eternity, supra-temporal eternity, and post-temporal eternity. Briefly these are:

1. God's eternality is pre-temporal (*vorzeitlich*): God was before time and was complete "in Himself" apart from time.[29] Time is of God's making, though Barth also affirms that "It is because God is pre-temporal that He does not owe us anything" and that "He could have done without it."[30] Though God wills to make time for us, He wills to make time primarily for "its center in Jesus Christ."[31] God determines God's self to be God for us in the election of Jesus Christ to be the God of time. Barth explains:

   > For this pre-time is the pure time of the Father and the Son in the fellowship of the Holy Spirit. And in this pure divine time there took place the appointment of the eternal Son for the temporal world, there occurred the readiness of the Son to do the will of the eternal Father, and there ruled the peace of the eternal Spirit—the very thing later revealed at the heart of created time in Jesus Christ.[32]

   And so for Barth, in God's past, in His "knowing and willing which preceded all time,"[33] God already is who He will be in the time of the man Jesus of Nazareth.

27. *CD* II/1, 664.
28. *CD* I/1, 483.
29. *CD* II/1, 621.
30. *CD* II/1, 621.
31. *CD* II/1, 622.
32. *CD* II/1, 622.
33. *CD* II/1, 622.

2. God's eternality is supra-temporal (*überzeitlich*):[34] God is not limited
by created time and so resides above it. But more importantly God is
with created and fallen time and enters *into* it. God walks in time and
alongside of time. Barth admits *mitzeitlichkeit* or *inzeitlichkiet* might
better express this theme.[35] "God's eternity accompanies [time]; and
it, too, may accompany God's eternity by which it is created and in
which it also has its goal."[36] Moreover time itself is fully established,
confirmed, and consciously constituted (for God and for us) in Jesus'
death on the cross and His resurrection from the dead. The cross is
the "middle point"[37] of time and exists as time's "hidden centre."[38] For
Barth, supra-temporality affirms that who God will be in our future, is
who He already was in this world as Jesus, just as He eternally determined Himself to be before our time began.

3. God's eternality is post-temporal (*nachzeitlich*):[39] "Just as God is before and over time, so He is after time, after all time and each time."[40]
Our time as we know it will end, but God's glory will continue to
endure and with Him will reside those free creatures who can know,
love, and experience God unveiled. Post-temporality means "Eternity
is also the goal and the end beyond which and over which another
goal and end cannot exist. All roads necessarily lead to it."[41] But the
God of our destination, the One whom we will meet then, will be the
same God who was before time and who showed us Himself in time
as Jesus Christ. In effect, we will experience God saying, "I am the
One who is, the same One who always was, and the One who will be
always still to come" (Rev 1:8).

The fact that "three moments are not alien to God's being as God" means
that God can be God again and again and again in our time, differently
or the same, without any threat to God's own being. It means that we will
encounter this God once, differently again, and now a third time in new but
same ways. "Same same but different," as I frequently heard while traveling
in Thailand, means God is free to move from one state to another; to go

34. *CD* II/1, 623–629.
35. *CD* II/1, 623.
36. *CD* II/1, 623.
37. *CD* II/1, 629.
38. *CD* II/1, 626.
39. *CD* II/1, 629–638.
40. *CD* II/1, 629.
41. *CD* II/1, 629.

from a *now* to a *then*; to have an alteration from a *this* to a *that*; to experience a succession from a *here* to a *there*; or to engage in a procession from a *one* to an *other*. It also means that God can be like this *and* like that. God's threefold repetition as Father, Son, and Holy Spirit and eternity's ongoing continuous relationship of this triune loving means that there is a threefold rhythm within the divine being. This rhythm is the foundation and source of our time. This triune and divine rhythm is shared with this world *as* time. The invitation, then, is to join this divine rhythm and let God's beat be the bass line to your life. Doing so puts you face to face with the one who was, who is, and who is to come. This then, is not a stairway to heaven bought by human science, logic, or reason; one that gives preference to the static rock and not to the dynamic roll. Rather, this way of thinking is an acceptance of the infusion of God's living grace into the world that takes knowledge of the triune God that comes through the rhythm of God's revelation as Christ as its starting point. And given that eternity's foundation is the One who says "Follow me," it seems the piper is not the most intriguing one calling you to join him.

Led Zeppelin: *Stairway to Heaven*

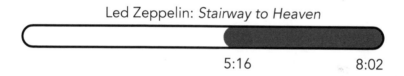

5:16   8:02

— 3 —

Revelation: So What'cha Want?

Who is the Bible? Where can you find God? Who is Jesus? When is revelation? These are some of the questions we are addressing in this chapter. When faced with such questions, it is sometimes useful to think alongside the great minds of Western civilization. Which is why I go the Beastie Boys:

Beastie Boys: *So What'cha Want*

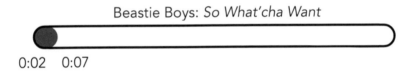

0:02   0:07

While not typically known for their theological profundity, the Beastie Boys distill the matter of this chapter into two provocative questions:

Beastie Boys: *So What'cha Want*

0:47   1:03

The first, concerning the origins of one's information, interrogates one's epistemic basis for one's outlook or stance. The second, concerning our ability to "front," suggests that revelation somehow unmasks our false pretenses and exposes us for who and what we really are.

"You think that you can front when revelation comes?" And in case you need the definitive answer ever-fresh from the five boroughs, the dropped conclusion is, "Yeah, you can't front on that."[1] So let us explore these deeper questions: What is revelation? And why can you not front on it? Barth's got the best extended answer I have seen yet.

I. The Word of God According to Karl Barth

In the realm of Christian theology, for most people the word "revelation" is thought of as either the last book of the Bible or the whole collection of books in the Bible. But for Barth, revelation's main definition is neither. For Barth, "God's revelation" is not the Bible. This means "the Word of God," which is so often used to describe the Bible, at least in American Christianity, is not its proper primary referent. For Barth, revelation is "the event of the presence of Jesus Christ."[2] Giving primary emphasis to John 1, Jesus Christ, not a collection of texts, is the Word of God. This simple corrective of relocating "the Word of God" from the documents of the Bible and onto the person of Jesus means revelation is *God's self-disclosure as Jesus Christ*. It turns revelation into a present tense: God showing up; God doing something; God showing you face to face who and how God is. As the radical black theologian James Cone says, revelation is "the Wholly Other God descending on humankind like a bolt from the blue, radically transforming the human situation."[3] On this point Cone well explains Barth's significance,

> In Protestant Christianity, because of the influence of the so-called Barthian school, the first half of this century will be remembered for the radical reinterpretation of the idea of revelation. Before this period, revelation was largely understood as divine information *about* God communicated to humankind through reason (natural theology) or through faith (assent to biblical truths).[4]

But as Cone goes on to teach, in light of Barth's thinking, revelation has "nothing to do with truths about God communicated through the church, scripture, or reason." Revelation is, rather "the existential encounter" of

---

1. Horovitz, "So What'cha Want."
2. *CD* I/2, 45.
3. Cone, *Black Theology of Liberation*, 45.
4. Cone, *Black Theology of Liberation*, 44.

God with us "in the person of Jesus Christ."[5] Or as Barth says, "the presence of Jesus Christ is God's time for us."[6] Thus, Christ is time.

Since revelation *is* the person of Jesus Christ living out God before us, Barth can say that "God is the constant subject of revelation."[7] This entails a few things that revelation is not. Revelation is not an impersonal disclosure of secondary facts about God.[8] Revelation is not a list of propositions, statements, or equations that have to be endorsed and repeated as timelessly and statically true. Revelation is not something that happens apart from both historical context and individual relationship. Revelation is, rather, a personal confrontation of God with a person or a group of persons. Revelation is God speaking to you and, in so doing, revelation is the opening of God's heart, God's "personality," God's character to you. This is God unveiling God's self; God in self-disclosure. This is not a revelation that has to be approved and advertised by us and our organizations as something we can distribute. It is revelation we, as individuals in community, have to trust and follow.

Revelation, then, is not like a jigsaw puzzle in which you need to collect different pieces that finally assemble into a whole, giving in the end finally a very different picture than what you had on each piece. Revelation is like a jigsaw puzzle in which on every uniquely shaped piece you get a different portrait of Jesus. However, "Even the man Jesus," writes Barth, "is always enigma." He continues, "If He is not only enigma, if as enigma He is also illumination, disclosure and communication, then it is thanks to His unity with the Son of God" and "the faith in Him effected by the Holy Spirit."[9] This is so because, for Barth, revelation, in each of its happenings, is a full and complete disclosure

---

5. Cone, *Black Theology of Liberation*, 45.

6. *CD* I/2, 45.

7. *CD* I/2, 1.

8. You, dear reader, should also read James Cone's book, *A Black Theology of Liberation*. If you do, you will see that, even more than the other authors, the name of Karl Barth keeps coming up. Indeed, if you read Cone's 1986 preface, you will discover that Cone himself admits that his book has an "inordinate methodological dependence upon the neo-orthodox theology of Karl Barth" (Cone, *Black Theology of Liberation*, xxiii). Cone cites this as the "fourth and last weakness" of his book but admits that at the time of the book's writing, Barth offered "the only theological system with which I was intellectually comfortable and which seemed compatible with the centrality of Jesus Christ in the black church community . . . I had to use what I regarded as the best of my graduate education" (Cone, *Black Theology of Liberation*, xxiii). As it so happens, Barth is also what I regard as the best of my graduate education. Treating his doctrine of revelation, as we are doing, will let you understand what Cone employs from Barth and should let you evaluate for yourself whether this is a weakness or a strength of Cone's passionate and unrelenting theology.

9. *CD* II/1, 56.

of God's self. In each revelation you get Jesus Christ, and if you haven't gotten Jesus Christ, you have not gotten God's revelation.

Barth's understanding of revelation, as complex and lengthy as it is, and over as many years as it was developed and refined, is designed from first to last to be faithful to the entire narrative of Scripture, including the claim of Ecclesiastes 5:2 that "God is in heaven, and you upon earth." For Barth, and his articulation is rigorously exegeted from the widest swath of biblical texts, God's self-revelation is a full triune event in each revelation. Each event is a full and personal disclosure of the triune God, though it is often not seen and understood as such. Revelation is then for Barth never a tip-of-the-iceberg type of thing. When God reveals God's self, God reveals God's whole self, not just a small fragment behind which something mysterious, unknown, and possibly very different is lurking. In Barth's understanding of the New and Old Testaments, God chooses to disclose God's nature and character as "Jesus Christ." It is as if when God takes time for humanity, God sets up the appointment on the calendar as Jesus Christ. Jesus Christ is God's appointment to the world; God speaking to us. Though we must be alert, for God humbles Himself so severely that "God Himself can be rejected in the grace of His condescension to the creature."[10] Jesus Christ is God's communication, *God's word* to humanity, a word that is not understood until we look to the cross and resurrection, and which, even after this, can still be rejected.

Finally, and I think most importantly, revelation is not something we "have." Revelation is not some*thing* we possess and control. It is not something that we can decide to distribute, hold on to, preserve, or alter. Revelation is instead some*one* who comes to us again and again; someone who again and again shows us that our control, our possessions, our plans, our "being, having and doing" as Barth says, are overturned. Since this someone is God, God remains Lord over the event of self-disclosure. Humanity never gains control over God and is never able to manipulate God for its own ends. On the contrary, humanity is always spoken to.

Note that Barth affirms that there is revelation, that there was revelation, and that we have good reason to hope there will be revelation yet again. Barth thus thinks that revelation is real. Not only did it happen, but it actually still happens. Revelation is not something purely subjective, not merely a wishful thinking on the part of humanity, not a deification of something we have chosen as precious and sacred. On the contrary, revelation is something historical. This means there is something *real, true,* and *objective* for us to gather around, to study, and to learn from. But the

10. *CD* II/1, 56.

historicity of revelation does not mean we gather around something that is of historical interest alone. Revelation is no merely interesting archeological tomb to excavate. Because Christ is God's revelation, and because Christ rose from the dead, He not only was, but is again. So the person of Jesus Christ is the real, true, and objective living one around whom we ought to gather, such that God can speak to us again, here and now.

Finally, the objective reality of revelation of God as Jesus Christ means we do not judge revelation and decide from a neutral standpoint whether revelation is good and acceptable to us. On the contrary, *the* revelation of God on the cross as Jesus Christ displays that we all are sinners and that revelation judges us. Fortunately this is disclosed by God as a judgment towards us of grace, forgiveness, love, and acceptance. But this finally means we are not the criteria for what is good, true, and beautiful. God's disclosure as Jesus is. In Christ we are shown what is good, what is true, and what is beautiful. It is not our calling to evaluate and critique this but to be obedient to it and to follow. And that the crucified and resurrected Christ is the archetype of all that is good, true, and beautiful means that all the world's conceptions of such things are thrown into KRISIS, a theme that arises with Barth's commentary on Romans and that runs strong through the *Church Dogmatics*.

What about the Book?

Over and against the notion that revelation is God's self-disclosure in Jesus Christ, we have the Holy Bible. What then is this book? What is this thing? What makes it special? Is it special? Barth's answer to the question of "is this book special" is "no" and "yes." And to the question of what makes it special, Barth gives his faithful answer, "Jesus Christ."

We will start with why, on the one hand, the Bible is not special. On the one hand, it is an object like all other objects in this world. Bibles are printed, bound, and sold; read, discarded, and ignored. True, in some ways "Bibles" form a slightly different class of things, because unlike most things you can buy at Walmart, these are a collection of interesting and ancient documents. But this too does not make it absolutely unique. After all, there are other books of ancient documents, and of course there were many other ancient documents. Like all the other documents that were signed, sealed, and delivered by FedEx in the ancient near east, these letters, reflections, and poems were also signed, sealed, and delivered by FedEx.[11] If we think of things divided into the sacred and the profane, it

---

11. The latter half of this claim is not true.

must be admitted that this is a collection of words, letters, and documents from within the latter. This Bible after all (imagine me waving my plastic wrapped duct-taped backpacking Bible) hardly looks sacred. So what makes the Bible special? Is it the ink?

For Barth, the Bible is special, unique, and authoritative because it is "a witness of revelation."[12] Now, as Barth reasons, a witness "is never identical with that to which it witnesses."[13] This seems fairly basic, as a witness is something that points to another thing. So it is with the Bible and revelation. The Bible is a witness, a *collection* of different witnesses, really, pointing forwards and backwards to the unique and unrepeatable event of God's self-revelation as Jesus Christ. So just as Exodus 3, for instance, is not *itself* a burning bush but is a witness to a revelatory encounter of God before Moses via a burning bush, so too the Bible itself is not revelation. It is a witness to events of revelation. The Bible is a pointing. To what does it point? For Barth, the answer is that it points to a hidden God revealed via objects in this world.

Dan Migliore's book points out, "Revelation literally means an 'unveiling,' 'uncovering,' or 'disclosure' of something."[14] Barth unpacks this at great length and in an impressive level of detail and sophistication, but the fundamental point is that for God to *unveil* God's self through something, God first veils God's self in that something. In order for God to take off a veil, God first puts on a veil.

Now Barth draws this all from the Bible, though it may seem to be from an unlikely place. The foundations of his veiling and unveiling dialectic are seen in verses such as Deuteronomy 6:4: "Hear O Israel, the LORD your God is one God"; Exodus 3:14, "I am who I am"; and Hannah's prayer in 1 Samuel 2:2: "There is no one holy like the LORD; there is no one besides you; there is no Rock like our God." How? You might ask: Does God's holiness relate to God putting on a veil of creaturely objects? For Barth, God's holiness (or in traditional philosophical jargon, God's *aseity*) means God is like only God's self and that God is not simply another object within this world. Indeed God is not even *like* any object in this world. And though traditional theology and philosophy often thought it could argue via analogy from the being(s) of this world to the being of God, Barth's consistent line about God's *total* and *complete* otherness breaks the permanent rational basis for an analogy of being. Again, no stairway to heaven can be thought. And yet, because of this holiness, freedom, and total otherness, Barth argues God

12. *CD* I/2, 463.

13. *CD* I/2, 463.

14. Migliore, *Faith Seeking Understanding*, 21.

can reveal God's self through any object in this world, since effectively God stands at an equal distance to all objects in this world. In a famous line, Barth acknowledges: "God may speak to us through Russian Communism, a flute concerto, a blossoming shrub, or a dead dog." God is free to use any element of this world. Or none. More importantly, Barth advises us, "We do well to listen to Him if He really does."[15]

The consequence of God's holiness, *aseity*, or otherness is that in revelation there is a dialectic of veiling and unveiling. God veils so that God can unveil. God hides so that God can *re*-veal. And in that veiling and unveiling of God there is an *indirect identification* of God with an object. If God speaks through a dead dog or a flaming shrubbery, then God makes it clear that God is not simply a dead dog or a flaming shrubbery. Moreover, taxidermy-ing the dead dog or uprooting the shrubbery and bringing it home would not put God in your hands, garden, or living room. Even if these are objects that God spoke through they, like a megaphone or radio, are effectively mute once the broadcast has ended. They are the speakers through which the voice comes. They are not the voice itself. Epistemologically speaking, God is mediately and indirectly present though them, not immediately and directly present in them. This prevents us from grabbing ahold of revelation, freeze drying it, and then serving it up later whenever we pop it in a micro-wave to satisfy our purposes (or not!). God is simply not under our control. Hence, "Thou shall not front."

Now just as the OT and NT give repeated witness to these kind of unveiling and revealing events, Barth thinks *the* final and decoding event of revelation is the presence of God's self in time as Jesus Christ. Barth writes, "God wills to veil Himself by becoming a man, in order by breaking out of the veiling to unveil Himself as a man."[16] In other words, God clothed God's self in something that was itself not-God, namely, a third-world infant born in poverty and destitution. God did so precisely so that God could unveil God's self through that medium. But if God can use the object of a struggling, political, dangerous infant body, the question we ought now ask (in fear and trembling, really) is what *can't* God use to unveil God's self? As I hope you now expect, the answer is, "God can use anything and everything."

This then allows Barth to have a very high view of Scripture, but this view does not arise because the text has a unique, sacred, and divine ontology in itself. The Bible is not holy because it dropped from heaven on golden plates, but rather because it faithfully points to the living God: "The Bible is not a book of oracles; it is not an instrument of divine impartation. It is a

15. *CD* I/1, 55.
16. *CD* I/2, 41.

genuine witness."[17] For Barth, this means that Scripture *can become* revelation when God speaks to us through it. As simply another object among objects, if we want to hear God's voice through Scripture, we need to invite God to use it again and again and are dependent upon God's actually coming to it and actually using it. Indeed, Barth recognizes, "A complete non-recognition of the Lord who has instituted and used this medium is possible."[18] Scripture can become revelation if God chooses to use it in moments of self-disclosure, but we must also be open to believing through it. We advance in hope and with faith.

Now if this sounds offensive, it should. For Barth has just ripped God out of my control, out of your control, indeed, out of human control. This is the reason why we cannot "front" when revelation comes, for God alone is God and we are not. This means we cannot control when, where, and what God uses to disclose God's self, a lesson Flannery O'Connor brilliantly exploits in her short story *Revelation*. We cannot control God or summon God on command because to do so would be to make ourselves more than divine. No longer can we flip open the Bible and hit somebody with God's revelation. No longer can we claim objective revelation on behalf of our political or social strategy. No longer can we style ourselves as unambiguous bearers of God's truth. What Barth wants to do is to put God in charge of God's self-disclosure. What Barth wants to do is to ensure that *Jesus Christ* is "the kingdom of God," not these texts, not our interpretation, not our translations, not our churches, not our seminaries, not our ideologies, not our governments, not our communal societies, not our theologies, not our philosophies, or even our _____ (←fill in the blank). If the heavens ever do speak, Jesus Christ is the last true mouthpiece.

How Do You Read This Thing?: The Question of Hermeneutics

Briefly then, let us deal with the question of hermeneutics—that is, *how* we are to read and understand the Bible. Given that we have said the Bible is a collection of diverse and secular media existing within the plane of things and alongside all other things in this world, it is worth asking, "What holds it together?" Through what lens ought we to understand it? At seminary, you will frequently hear that it is important to understand Scripture in light of its context. The debate then becomes what context governs all others? Ought we understand Scripture from within power narratives of social oppression?

17. *CD* I/2, 507.
18. *CD* II/1, 55.

From within the socio-political context of second temple Judaism? From within a context of post-exilic religious syncretism? From within the norms of Roman law? From within Greek myth? From timeless mathematical rules that can govern rational ethical behavior?

For Barth, the context that ought to govern our interpretation and understanding of Scripture is the historical event of the resurrection of Jesus Christ. *He* is the historical event that prompts Matthew, Mark, Luke, John, and Paul to hit their desks and start typing. He is the point in history that governs what and why they write. And it is in trying to describe this event and its ramifications that they borrow and bend their words and concepts. The resurrection of the crucified Jesus is the ultimate anchor event that interprets, governs, founds, and grounds the existence of the New Testament. It is what holds all these other diverse and sporadic witnesses together, including the diverse and sporadic witnesses of the Old (and New!) Testament. Indeed, as Barth argues, the resurrection event is the midpoint and fulfillment of not only biblical history and testimony, it is the fulfillment of all time itself.

For Barth, then, if there is proof that there is a creation event and that this creation is good; if there is proof that the Israelites went through the genuine life-threatening gulf of the Red Sea, and did not just wade through some ankle-deep puddle (or make the whole saga up); if there is proof that Jonah did survive his descent to the depths in the dark foul belly of some great and deadly beast; and if it is true, as Cone argues, that God is *the* God of liberation and freedom who slays all powers of hatred, violence, enslavement, and death; all these are true and only true because of the fact that God raised Christ from the dead. These other events are called to serve as witnesses to that reality, but it, the resurrection of Christ from a deadly death, is the foundation upon which they sit. This means that without the resurrection, even if these other events still happened, they would be worse than false, they would be meaningless, arbitrary, chaotic, and untrustworthy. They would be *random*.

II. Natural Theology

We now come to the matter of general revelation and natural theology. As we encountered in the last chapter, these terms refer to the question of whether we can know anything about God from the natural order, perhaps via our reason, perhaps by looking at history, or perhaps by investigating nature through science.

Traditionally, Christian theologians affirmed that though biblical revelation shows us a completed picture of God, humanity could, on its own, begin to form an accurate picture of the divine before and apart from "special revelation." Theologians like Augustine and Aquinas, for instance, affirmed that humanity can know that a god exists, that such a god is good, unchanging, not made up of any thing that is not divine, and that this world is in dependence upon that god for its existence. Such a "natural knowledge" of God often also warranted a knowledge of a moral order, through what is often referred to as "natural law."

The great protestant reformer, John Calvin, also affirms our reason and experiences: "wherever you cast your eyes, there is no spot in the universe wherein you cannot discern at least some sparks of his glory."[19] These "sparks" are God's "insignia" that are "engraved" in creation such that "therein lies an attestation of divinity so apparent that it ought not to escape the gaze of even the most stupid."[20] However, and this is the key that distinguishes him from similar Catholic theologians, Calvin denies that these sparks do anything productive for us in our knowledge of God. For rather than building upon our knowledge in a positive and cooperative way towards what is subsequently and accurately known in revelation, humanity's "ungratefulness" and "madness" bends and distorts them such that we become "deluded by vain error."[21] Calvin exegetes Romans 1:18–23 in a way that most of his supporters actually fail to recognize. Calvin argues that whatever natural revelation there is from God, it is inevitably distorted by fallen human beings and leads only to superstition, error, and idolatry. So for Calvin, natural knowledge of God does nothing to help us along an upward path to a true and salvific knowledge of God. Indeed, because we misunderstand and misuse it, it serves as a block and detriment to a true and salvific knowledge of God. Hence in Calvin, whatever natural knowledge of God we have actually makes our condition worse.

Now, because James Cone suggests that "Every student of theology knows of Karl Barth's merciless attack on natural theology,"[22] and because I wish this was so, I want to spend a few minutes on Barth and how he ups the ante, as it were, from Calvin and those before him.

Whereas for Augustine and Aquinas I think it can be said that natural theology has a status as "good", in Calvin it has a status as "bad" and in Barth

19. Calvin, *Institutes*, 52.
20. Calvin, *Institutes*, 53.
21. Calvin, *Institutes*, 55, 67.
22. Cone, *Black Theology*, 51.

natural theology is simply "impossible." We do not and cannot have any. Here are a few reasons why:

1. For Barth, there is no such thing as an impersonal knowledge of God. For Barth, all knowing related to God is a personal/relational knowing of an I (the human) to a Thou (God), and never an I (the human) to an it (God). This relational knowing finds its origins in the fact that God only knows God's self in the give-it-away-ness of the triune relations of Father, Son, and Holy Spirit. This triune knowledge is not an impersonal, factual, objective, external form of knowing. It is not a cold, scientific knowledge of a body of data. On the contrary, in the triune fellowship, God's self-knowledge is relation of grace, love, giving, service, dependence, and faithfulness. This kind of knowing is the kind that is extended to us. We are invited to "know" God as the Son knows the Father. But this is knowledge born in and from relationship in active discipleship, not passive reflection; from service and suffering as we follow, not from distant cognition and inconsequential fact collection.

2. Through passages like Psalm 19:1 ("The heavens declare the glory of God"), which might seem to offer a general knowledge of God through nature, Barth argues from a basis of covenant. The Psalmist, Barth argues, is only able to proclaim such a thing because she is already a part of the specially revealed covenant that forms this confession's basis. She is not a secular pagan philosopher exerting her reason, but a believer already living within a community that has been called; she is amidst a response of faith that is both communal and individual. That "the heavens declare the glory of God" is not an axiom of *a priori* reason but an *a posteriori* confession of faith and a response of worship. Likewise against Romans 1:20,[23] Barth turns to I Corinthians 1:21.[24] This passage seems to explicitly deny the inferences interpreters often draw from Romans 1, which is that human reason, through philosophy or the sciences, can provide a true and accurate counterpart to God's self-declaration as Jesus Christ. In I Corinthians, Paul tells us that Christ is the wisdom of God and, until we know Christ crucified, which is

---

23. "For since the creation of the world God's invisible qualities—his eternal power and divine nature—have been clearly seen, being understood from what has been made, so that people are without excuse."

24. "Where is the philosopher of this age? Has not God made foolish the wisdom of the world? For since in the wisdom of God the world through its wisdom did not know Him, God was pleased through the foolishness of what was preached to save those who believe."

foolishness to the Greeks, we do not know God. *At all.* I Corinthians
1, which seems to have been wildly overlooked by pro-natural-knowl-
edge-of-God exegetes of Romans 1, proclaims that we do not know
God via our wisdom, no matter how much we love it.

3. Barth exegetes John 1 to the effect that, as the Word of God, Jesus
    is *the* Word of God and not simply *a* word among many that God
    speaks. Over and against the Adolfs of this world who would pro-
    claim themselves to be an additional, corollary, and even cooperat-
    ing divine revelation, Barth argues that as *The Word,* Jesus Christ is
    the ultimate, first and final, eternal, one Word of God. This means
    the person, identity, and character of Jesus is perpetually God's word
    to the world and not simply a passing expression of a divine fashion.
    Future revelation thus can only show us again that Jesus Christ still
    lives, still loves, and still reigns. "God is One" means "God is Jesus."
    Here is a classic passage:

> Knowledge of God in the sense of the New Testament
> message, the knowledge of the triune God as contrasted
> with the whole world of religions in the first centuries,
> signified, and still signifies, the most radical "twilight of
> the gods," the very thing which Schiller so movingly de-
> plored as the de-divinisation of the "lovely world." It was
> no mere fabrication when the Early Church was accused
> by the world around it of atheism, and it would have been
> wiser for its apologists not to have defended themselves so
> keenly against this charge. There is a real basis for the feel-
> ing, current to this day, that every genuine proclamation
> of the Christian faith is a force disturbing to, even destruc-
> tive of, the advance of religion, its life and richness and
> peace. It is bound to be so. Olympus and Valhalla decrease
> in population when the message of the God who is the one
> and only God is really known and believed. The figures
> of every religious culture are necessarily secularised and
> recede. They can keep themselves alive only as ideas, sym-
> bols, and ghosts, and finally as comic figures. And in the
> end even in this form they sink into oblivion. No sentence
> is more dangerous or revolutionary than that God is One
> and there is no other like Him. All the permanencies of
> the world draw their life from ideologies and mythologies,
> from open or disguised religions, and to this extent from
> all possible forms of deity and divinity. It was on the truth
> of the sentence that God is One that the "Third Reich" of
> Adolf Hitler made shipwreck. Let this sentence be uttered

in such a way that it is heard and grasped, and at once 450 prophets of Baal are always in fear of their lives. There is no more room now for what the recent past called toleration. Beside God there are only His creatures or false gods, and beside faith in Him there are religions only as religions of superstition, error and finally irreligion.[25]

Or as the Barmen Declaration puts it:

8.11—Jesus Christ, as he is attested for us in Holy Scripture, is the one Word of God which we have to hear and which we have to trust and obey in life and in death.

8.12—We reject the false doctrine, as though the church could and would have to acknowledge as a source of its proclamation, apart from and besides this one Word of God, still other events and powers, figures and truths, as God's revelation.[26]

Against natural theology, Barth argues that God is not known through isolating of any element of this world and then maximizing it up as a stairway to heaven. As an act of human exaltation, such stairways can only yield idols and false gods. On the contrary, God is known via revelation as Jesus Christ. This is a revelation who comes to us, who sets us free from our idols and false gods, and who offers us a lasting relationship with the eternally triune God, the true God, the Holy One of Israel.

Conclusion

I began by asking "Who is the Bible?" and "When is Revelation?" And I suggested this means, at its heart, we are asking, "Where'd you get your information about God from?" I have suggested, alongside Barth, that we should understand "revelation" as God's self-disclosure as Jesus Christ and that the Bible is the faithful and reliable witness to this living God. This transcends questions of textually inerrancy or factual accuracy and suggests that if the Bible is to become revelation, God must come to it and use it, allowing it to become a medium of revelation once again.

As for the question, "Where can I find God?" this means we very well might *not* find God within the pages of the Bible, especially when it is read from a position of unbelief, skepticism, or worst of all, critical neutrality. "Revelation occurs for faith, not for unbelief. God exposes Himself, so to

25. *CD* II/1, 444.
26. "Theological Declaration of Barmen," 249.

speak, to the danger that man will know the work and sign but not Himself through the medium of the work and sign."[27] Hence, to know God means we might very well need to find the God of the past, alive in our present, out in the wild, walking the same kinds of country roads, healing the same kinds of broken people, and having mercy on the same kinds of hungry crowds. But this means God is not frozen and stuck within the pages of the Bible. The Bible is not God. This does mean the biblical God is alive and that we need to use the Bible and ask the Spirit to guide us to the place, perhaps especially to a place we would rather not go, in order to find the One who alone deserves the title of "My LORD and My God" (John 20:28). And isn't that really what'cha want?

Beastie Boys: *So What'cha Want*

3:02   3:37

---

27. *CD* II/1, 444.

— 4 —

Creation: Alive

When I stepped off the bus, three things hit me. The first was the heat. The bus had been air-conditioned and, though I knew it was hot outside, the wall of heat I walked into was shocking. It was mid-day, the sun was high, the asphalt melting. The heat was so intense I could feel my body being radioactively fried up and dried out. I put on my sunglasses and hat as I moved to let others behind me off the bus. But I was already thinking about turning around and getting back into the A/C. The second thing that hit me was the wilderness. This was not what I had been expecting.

I was on a trip to Israel and I had been excited to get out and see the Judean wilderness. At the time I was a junior in college and back home I had become enamored with the great outdoors. With the freedom of the college schedule, bags of old (mostly stolen) bagels, and a Toyota loaded with mountain bikes, climbing gear, skis, and backpacks, the mountains of Montana and Colorado were always the place I was trying to get to. Western excursions were adrenaline-fueled fun, but they also had a spiritual component. I had become a Christian after my freshman year in college while on a mountaineering trip in British Columbia. God and wilderness were inseparable in my head and heart. The Coast mountains of British Columbia are lush, and steep temperate rain forests jut up out of the saltwater inlets, rising up to shattered glaciers and sharp granite summits. It was a demanding environment, with slippery slopes, massive granite walls, and often only a narrow path to hike upon. But the wilderness of BC, like the lusher parts of Montana and Colorado, also had an Edenic sense about it. For one, wherever you were in that wilderness, you could always hear water running. Cold, freshly melted, *pure* water was always available. One only had to stop, unbuckle the water bottle from the pack, and choose which spigot off rock or root looked best. Even the standing pools and puddles of water, once one was in the alpine, were clear, pure, and completely potable. A few years later I went back to guide for two seasons with the same program, Young Life's Beyond Malibu. I stopped purifying my water after the first week and never got slightly ill.

But now in the heat, this Judean wilderness was just the opposite. Not only was it hot, it was totally dry. The craggy hills showed no sign of vegetation. They struck me as piles of rock, gravel, and dust. This Judean wilderness was as dry as cardboard, jagged as a broken tooth, and hotter than Hellgate (a high school in Missoula, Montana) in August. So the second thing that hit me was, "This wilderness is no good—you can't survive out here by yourself." And of course, that is when the third thing hit me. But we will get to that third realization in a moment. Before we do that, we need to contemplate existence, the nature of the universe, and the fact that we are alive.

Pearl Jam: *Alive*

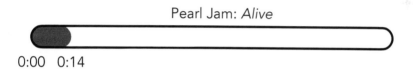

0:00   0:14

In their era-defining grunge anthem, Pearl Jam poses the uncertainty fundamental to human existence. Take a listen:

Pearl Jam: *Alive*

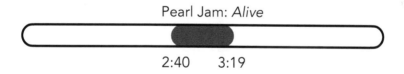

2:40   3:19

We are alive. We learn this fact most fully through interactions with others. But why are we alive? Do we deserve to be? Is this even the correct question? And if so, who can answer it? Let us take these moshing matters to three great minds in the Christian theological tradition. We will ask them why there is something rather than nothing to see if we can discern why we are alive. From there we will head back to the wilderness to tie it all up.

I. Creation by Formation: Plato's *Timaeus*

Though Plato predates the New Testament and was not a Hebrew (he was an Athenian philosopher), next to Genesis probably no other text has been as influential in the West on the matter of creation as has the *Timaeus*. The *Timaeus* is delivered as a conversation between Socrates and Timaeus and is not only his account of the creation of the universe, it is also Plato's explanation for why the universe is intelligible and why it came to be.[1] It is equal parts geometry (triangles and circles, in particular), philosophy, anatomy (including an explanation of why we walk forward), and astronomy, optics, and medicine. It even goes into politics and includes Plato's account of the lost island Atlantis, great deluges of old, and a brief summary of his ideal political state in which "all wives and children" are "to be in common," and in which "the children of the good parents were to be educated, and the children of the bad secretly dispersed among the inferior citizens."[2] The *Timaeus* really has it all. It literally is about everything and anything.

In its opening, Plato, through the mouth of the character Timaeus, begins with *the* classic question:"I am asking a question which has to be asked at the beginning of an inquiry about anything—was the world, I say, always in existence and without beginning, or created, and had it a beginning?"[3]

In response, Socrates, via Plato, reasons that as the world is "visible and tangible and having a body," it must be created. The universe must then "of necessity be created by a cause."[4] But just in case you are curious, Plato holds, "the father and maker of all this universe is past finding out, and even if we found him to tell of him to all men would be impossible."[5] Now Plato argues that in creating the universe, God's motive is to make "a copy"[6] of something intelligible, good, and eternal, and so formed this world as a "moving image"[7] in the "pattern of the unchangeable."[8] In this fabricating, God, or the Demiurge as Plato calls it, looked to the eternal forms such as pure goodness, total equality, absolute truth, perfect beauty, and then crafted the universe to mimic them. Thus the universe is rational, intelligible, and good because it is formed to reflect the eternal and

1. Plato, *Timaeus*, 1151.
2. Plato, *Timaeus*, 1154, 19a.
3. Plato, *Timaeus*, 1161, 28b.
4. Plato, *Timaeus*, 1161, 28c.
5. Plato, *Timaeus*, 1161–1162, 28c.
6. Plato, *Timaeus*, 1162, 29b.
7. Plato, *Timaeus*, 1167, 37d.
8. Plato, *Timaeus*, 1162, 29a.

unchanging pattern of the supreme good. And yet, of key importance, matter itself exists perpetually, or eternally, and the Demiurge merely fashions it toward the good because "he desired all things should be as like himself as they could be."[9] Here's a bit more:

> God desired all things should be good and nothing bad, so far as this was attainable. Wherefore also finding the whole visible sphere not at rest, but moving in an irregular and disorderly fashion, out of the disorder he brought order.[10]

Now it is also to be noted, as a major divergence from the Christian tradition, that for Plato this universe of order itself has an intelligence and a soul. So the universe is itself a living rational creature:

> When he was framing the universe, he put intelligence in soul and soul in body, that he might be the creator of a work which was by nature fairest and best. On this wise, using the language of probability, we may say that the world came into being—a living creature truly endowed with soul and intelligence by the providence of God.[11]

The takeaway point I believe, for our purposes, is that in the *Timaeus* the fabricator of the universe forms co-existing matter into the likeness of the eternal unchanging forms. The Demiurge did this by first condensing the body of the universe into the four elements of fire, earth, air, and water. But the key is that the Demiurge sits below the eternal forms, contemplating them, as it were, and then crafting things in their image out of an ever-existing matter that is mutually existing with, though independent of, its own being.

II. Creation by Emanation: Meister Eckhart

Meister Eckhart (c. 1260–1327) is unique amongst medieval theologians and mystics in that he was the *only* theologian tried under the Inquisition.[12] Eckhart died while the trial was ongoing, but upon its conclusion seventeen of his statements, whittled down from an initial list of nearly 150, were declared to have "the error or stain of heresy."[13]

9. Plato, *Timaeus*, 1162, 30a.
10. Plato, *Timaeus*, 1162, 30a.
11. Plato, *Timaeus*, 1163, 30b.
12. McGinn, *Mystical Thought*, 1, 15.
13. Eckhart, *Essential*, 80.

These first three condemned articles were a product of Eckhart's view that creation was the result of God's *ebulliat,* God's "boiling over."[14] Both an essential part of Eckhart's thought and one of the more controversial, *ebulliat* was founded on, or at least embodied, the first half of the Neoplatonic notion of procession and return.[15]

Eckhart saw the process of creation as "conferring of existence"[16] from God to the material reality. Since existence or *esse* exists originally, formally, and ultimately *in* God, for the universe and its contents to come into being, God must share God's own existence *with other things* by "pouring forth into the created universe."[17] As Eckhart taught, all things are contained within God, "the One," and from God's *being* comes the *being* that constitutes all things. It might be said that God *pulls out* all of creation's existence from within God's own existence.

A corollary of this for Eckhart is his view that humanity's soul and God's soul are one and the same in essence. In his writings, Eckhart refers to this theme as the *grunt;* the ground, essence, origins,[18] or "innermost of the soul."[19] This innermost essence is such that "Here God's ground is my ground and my ground is God's ground."[20] Thus Eckhart boldly claims the essence of our being, our soul or spirit, is one and the same as God's soul or spirit. As he says in this zinger of a sermon snippet: "God's being is my life. If my life is God's being, then God's existence must be my existence and God's is-ness is my is-ness, neither less nor more."[21] The direct identification of God's being with his own being correlates to biblical concerns about blasphemy and certainly set off alarms in Rome.

That God's being is shared equally between divinity and creation enables Eckhart to affirm the goodness and accuracy of philosophy: "Moses, Christ, and the Philosopher [i.e., Aristotle] teach the same thing, differing only in the way they teach."[22] So Eckhart could affirm that one did not need Christianity to either understand the cosmic order or to achieve salvation. Yet, Eckhart also wanted to keep the forms and language of Christianity, and so he put a trinitarian and christological spin on the unification of our

---

14. McGinn, *Mystical Thought,* 73.

15. Eckhart, *Essential,* 41.

16. Eckhart, *Essential,* 87.

17. McGinn, *Mystical Thought,* 100.

18. McGinn, *Mystical Thought,* 39.

19. McGinn, *Mystical Thought,* 41.

20. Eckhart, *Essential,* 183.

21. Eckhart, *Essential,* 159.

22. McGinn, *Mystical Thought,* 3.

being with God's being. Eckhart did this by collapsing trinitarian notions of the Son's "being begotten" into the act of creation. As Eckhart writes in his *Commentary on Genesis*, "in one and the same time in which He was God and in which He begat His co-eternal Son as God equal to Himself in all things, He also created the world."[23]

"Nothing seems to have annoyed his opponents more"[24] than Eckhart's preaching concerning the equivalence of God's Son with "every good and divine man."[25] This teaching of direct identity or "indistinct union"[26] comes as a junction of Eckhart's doctrines of *ebulliat* and *grunt*. The schema is something like this: God creates via an overflowing of God's self into additional objects and, since God is non-temporal, Eckhart believed "he still, without ceasing creates it."[27] Eckhart also believed "the Father gives birth to his Son in the innermost ground."[28] This too is a continual process, as "whatever God did or created a thousand years ago or [will create] a thousand years hence he is doing now; it is simply all one work."[29] Eckhart did not shy away from the consequences of his thought:

> He must do it whether he likes it or not. The Father gives birth to
> his Son without ceasing; and I say more: He gives me birth, me,
> his Son and the same Son. I say more: He gives birth not only to
> me, his Son, but he gives birth to me as himself and himself as
> me and to me as his being and nature. In the innermost source,
> there . . . he gives me, his Son, birth without any distinction.[30]

Since our soul and God's are one in *grunt*, for Eckhart, God's continual birthing of the Son happens within us and to us. We are not only a by-product, even more so we are an eternally equal co-product of the eternal generation of the Son from the Father.

Now if you think it is slightly unfair of me to use Eckhart as an example, given that he was the subject of a heresy trial, and given that seventeen statements of his were condemned with the papal bull *In agro dominico* (March 27, 1329, by Pope John), then consider the following. In 2010, Timothy Radcliffe, Master of the Dominicans, announced:

23. Eckhart, *Essential*, 155.

24. Eckhart, *Essential*, 52.

25. Eckhart, *Essential*, 78.

26. McGinn, *Mystical Thought*, 148.

27. Eckhart, *Essential*, 229.

28. Eckhart, *Essential*, 182.

29. Eckhart, *Teacher and Preacher*, 298.

30. Eckhart, *Essential*, 187, 188.

> I wonder whether you know that we tried to have the censure lifted on Eckhart and were told that there was really no need since he had never been condemned by name, just some propositions which he was supposed to have held, and so we are perfectly free to say that he is a good and orthodox theologian.[31]

So, at least in some circles, the question remains an open one regarding whether creation via emanation is orthodox or not. Regardless, here are some consequences and implications:

1. Eckhart's understanding of creation via emanation affirms the goodness, and even the divinity, of the natural order. The question is whether it does so to the point of denying the reality of evil. Is not everything totally divine?

2. Eckhart's affirmation of the divinity of the natural order means you can affirm Christian language and traditions while not being bound by them. You can have a Jesus on the cross and a gathering of the church as believers if you like, but you do not need them. A re-unification of our being with God's can also be had via some metaphysics, Monads, Macrobius, and heck why not, even McDonald's.

III. Augustine and *Creatio ex nihilo*

The third model we now turn to is that of *Creatio ex nihilo*; that is, creation from absolutely nothing. For an articulation of this, we go to Augustine.

In Book 11 of *The Confessions,* Augustine wrestles with such questions as how God created, what it means that God created by the word, and what God was doing before creation. To the later question, that is, "What was God doing before He made heaven and earth?" Augustine resolutely and boldly declares, "Before God made heaven and earth, He did not make anything. For if He did, it could have been nothing else except a creature."[32] Augustine's firm conclusion, then, is that "before there was any creature in existence, there was no creature in existence." This is pretty good logic; before there was anything, there was not anything.

Augustine then goes on in Book 12 to advance and articulate a notion of creation out of nothing. *Creatio ex nihilo* means primarily three things for Augustine. The first is that matter is not co-eternal with God. Only God is eternal. Contrary to the Platonic notion of the permanence of matter, God

---

31. See "Eckhart: the Man."

32. Augustine, *Confessions,* 260.

and matter do not exist in an eternal dualistic relationship. Matter, form, physics, and time all have a starting point—God's act of creation. On this matter Augustine effectively reasons himself into a big bang cosmology— that all matter, energy, space, and time originate from nothing—almost two-thousand years before such thinking became empirically corroborated. As physicist Robert Jastrow put it,

> For the scientist who has lived by his faith in the power of reason, the story ends like a bad dream. He has scaled the mountains of ignorance; he is about to conquer the highest peak; as he pulls himself over the final rock, he is greeted by a band of theologians who have been sitting there for centuries.[33]

Long before Hubble space telescopes, the deep field photographs, the red shift, or cosmic microwave background radiation, Augustine reasons that God alone is primary and first, and all must erupt from nothing, nothing that is except God's good will.

A second thing that *Creatio ex nihilo* means for Augustine is that we are not made up of God. Rejecting the very position Eckhart later endorsed, Augustine reasons,

> You *created heaven and earth*; but you did not create them out of yourself. If you had, they would be equal to your only-begotten Son and therefore to yourself too, and it could not possibly be right that something not-proceeding from you should be equal to you. And there was nothing else in existence besides you from which you might create them, God, three-in-one and One-in-Three, nothing. You created a great thing and a little thing—a great heaven and a little earth. You were and nothing else was and of nothing you made heaven and earth, two things, one close to you, the other close to nothing, one which has only you superior to it, the other which is of all things, the most low.[34]

Wanting to do justice to the fact that Genesis 1:2 says, "Now the earth was formless and empty, darkness was over the surface of the deep, and the Spirit of God was hovering over the waters," Augustine reasons that God first created a formless matter out of nothing and then shaped that into the things that are. As he says, "For you, Lord, made the world out of a matter which was without form, and it was from nothing that you made this formless matter, this next-to-nothing."[35]

33. Jastrow, *God and the Astronomers*, 116.
34. Augustine, *Confessions*, 288–89.
35. Augustine, *Confessions*, 288–89.

A third thing that *Creatio ex nihilo* means for Augustine is that the material is good. It is not something with which God is in eternal opposition, but something that God calls into existence as a something that is good in itself. Over and against the Manichees, who wanted to affirm the goodness of spirit but the corrosive nature of the material, Augustine sought upon his conversion to Christianity to be able to affirm that matter itself is not an evil anti-God but is something good that God wills out of nothing, employs for redemption, and saves from negation and disintegration.

Wrapping up this element of today's topic, we thus have three views on creation: (1) Plato and creation by the formation of eternal matter, which is itself not-god; (2) Meister Eckhart and creation by the emanation of God's own being into other forms; and (3) Augustine's *Creatio ex nihilo* wherein we see God's institution of a domain that simply was not in any way before it was.

For now, we will leave unanswered questions standing in queue because there is something greater at stake. Nor will we attempt to briefly investigate Barth's take on creation, as even a most basic commentary on his foundational commitments, regardless of a summary of the four volumes he gives creation in the *Church Dogmatics* (well over two-thousand pages), would take us too far afield. The orientation of his thinking will emerge as we progress in future topics, even as some of his conclusions to today's matter may already be discerned from our earlier treatments. Instead, let us get back to the Judean wilderness.

IV. Into the Wild

You will recall the heat was the first thing that hit me. The second thing was the feeling, "This is no good. You can't survive out here." That is when the third thing immediately kicked in: "Oh. Yeah. I guess that's the point." The point of this hostile and wild Judean wilderness is to show us we cannot survive by ourselves and we need to rely upon God. The point of being taken into the wild is that we are to rely upon the trustworthy, dependable, faithful, reliable provider and cook, who is Our Heavenly Father.

Think of the Exodus with its manna, quail, and sweet water from bitter water. Think of Elijah being delivered meat and bread by the ravens. Think of Jesus being tempted in the desert and being sustained only by the Spirit. Think of the feeding of four thousand and five thousand—feedings that happened out in the middle of nowhere—out where there was *nothing*, no help, and no one to rely upon but God. Think of Hagar with her son, Ishmael, about to evaporate into death after being evicted by Abram and Sarai. The Judean wilderness: this is the kind of place where you do not want to fend for yourself. This is the kind of place where you *cannot* fend for yourself. This is a place where a rational decision is to look for the quickest form of death. This is why God takes you there; so that you can be taken care of and so that you can *know* you are being taken care of. Once you realize this God is good and can be trusted with your life, then you are taken back into the marketplaces, the cities, the villages, the promised land, and the places where you have to choose to depend upon God; where you have to choose to not rely upon on your own resources. That is the point of the wilderness. It is the place where you learn what Friedrich Schleier-macher called *the feeling of absolute dependence*. The wilderness confronts you with the harsh reality that you are *a being in absolute dependence*. You are a creature. You have needs. You must be provided for. If you are not, you whither. You fade. You perish. You crumble. You ride the downward spiral and disintegrate into nothing. This means the wilderness tells us the truth about ourselves, one that creation itself might already know: that we rely on the grace, mercy, love, and glory of God for our existence. Why are we alive? Do we deserve to be? Who answers such questions? We exit with Augustine and a touch of Barth:

> And what is this God? I asked the earth, and it answered me, "I am not He," and all the things that are on the earth confessed the same. I asked the sea and the deeps, and the creeping things with living souls, and they replied: "We are not your God. Look above us." I asked the blowing breezes, and the universal air with all its inhabitants answered: "Anaximenes was wrong. I am not God." I asked the heavens, the sun, the moon, the stars, and "No," they said, "we are not the God for whom you are looking." And I said to all those things which stand about the gates of my senses: "Tell me about my God, you who are not He. Tell me something about Him." And they cried out in a loud voice, "He made us." My question was in contemplation of them, and their answer was in their beauty.[36]

An alternative theological rendering in the key of Karl has it go like this:

> This is their secret that will one day come out and be revealed. . . . The creature has no voice of its own. It does not point to its own picture. It echoes and reflects the glory of the Lord. It does this in its heights and its depths, its happiness and its misery. The angels do it (and unfortunately we have almost completely for-gotten that we are surrounded by the angels as crown witnesses

---

36. Augustine, *Confessions*, 207.

to the divine glory). But even the smallest creatures do it too.
They do it along with us or without us. They do it also against
us to shame us and instruct us. They do it because they cannot
help doing it. They would not and could not exist unless first
and last and properly they did this and only this. And when man
accepts again his destiny in Jesus Christ in the promise and faith
of the future revelation of his participation in God's glory as it
is already given Him here and now, he is only like a late-comer
slipping shamefacedly into creation's choir in heaven and earth,
which has never ceased its praise . . .[37]

Doctrines aside, this is what we should hold most dearly as we encounter
creation: extreme awe at the existence and beauty of the world should bring
us to our knees in overwhelming gratitude for still being alive.

Pearl Jam: *Alive*

3:31   5:40

37. *CD* II/1, 648.

Sin: To Live Is to Die

Metallica: *To Live is to Die*

0:00   0:18

I n June of 1916 two Swiss pastors met in the small village of Leutwil for a bit of holiday.

Metallica: *To Live is to Die*

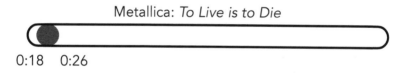

0:18   0:26

They were a few years out of seminary and both had pastorates in small villages.

Metallica: *To Live is to Die*

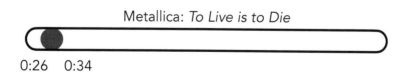

0:26   0:34

They had been armed in school with the latest and the greatest theology. But, in their conversations, both admitted they needed something additional to boost their preaching.

Metallica: *To Live is to Die*

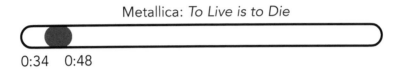

0:34   0:48

Both had become inclined to think that their pastoring, and not just their preaching, also needed something new, something different, something to give things a little spice. Their wives were along on the trip and the two women, Marguerite and Nelly, were musicians. Though they were not fans of the Red Hot Chili Peppers, their music occasionally made the one pastor feel "moved by the Spirit" giving him an urge "to join in making music with them in the wildest ways."[1] *Ahem.*

Metallica: *To Live is to Die*

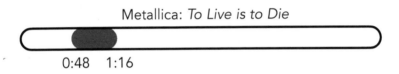

0:48   1:16

The two pastors wondered how they might bring some of *that* vibrancy into their Sunday sermons. Reflecting on what kind of *something* they could add to their preaching, they debated whether they should return to academic theology in order to try and learn something new. One of the pastors, Eduard, suggested that perhaps a study of the philosophy of Hegel would jumpstart their ministry? The other countered with the idea that perhaps Kant would be better? Thankfully for the parishioners, nothing came of either suggestion. Eduard suggested they find something totally different, "a wholly other theological foundation"[2] than what they had read in seminary. But where might something like that be found, if not in Western philosophy? In the end, the two decided to do something much more basic. Remembers the one, "In fact we found ourselves compelled to do something much more obvious. We tried to learn our theological ABCs

1. Busch, *Karl Barth*, 97.
2. Busch, *Karl Barth*, 97.

all over again, beginning by reading and interpreting the writing of the Old and New Testaments, more thoughtfully than before."[3]

Metallica: *To Live is to Die*

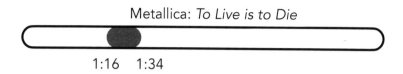

1:16 1:34

What happened when they set out to investigate the Scriptures afresh?: "Lo and behold, they began to speak to us."[4] One of the pastors had learned in confirmation class as a youth (note: *not* in seminary) that Paul's Epistle to the Romans was "of crucial importance" to the New Testament. In a letter, he recounts, "I sat under an apple tree and began to apply myself to Romans with all the resources that were available to me at the time. . . . I began to read it as though I had never read it before. I wrote down carefully what I discovered, point by point. . . . I read and read and wrote and wrote."[5]

Metallica: *To Live is to Die*

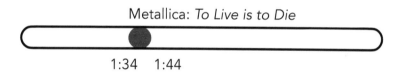

1:34 1:44

In Paul's Epistle to the Romans, this young pastor found something strange:

> During the work it was often as though I caught a breath from afar, from Asia Minor or Corinth, something primeval, from the ancient East, indefinably sunny, wild, original, that somehow is hidden behind these sentences. Paul—what a man he must have been . . . And then *behind* Paul: what realities those must have been that could excite the man in such a way! What a lot of far-fetched stuff we compile about his remarks, when perhaps ninety-nine percent of their real content escapes us![6]

3. Busch, *Karl Barth*, 97.
4. Busch, *Karl Barth*, 97.
5. Busch, *Karl Barth*, 97–98.
6. Busch, *Karl Barth*, 98–99.

Metallica: *To Live is to Die*

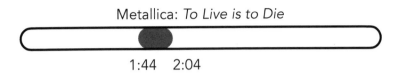

1:44   2:04

Gradually, a "first notebook with comments" was filled, but then a second and a third with "copybook exercises," until by September 1916, having reached only Romans 3, "quite a thick book" was already in hand.[7] By this time, our young pastor was so enthralled that he had gone a bit overboard, to the point of needing to beg for time off from his church's council after getting sick from overwork and exertion. By March of 1917— nine months after he had started—he had made it to chapter 5. And that is when his discovery of "The Strange New World within the Bible" began to have real consequences.

Metallica: *To Live is to Die*

2:04   2:12

The village in which our pastor lived, Safenwil, was a textile producing town and conditions in the factories were not ideal. The textile workers, under the influence of socialist thinking, wanted to organize into trade unions in order to advocate for better working conditions. The factory owners were against them.[8] The pastor sided with the workers. He recalls, "The aspect of Socialism that interested me most in Safenwil was the problem of the trade union movement. I studied it for years and also helped to form three flourishing trade unions (where there had been none before)."[9] By August and September of 1917, things in Safenwil were combustible. Public demonstrations and clashes were happening over the existence of these unions and the demands they were making. The "red pastor," as was his new nickname, participated in these demonstrations and even paid a personal visit to the owner of one of the knitting mills, recounting that "in his villa, like Moses with Pharaoh, asking him to let the people go out

7. Busch, *Karl Barth*, 101.

8. Busch, *Karl Barth*, 103.

9. Busch, *Karl Barth*, 103.

into the wilderness."[10] The conversation ended with a "flat rejection and a declaration of war" from the mill owner "in which I was told that I was the 'worst enemy' he had had in his whole life."[11] As tensions rose in Safenwil, church attendance dropped in protest of the red pastor, *except* that the textile workers began to come to church. "They came to me at the parsonage. But they also came to church. The socialists were the keenest audience for my sermons, not because I preached socialism but because they knew that I was the man who tried to help them."[12]

Metallica: *To Live is to Die*

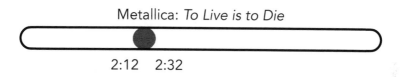

2:12   2:32

You know of whom I speak.

Metallica: *To Live is to Die*

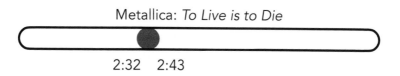

2:32   2:43

I tell you all of this because, (1) it is a great story, (2) it is even better to Metallica, and (3) it warns of what can happen if you leave behind the eggshells of shallow teachers, open the Bible, and read it like you have never read it before. More fully, this is a warning lest you discover in the Bible a deep understanding of *sin*. For this is what Romans 1, 2, 3, 4, and 5, the chapters he was working on at the time, are about. And Karl Barth's discovery of *sin* is what prompted both his tremendously radical commentary on Romans *and* his tremendously radical work on behalf of textile workers. In Romans 1–5, Karl Barth discovered sin (said with my best heavy metal growl).

Certainly, having grown up in a Christian home and having been trained for the pastorate, Barth had learned something *about* doctrines of sin. But given the *metanoia* his career takes and the fuse he lights with his commentary on Romans, and given his next fifty years of tremendously intellectual

10. Busch, *Karl Barth*, 104.

11. Busch, *Karl Barth*, 103–4.

12. Busch, *Karl Barth*, 104.

devotion to God's grace, it is obvious, to me at least, that sitting under that apple tree is when Karl first began to be taught *by God* what sin is.

Metallica: *To Live is to Die*

2:43 3:05

I too, had an experience with Romans 3. I had grown up in the church. I had parents who were (and are) Christians. My dad was ordained, came here to Princeton, in fact, and taught New Testament at two different Presbyterian colleges. So I "knew," or at least thought I did, a fair amount about Christianity. But as I got into high school and college, I also knew that I did not like Christianity. I thought it was boring, dead, and rule-ridden. I wanted some adventure, something new and different. I wanted something wholly other than what I had grown up with. I will spare you the whole story, but the short of it is, a long-haired guitarist named Jonah Werner gave me his spot on a mountaineering trip to British Columbia with his punk high school friends. He knew that I was not a Christian and he felt led to give away his spot so that I could go experience God. I went. I did. On the fifth day of the trip, our guides put us on a solo for twenty-four hours. No food, no tent, just a pad, a Bible, some sunscreen and the most beautiful granite living room you can imagine. I was alone, looking out over peaks, glaciers, and thousands of miles of pure wilderness. At some point I opened the Bible and read Romans 3. It changed my life. Not instantly, but in under ten hours. For one, it confronted me with the reality that no matter how good and decent I thought I was, it was not going to cut it. Out there in the wilderness, using Romans 3 and all the punks with whom I was surrounded, I think *God* taught me something about sin. God taught me that I was in it, there was nothing I could do about it, and that Jesus had fixed it. I do not think following God is boring, rule-ridden, and dead anymore. Just the opposite.

Metallica: *To Live is to Die*

3:05 3:22

By now, perhaps you have encountered enough of Cone and Calvin to show the radical character of their theology.[13] Those two! Talk about "tremendously radical." I keep asking myself what would happen if you put the two of them in a class together. That would ride the lightning, for sure.

Metallica: *To Live is to Die*

3:22   3:33

If you haven't read Cone or Calvin, you should. If you have read them, but cannot make sense of them, keep trying. They are important. But also realize, it is okay to admit that they are *totally* foreign to you. If so, you would not be alone.

After Karl's discovery of sin under the apple tree and of the God who has annihilated it in Jesus Christ, Barth's commentary on the Romans made him famous. He was invited to teach at the university in Germany's Göttingen. Only there, as a theology *professor*, mind you, did Karl begin to read Calvin. This was his response:

> Calvin is a cataract, a primeval forest, a demonic power, something directly down from the Himalayas, absolutely Chinese, strange, mythological; I lack completely the means, the suction cups, even to assimilate this phenomenon, not to speak of presenting it adequately. What I receive is only a thin little stream and what I can then give out again is only a yet thinner extract of this little stream.[14]

Metallica: *To Live is to Die*

3:33   4:01

Indeed, John Calvin can be a real headbanger, especially on the topic of sin, free will, and our ability to choose the good that God wills for us.

13. See Calvin, *Institutes* I.xv, II.i–ii; Cone, *Black Theology*, 87–115.
14. Barth, *Revolutionary Theology*, 101.

For Calvin, we have a free will that gives us a choice between sinning and not sinning, except that we cannot choose not sinning because we have inherited Adam's guilt and love of evil. So we always sin, except when by the grace of God we choose the right thing. Okay. Fine. That makes sense, right? We do not have to do it, except that we do, except when we do not, except that then it is not us, because we cannot. Now maybe that is the "right" way to think about sin, and in some ways that does match Paul's corkscrew logic of Romans 7:7–25. Maybe Calvin does have Scripture just as accurately exegeted as he should. But I, for one, am not so sure. For instance, is it really the case that we have to first think like Aristotle in order to truly understand sin? Reason, understanding, prudence, judgment, choice, appetite, will, mind, etc. Who thinks like this anymore, besides my Thomist friend, John? So this is my one problem with Calvin—it is so old, so out-of-date, so mechanistic, so different, so fully explained, so confident, and so contextual. And I am not in that context. I cannot fully adopt Calvin's doctrine of sin, though I do think it is worth trying to understand it, and I would encourage you to attempt at deciphering it in long hours of dedicated study, because we do not think and talk and live in Calvin's world. It is not necessarily that I think Calvin is *wrong*. Even if Calvin was 100 percent right, what he said *then now* needs to be said again in a new way. Just as we need to do with the church councils, we need to figure out what the past, Calvin in this case, was trying to affirm and then attempt to scrutinize it in light of Scripture and the revealed life of God as Jesus Christ. Then, we need to affirm the same thing in our own way in our own time.

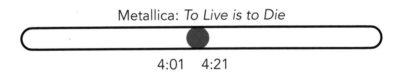

Metallica: *To Live is to Die*

4:01   4:21

But here is a bigger problem with Calvin's *moral* understanding of sin: suppose we always chose the right thing. Suppose we are always good. We still would not be God. We still would not necessarily be *with* God. We could be the perfect little human, and someday we will likely program or bio-synthesize an android to be one, but we still would be *apart* from God. We still would be *not-god,* an independent free floating autonomous "perfectly moral" being drifting off in ethical space all by ourselves. In this case, morality is not the problem, for no matter how *good* we are, we still would be un-god and un-with god. But if this is so, then even *goodness,* however it is construed, needs God to come, to build a bridge to it, to accept it, adopt it, and draw it in. Even *goodness* is dependent upon the gracious act of God bringing us into the eternal divine fellowship. In the language of Genesis 1, even *unfallen* Adam and Eve still needed God to come to them, to *walk* with them, and to *instruct* them on how to live. Even *unfallen* Adam and Eve still needed to be obedient to the divine guidance. And they already had God's blessing as being "very good." That they did not remain this way seems to have introduced sin and death into the world. Even in their unfallen morally perfect state, God's presence does not seem to be one that they control. They are still at the mercy of God wanting their company.

Metallica: *To Live is to Die*

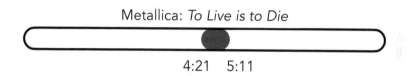

4:21   5:11

I have intentionally not given you a checklist of things to believe about sin or a history of the concept. I am not saying that such a checklist is impossible or unimportant. I have read a bunch of good ones this week that go something like, "A good doctrine of sin must include and account for . . ." Likewise it is worth investigating what it is previous Christians thought we were being redeemed from, something I have not provided you with (yet). But here is the greater question that I hope has risen to the center of your consciousness: What is it that *I* am, that *we* are, and that *this world* is being redeemed from?

What I would suggest is that we need to learn anew what sin is.

Metallica: *To Live is to Die*

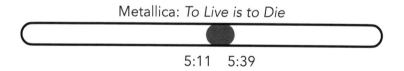

5:11   5:39

James Cone insists that you (we) should not listen to the privileged and their understanding of sin. There is great truth in this. If there are oppressors, do not let them define the terms of oppression. But Friedrich Nietzsche (*Genealogy of Morals*) and Elie Wiesel (*Dawn*) also share the powerful insight that the oppressed can just as easily divide the world up into an *us-versus-them* and manipulate the situation so as to turn the tables. In this way, the Servants become the Masters and become the ones who wield the power of oppression, even if, strangely enough, from below.

So I would suggest that, over and against learning about sin from me, or from Calvin, or from Barth, or from Cone, we bust open Romans and ask *God* to show us what in the hell sin is. If there is a God, he has done it before. Perhaps God will do it again, now, even if in a small way. Here, frankly, I recommend that you create your own checklist about the nature of sin based on Romans 1–8. What is it that you find?

Metallica: *To Live is to Die*

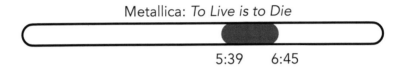

5:39   6:45

I. Is Sin Universal? How? Why?

Once you think you have gotten a hold on some of what sin is, let us ask: Is sin universal? Is it the case, that to live is to die? For all of us? How? Why? Here are three options:

Augustine and Sin as Hereditary

In the *City of God*, Augustine set forth what became the definitive articulation in Western Christianity for how original sin was passed along. He did so via the biologically hereditary nature of sin and death, writing:

> Their nature was deteriorated in that proportion to the greatness of the condemnation of their sin, so that what existed as punishment in those who first sinned, became a natural consequence in their children. For man is not produced by man, as he was from the dust. For dust was the material out of which man was made: man is the parent by whom man is begotten. Wherefore earth and flesh are not the same thing, though flesh be made of earth. But as man the parent is, such is man the offspring. In the first man, therefore, there existed the whole human nature, which was to be transmitted by the woman to posterity, when that conjugal union received the divine sentence of its own

condemnation; and what man was made, not when created, but when he sinned and was punished, this he propagated, so far as the origin of sin and death are concerned.[15]

In Augustine's eyes, the consequences of the disobedience actively chosen by the first parents was passed along in an hereditary way (via conjugal union) to all who come after. The guilt of original sin is both inherited by us and confirmed anew by our sinful actions. Thus Augustine suggests the fall in Eden has an effect on all human nature and that the sin of Adam and Eve has been transmitted to all of humanity via the "conjugal union." In doing so, he proposes a historical origination to sin and a temporal/biological mechanism by which sin is transmitted from Adam and Eve to others, assuming they are in the lineage of Adam and Eve. In this sense, sin can be seen as the fault of Adam and Eve. Had neither sinned, according to Augustine, we very well might still be kickin' it holy style in the Garden of Eden. As Augustine writes, "[T]hose first men in Paradise were blessed previously to sin, although they were uncertain how long their blessedness was to last, and whether it would be eternal (and eternal it would have been had they not sinned)."[16]

Metallica: *To Live is to Die*

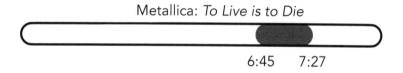

6:45   7:27

Schleiermacher and the Social Transmission of Sin

Contrary to Augustine's biological-historical view is Friedrich Schleiermacher's articulation of sin as a sociologically, psychologically, and culturally transmitted reality. In his account of the origin and transmission of sin, Schleiermacher (1768–1834) seeks to explain the presence of sin without recourse to either an historical narrative or a temporal process that initiates with Adam and Eve alone. While claiming agnosticism about our first parents, he thus is able to formulate a novel proposal as to how sin is transmitted without necessitating the existence of either a historical moment of origination or a singular mechanism of individual transmission. Quite

15. Augustine, *City of God*, 413–414.

16. Regarding the blessedness of Adam and Eve, see Augustine, *City of God*, 357.

plainly then, Schleiermacher does not need a literal reading of Genesis. He rather seeks to explain the origin of sin both individually and corporately, yet without recourse either to an individualized historical event or to a particular change in human nature. What he is able to build, therefore, is a sort of psychology of sin, one that makes all humanity responsible for sin, even original sin. No longer is the origin of sin "woman's/Eve's fault." No longer is the transmission of sin "man's/Adam's fault." Rather, *all* humanity is implicated in both the origin and transmission of sin. While certainly clever, the real genius is even deeper.

Schleiermacher is wary of a positive definition of sin-in-itself, what he terms an "objective elucidation of sin."[17] Instead he offers a number of definitions of sin that are constructed solely by their relation to grace. This strategy is evident in the following:

- "the only course open to us is to reckon everything as sin that has arrested the free development of the God-consciousness"[18]

- "sin consists in desiring what Christ condemns and *vice versa*"[19]

- "the consciousness of sin never exists in the soul of the Christian without the consciousness of the power of redemption, the form is never actually found without its complementary half which we are to describe later, and, if taken by itself alone, represents only that state of a hopeless incapacity in the spirit, which prevails outside the sphere of redemption"[20]

- sin is the "result of the unequal development of insight and will-power"[21]

To put it plainly, for Schleiermacher sin is not whatever is wrong in-itself, but whatever stands in the way of grace, even if that be "good" things. If that sounds relativistic or subjective, it is. For sin is that which is opposed to God, rejects God, and prefers itself even by good means. Schleiermacher's discussion of sin is necessarily, then, tied up with the experience of it in the Christian life. Indeed, central to the foundation of Schleiermacher's doctrine is our first-person struggles both with ourselves and the world around us. Indeed, any consciousness we have of God is comprised of the antithesis of sin and grace, neither of which can be divorced from the other.

17. Schleiermacher, *Christian Faith*, 271.
18. Schleiermacher, *Christian Faith*, 271.
19. Schleiermacher, *Christian Faith*, 273.
20. Schleiermacher, *Christian Faith*, 272.
21. Schleiermacher, *Christian Faith*, 275.

Schleiermacher is able to start quite minimally with the simple observation that none of us fully know God. Whatever it is that has impeded our knowledge of God can be called sin. Moreover, life itself can be characterized by the struggle, ongoing within us and around us, to both know and not know God. An analysis of this struggle leads to a twofold conclusion. On the one hand, we will realize that "the sin of the individual has its source in something beyond and prior to his own existence."[22] Thus, in some sense, sin is not our making and it resides in some outside source. On the other, we will realize that we are not the only pure thing in an otherwise dirtied world and that "every single sin of the individual must necessarily have its source in himself." In this sense, sin begins within and has its source in us. With this existential starting point, Schleiermacher is thus poised to construct full doctrines of both original and ongoing sin without reference to Eden. Let us look first at what he does with original sin, a doctrine that is not in relation to a historical Eden.

Schleiermacher maintains that "original sin is the sufficient ground of all actual sins."[23] While original sin is prior to actual sins, it nonetheless cannot be understood independently of the actual sins that it manifests itself in. In fleshing out what this means, Schleiermacher turns to language previously reserved for Adam and Eve's first sin. All of us, in fact, are equally guilty and responsible for the original sin that others are under, for in all of us there is an "originating original sin" which "brings forth and increases sin in oneself and others."[24] Original sin, therefore, is not simply the fault of Adam and Eve and can, in fact, be accounted for without reference to them. This is not simply to say that, had we been in Eden, we would have done the same as Adam and Eve did. It is, in fact, to say that each and every human is genuinely (not just hypothetically) guilty for the origin of sin into the world. Not only would we have done the same, we do do the same, introducing sin into realms where it was not. Conversely, this is not to say that we all are born in a state of original perfection. It is, however, to say that there is a point in every one of our lives where we forsake the God-consciousness we have and the relationship with God available to us and "voluntarily perpetuate"[25] the un-Godly option that resides within or around us. Moreover, every opportunity that we do not seek to maximize our God-consciousness is one that becomes victim to sin. This fallen moment is then transmitted on to the future.

22. Schleiermacher, *Christian Faith*, 279.

23. Schleiermacher, *Christian Faith*, 287.

24. Schleiermacher, *Christian Faith*, 287.

25. Schleiermacher, *Christian Faith*, 280.

With such a proposal, Schleiermacher is able to essentially solve, or at least redefine, the question of how original sin is transmitted to future generations. Contrary to Augustine's proposal, which locates the mode of transmission in sexual union, Schleiermacher is able to explain the transmission of original sin via simple social interaction. He writes, "it is transmitted by the voluntary actions of every individual to others and implanted within them."[26] Because all of our actions are a product of original sin and flow from it as their source, no action, however small or innocent, is untainted by sin. Like a dialect that is being passed along in language, sin is passed via all that we do, both in relation to ourselves and to others. The transmission of sin, therefore, is not traceable to any particular mechanism with a historical point of origin. It is, rather, atmospheric and embedded in the very fabric of every interaction between humans.

Moreover, as for historical commitments, this view needs only two or three generations of humanity. All that is required is empirical analysis of "the relation between each earlier generation and the one immediately succeeding it."[27] Since sin is transmitted in all deeds to all people, what such analysis reveals is that:

> the actual sin of the earlier is always the originating original sin for the later, while the sinfulness of the later generation since it produces the actual sins thereof, is also original sin, while yet as dependent upon the sin of the earlier it is originated, and thus is originated original sin as well.[28]

In other words, the actual sins of a previous generation set the stage for the inevitability of actual sin in a later generation. This "setting the stage" is what is properly called original sin, since it is the ground and basis that will affect all individual actual sins of that next generation. Finally, since each generation undergoes this anew, each generation can properly be held responsible for both original and actual sin in the world. Schleiermacher has thus constructed an account of the origins and transmission of sin without reference to a historical Eden or even a semi-literal reading of Genesis.[29]

26. Schleiermacher, *Christian Faith*, 287.

27. Schleiermacher, *Christian Faith*, 304.

28. Schleiermacher, *Christian Faith*, 304.

29. Thanks to the Wikipedia article on . . . *And Justice for All* (last accessed Oct. 10, 2019) I learned that in the following clip, the spoken word is comprised of lines by the seventeenth-century German Lutheran theologian and poet Paul Gerhardt ("When a man lies, he murders some part of the world"), the American sci-fi writer Stephan R. Donaldson ("These are the pale deaths which men miscall their lives"), and Metallica bassist Cliff Burton ("All this I cannot bear to witness any longer. Cannot the kingdom of salvation take me home?") who died in a tour band bus accident before the recording of . . . *And Justice for All.*

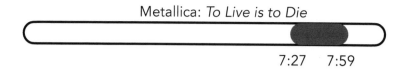

Metallica: *To Live is to Die*

7:27   7:59

II. Barth's Ontological Notion of Sin

As we turn from Augustine and Schleiermacher to Barth, let us start with Paul's statement in Galatians 5:17: "For what the flesh desires is opposed to the Spirit, and what the Spirit desires is opposed to the flesh; for these are opposed to each other." Here we have a binary opposition between flesh (σάρξ) and Spirit (πνεῦμα). This opposition is head to head. The one is ungodly, the other is godly. The one is bad, the other is good. Where does such binary opposition come from? Any guesses? I will give you a clue: it does not originate with Metallica.

In an attempt to build a christological understanding of sin, we may read the spirit/flesh binary out of John 1:1. Noteworthy in John 1's "In the beginning was the Word, and the Word was with God, and the Word was God. He was in the beginning with God" is the small Greek preposition πρός, which appears twice and simply means "to; towards." You do not see "towards" in the NRSV translation above because it is almost always translated in this verse as "with." And yet everywhere else, it generally means "towards." John 1's "the Word was *with* God" should really read "The Word was toward God." What does this mean?

If you recall Barth's construction of the Trinity as a threefold "give-it-away-ness," then there is something of that πρός; that *towardness*; that head-to-headedness; that face-to-faceness within the very being of God. There is an "otherness" of Father and Son, though each divine Other is oriented toward the other divine Others. Remember that? Now remember that the Word (λόγος), which is πρός God, is the Son. That λόγος that is πρός "the God" is, as John's prologue goes on to tell us in verse 14, Jesus Christ. The Greek word πρός has connotations of a vector (for example, Paul's Epistle πρός the Romans), of a relationship that exists "for the sake or purpose of," and even of beings that are in antithesis. Uniquely, πρός has the grammatical flexibility of "denoting a friendly or hostile relationship."[30] It can mean "for" *and* "against." Think of Jesus going πρός Jerusalem. Think of Jacob and Esau on a hostile

---

30. *Shorter Lexicon of the Greek New Testament*, v.s. "pros."

collision course in Genesis 33, except that their going πρός each other ends in an embrace of reconciliation, not retaliation.

In his treatment of the Trinity, Barth suggests that Father and Son stand before each other in a spirit of peace, service, and unity *for* and *towards* each other.[31] They stand before each "Other"[32] in the spirit of their love; their Holy Spirit. But here is where that dual capacity of πρός has import. For we are made to be in the image of God; an image that Christ alone defines, embodies, and fully lives out. This means we are made to be in a relationship to the Father as Jesus Christ is in relationship to the Father. This means we are supposed to live, not by our own abilities, powers, skills, and desires. Rather we are supposed to live "by the Spirit." That is, we are to live, not *independent* of God, but *in dependence* upon God. When we do so, we exemplify the harmonious, loving, peaceful mode of being πρός God, as Jesus was. When we live by our own desires, abilities, and powers, we necessarily, consciously or not, exemplify the hostile and rebellious mode of being πρός God. Regardless, all independence from God is sin. That sin is the natural and default position of this world is simply analytic to being "other" than God. Sin is basic to being a creature that is created by God as something distinct from God. We are by nature not-God and so we are by nature ungodly, even though, and this is the kicker, we are good. We are πρός God in fundamentally independent, and thus hostile ways, intentionally or not, immorally or not, because we do not know God as the Son knows God; because we do not live in total and absolute dependence and obedience toward God the Father, as does the Son. Because we try to support ourselves and keep ourselves upright, we fall over, over and over and over again. Remember the wilderness? This is why wilderness is so important: it shows us that we are beings dependent upon God. And the wilderness shows us that God is πρός us in a faithful way.

If we live by and rely upon God's Spirit, we will not be as Galatians 5:17 says, "opposed to each other." We will be at peace with each other. God the provider, we the provided for. Under Barth's conception, sin is not primarily about our moral standing, our goodness or badness: it is simply about our being separate and separated from the triune κοινωνία; our being other than God; our being creatures who are not the Creator; our being ungodly and not-God; our being of flesh and not of Spirit. Our

---

31. See for instance, *CD* IV/2, 352–53.

32. For instance: "God is One. That He is Father, Son and Holy Spirit, and that in this Trinity He is the epitome and sum of all riches, does not mean that His being is inwardly divided. The older dogmatics spoke here of the *perichoresis* of God's three persons or modes of being. It meant by this that He is always the One, not without the Other, but in and through the Other" (*CD* III/4, 32).

otherness means that no matter how good and moral we may be, we need the kingdom of salvation to come take us home. In this we hope that God reconciles our hostile and dissonant ungodliness into the beautiful melody that is the pure triune κοινωνία. Nothing else matters.

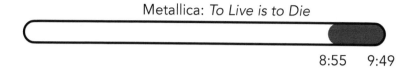

Metallica: *To Live is to Die*

8:55   9:49

— 6 —

Christology + Humanity: Patience

W hat are you?

In case you think that is a silly question, please consider that a *good* answer to it remains one of the most elusive holy grails in human questioning:

For instance, in this *New York Times* article, we find this about "The Riddle of the Human Species" by Harvard biologist E. O. Wilson:

> The task of understanding humanity is too important and too daunting to leave to the humanities. Their many branches, from philosophy to law to history and the creative arts, have described the particularities of human nature with genius and exquisite detail, back and forth in endless permutations. But they have not explained why we possess our special nature and not some other out of a vast number of conceivable possibilities. In that sense, the humanities have not accounted for a full understanding of our species' existence. So, just what are we?[1]

This is the question we are taking up here. Now our topic is formally on christology. Christology discussions have traditionally been on the question of how the divine and the human are related in the person of Christ. Here, I want to talk about christology and anthropology under the same heading. That is, here we are not only asking how Christ was God and human but also, even more basically, "What is a human?" In a way we are asking, "Who do you say that I am?" about both God and ourselves.

Here are three moments in the life of Jesus:

1. Jesus in the womb of Mary: "He [Joseph] went there to register with Mary, who was pledged to be married to him and was expecting a child" (Luke 2:5).

1. Wilson, "Riddle of the Human Species."

70

2. Jesus walking uphill: "After six days Jesus took Peter, James and John with him and led them up a high mountain" (Mark 9:2).

3. Jesus hanging on the cross and crying his last words: "My God, my God, why have you forsaken me?" (Matt 27:46).

Christology, as we have said, is the problem of how Jesus was both God and human. So the question is, are these events in the life of the human Jesus or are they events in the life of God? The tradition has been nearly uniform in that since God is immutable (cannot change), infinite (and so cannot move from one space to another—God is already everywhere), and impassible (not able to suffer), the above are events that play out on the *human* side of Jesus' two natures, but they do not make contact with the other divine nature of Jesus. If the divine nature is really a part of these events at all, it is along for the ride in an immutable, infinite, and impassible way. What this really meant, when push came to shove, is that a lot of traditional theology assumes a slight modalism, where the human aspect of Jesus is really a mode or front for revealing something about God, but that divine something/someone ultimately resides above, behind, beyond the actual robed figure of Jesus. Yet modalism is a heresy. While Arianism has been easy to avoid in formal creedal affirmations on the Sabbath, an Ebionite tendency towards adoptionism has been harder for the tradition to swear off on the other days of the week.

It is the thesis of this chapter that there is an understanding of the two natures that can avoid this modalistic tendency and that can articulate how the above events are to be attributed to both the human and the divine sides of Jesus. Now, if you are wary of saying that it was the divine eternal being of God as the second person of the holy Trinity in Mary's bubbling tummy, you would find good company with many, if not most, Christian intellectuals. But keep in mind, if it is not God in the belly, how can it be God on the cross? And if it ain't *God* on the cross, then how was the Son of God resurrected from the dead? And if it was not the Son of God who was raised, then we might as well all pack up, close the churches, and go be ski bums. See I Corinthians 15.

A primary danger here, one that the tradition has never sought to avoid, is that if we define divine nature and human nature in advance of our encounters with Christ, we put a pre-conceived straight jacket on God, and in the end, humanity as well. If we do not want to do this, we might follow Barth and let the *lifetime* of Jesus be constitutive and instructive of both the human nature and divine nature of Jesus. Let us deal first with the problem of Jesus' humanity. Then we will deal with the problem of His divinity.

I. Barth on the Humanity of Jesus

We start with that small opening phrase in the Chalcedonian Creed, one you might have thought was just pious but empty holy speak:

> We, then, following the holy Fathers, all with one consent, teach people to confess one and the same Son, our Lord Jesus Christ, the same perfect in Godhead and also perfect in manhood; . . . truly God and truly man.[2]

"Truly God and truly [hu]man . . ." is a powerful little phrase, and if we take it seriously, it is going to flip our whole world right side up. Here is how:

For Barth, Jesus shows Himself to be the truth about humanity "most particularly" and subsequently about humanity "in general" as well.[3] Given this, it is *not* the case that humanity is a general category that must be conceptually defined and filled out *in abstracto*, a category which then Jesus becomes a part of as its chief example or instantiation.[4] If this were the case, this could (and would) fuel a most vicious form of natural theology in which *we* would be free to define the humanity of Christ according to whatever we do or do not like about ourselves. This is what the tradition has basically always tried to do. Barth shuts down this opportunity, arguing "it is not possible for us to know in advance" what "human nature" truly is.[5] Barth intends, then, to go in quite the opposite direction. Barth turns to God's revelation as Jesus Christ for the definition of a human. Human nature "is to be explained by Him, not He by it."[6] This means a reversal of the traditional route:

---

2. Schaff, *Creeds*, 62.

3. *CD* III/2, 3.

4. In Barth's view such was the problem with previous articulations of predestination. For instance see *CD* II/2, 76: "We found previously that the doctrine of election must not begin *in abstracto* either with the concept of an electing God or with that of elected man. It must begin concretely with the acknowledgement of Jesus Christ as both the electing God and elected man." Likewise, *CD* III/2, 59: "Even in relation to Him, therefore, do we not have to take account of a universal humanity? Indeed we do, but not a humanity prior to or outside His earthly history in which He was participant in this history under specific limitations and conditions; not a neutral humanity in which He might have had quite a different history; not a humanity which we can seek and analyse in abstraction from or otherwise than in His work. These are conceptions of the humanity of Jesus which the New Testament not only does not encourage but forbids us to entertain."

5. *CD* III/2, 59.

6. *CD* II/2, 59.

> In so doing, we leave the traditional way, . . . Thus, contrary
> to the usual procedure, we must first enquire concerning this
> one man, and then on this basis concerning man in general.
> In His own person He is God's Word to men, of divine and
> human essence, man in immediate confrontation and union
> with God, and therefore true man, and the revelation of the
> truth about man.[7]

Because the figure of Jesus is, for Barth, "both true God and true man,"[8] this one individual is *the* true definition of humanity. "*Ecce homo*"[9] ("Behold the Man," John 19:5) though spoken mockingly by Pilate, is in fact the truth: *Ecce homo,* says Barth, means "Behold, *This* man *is* man"[10] and "Nowhere but in this man" is human nature "primarily and properly established and revealed."[11] For Barth, Jesus alone defines what human nature really is, for "He alone is primarily and properly [hu]man."[12] In Jesus' life before us as the "true man,"[13] all "vague ideas"[14] and "other theories"[15] of what human nature is and might be are finally relativized. They become "possible and useful only in connexion" with the "human nature of Jesus" which demonstrates itself to be the "exhaustive and superior"[16] definition of the true form of humanity.

Here is an example. When my son, Elias, was in pre-school he brought home a big block letter M with magazine images of "m" words pasted on it. Among the variety of pictures smudged on the big M was Richard Nixon, who represented "man." While Nixon might be an acceptable example of a sinful human, for Barth, only Jesus of Nazareth can be called the true instantiation of humanity. No one truly defines humanity but Christ.

If Jesus is "the truth of man"[17] in particular, and therefore the truth about all humanity in general, then here is the kicker. This means we are

---

7. *CD* III/2, 44.

8. *CD* II/2, 53.

9. See *CD* III/2, 44–46 for Barth's fine print exegesis of the phrase. Barth insists that in discussions of humanity, "It is exegetically not merely legitimate but imperative to recall at this point the saying of Pilate."

10. *CD* III/2, 43. Emphasis restored from German: "Dieser Mensch ist der Mensch" (*KD* III/2, 49)

11. *CD* III/2, 42. See also II/4, 42–43.

12. *CD* III/2, 43.

13. *CD* III/2, 43, 44, 50, 53.

14. *CD* III/2, 43.

15. *CD* III/2, 47.

16. *CD* III/2, 43.

17. *CD* III/2, 54.

not true humans. Because, for Barth, human nature is found definitively in Jesus, it is not found definitively in us. Yet Barth argues, compellingly I think, this is good news and is to our benefit, for Jesus stands as "an effective protest" against our "self-contradiction and all the self-deception in which we try to conceal it."[18] The true form of humanity in Jesus shows us that our human nature is only a shadowy and "debatable quantity."[19] Our humanity is an imperfect "concealed copy"[20] of that which exists perfectly in Jesus. Our lives are instead "dialectical" and "in antithesis," having "no unity."[21] In and of ourselves, we exist in a "striving to attain real humanity" but instead only find an "unrest" that exemplifies the "hopelessness of our illusions" and the "self-contradiction" of our failed "attempted solution."[22] But, and herein is another reason why proclamation of the true humanity of Jesus is good news, Jesus Christ as true God and true [hu]man is the annihilation of our self-contradiction. This is owing to the fact that "In Him is human nature without human sin" and when "He becomes what we are, He does not do what we do, and so He is not what we are."[23] Hence, it is in this one man of Jesus that "Here God finds human nature blameless."[24] This exchange means that "The human nature of Jesus spares and forbids us our own. Thus *he* is our justification."[25] There is then, for Barth, in Jesus Christ a great exchange between His true humanity and our false humanity.

Barth's goal is to ensure that human nature must be defined by the individual Jesus and that "we are partakers of human nature as and because Jesus is first partaker of it."[26] Our *being human,* if in fact we have any humanity at all, is then because "we derive wholly from Jesus."[27] Of the source of true humanity, then, we must confess, "primarily it is His and not ours."[28] Jesus, and Jesus alone, is the not only the "prototype"[29] but the "free

18. *CD* III/2, 47.

19. *CD* III/2, 47.

20. *CD* III/2, 50.

21. *CD* III/2, 47.

22. *CD* III/2, 47.

23. *CD* III/2, 48.

24. *CD* III/2, 48.

25. *CD* III/2, 47.

26. *CD* III/2, 50.

27. *CD* III/2, 50.

28. *CD* III/2, 50.

29. *CD* III/2, 50.

demonstration"[30] by God of "the true nature of man."[31] So if we want to understand humanity in general, or indeed our own humanity in particular, we need to ask, "What is *His* humanity?"[32]

The answer is that "humanity" is not then primarily an organic, biological, physical, or psychological category. A human is not simply an isolated and or independent "thing." On the contrary, the humanity of Christ shows us that humanity is a relational category, a kind of *being-with-and-for-others*. But even this is too vague. Humanity is not primarily a sociological, cultural, or co-creaturely relation; it is a theological relation, one that requires our looking to God's self-revelation in Jesus in order for it to be understood. What humanity is, says Barth, "is decided by the primary text, i.e., by the humanity of the man Jesus."[33] This means that humanity is primarily a *theological* relation. It is a being that relates to God. Let us be even more specific.

Based on the life of Jesus, Barth makes it clear, we can say "basically and comprehensively" that to be a human "is to be with God."[34] For Barth, to be human means to be a being in "dependence" on God;[35] to be elected for grace, and conversely to be preserved "from nothingness";[36] to be a being in "gratitude" toward God;[37] to be a listener who lives in "response to the

30. *CD* III/2, 40.

31. *CD* III/2, 51.

32. *CD* III/2, 55.

33. *CD* III/2, 225.

34. *CD* III/2, 135–36: "If it is not indifferent, incidental or subordinate, but ontologically decisive, that one man among all others is the man Jesus; if to be a man is to dwell with this man who is our true and absolute Counterpart; if to be a man is to be concretely with this man who is like us for all that He is so unlike in the full majesty of God, then the fact that we are with God is not merely one of many determinations of our being, derivative and mutable, but the basic determination, original and immutable." Based upon this, Barth will boldly say Godlessness is an "ontological" impossibility for man.

35. *CD* III/2, 140: "If human being is a being with God, we have to say first and comprehensively that it is a being which derives from God. It is a being dependent on God."

36. *CD* III/2, 143: "What is this will of God? We may express it most simply as follows. It is the will of God that the Yes which He as the Creator has spoken to His creation should prevail; that all men and all creatures should be delivered from evil, i.e., from that which God the Creator has rejected, and preserved from its threat and power."

37. *CD* III/2, 166: ". . . the being of man can and must be more precisely defined as a being in gratitude." See also *CD* II/1, 669: "This creature is grateful. It knows God, and itself becomes a new creature, by being thankful. To believe in Jesus Christ means to become thankful. This is to be understood as *radically as it must be in this context*. It is not merely a change of temper or sentiment or conduct and action. It is the

Word of God";[38] to be a being that lives in "obedience" to the command of God;[39] to be a being that lives "in responsibility" to the "judgment of God";[40] and finally to be a being in obedience, humility, and freedom before God.[41] More should be said about each one of these, and I would encourage you to read the examples I have cited below in the footnotes, or all seven-hundred pages of *Church Dogmatics* III/2. Briefly, to be human means to live in daily self-willed dependence, gratitude, and joy towards the God who provides for every need. It is to live like Jesus who "entrusted Himself to the providential care of His Father."[42] Throughout his anthropology, Barth makes it clear this is what it means to be human because this is how Jesus Christ lives before God. Such is the way that within the triune God there was, is, and will be a human. This means the young, the ill, the old, the incapacitated are not less human. On the contrary, they show us more truly what it means to

change of the *being* of man before God brought about by the fact that God has altered His attitude to man. It is the change from the impossible and dangerous position of ingratitude to that of gratitude as a new and better position before God which alone is possible and full of hope. *Gratitude is to be understood not only as a quality and an activity but as the very being and essence of this creature.* It is not merely grateful. It is itself gratitude. It can see itself only as gratitude because in fact it can only exist as this, as pure gratitude towards God."

38. *CD* III/2, 176: "1. As human life is a being in responsibility before God, it has the character of a knowledge of God. We have stated that the being of man as responsibility is response, being in the act of response to the Word of God. But if it is as it responds, then it is a being which knows, accepts and affirms the Word of God and therefore God Himself. It responds as it hears the Word of God as such, and receives what it declares."

39. *CD* III/2, 179: "2. As the being of man is being in responsibility before God, it has the character of obedience to God." See also II/2 §36.1 *The Command of God and the Ethical Problem*, especially page 535: "But the problem of obedience is the problem of human behaviour," and page 539: "Therefore 'to become obedient,' 'to act rightly,' 'to realise the good,' never means anything other than to become obedient to the revelation of the grace of God; to live as a man to whom grace has come in Jesus Christ." Likewise, one can turn to §37, *The Command as the Claim of God* in which one can read that, "Obedience to God always means that we become and are continually obedient to Jesus." (II/2, 568)

40. *CD* III/2, 191: "To come from God and therefore to go to Him is thus to submit oneself utterly to the judgment of God. There is no way to God which avoids this narrow defile. Man cannot come to God otherwise than by laying himself upon these scales. All gratitude and responsibility, all knowledge and obedience in the fulfilment of human being, if it is genuine and is really related to the true and gracious God, must consist and finally be expressed in the fact that in all these things man appeals to the judgment of the gracious God that he may receive in His Word and pronouncement not only the foundation of his being but also its confirmation and consummation."

41. *CD* III/2, 179, 190, and 192: "4. As the being of man is a being in responsibility before God, it has the character of the freedom which God imparts to it."

42. *CD* III/2, 67. For an alternate brief treatment of what it means to be human see II/2, 175–180, especially p. 178 and III/4, 43–44.

be human. It is then the most powerful, the most independent, the most autonomous, the most selfish who are actually the most inhuman. Amen. Now, we will turn to the divine side of things.

II. Barth on the Divinity of the Son

More radical than deriving anthropology from christology is Barth's novel claim that Jesus brings His humanity with Him from eternity. Christ's humanity, then, is not something that primarily pertains to the creaturely side of Jesus, it obtains on His very divinity itself. How can Jesus be the eternal human? We dive in.

For Barth, categorical definitions of humanity are dependent upon the way in which Jesus lives before the Father. Moreover, it is because Jesus lives in these specific ways that there is in fact any such thing as "humanity" in the first place. Jesus, not Adam, is then really the first human. Not the first human creature, mind you (that would be Arianism), but the first being that has a human relation to God the Father. But if you have been paying attention, then you will realize that Jesus is the first human because He is the Son of God, not because He became a birthed organic thing with legs and a brain. Says Barth, Jesus "is not a real man in spite but *because* of the fact that He is the Son of God."[43] "He is the Son of God as He is man and man as He is the Son of God."[44] The humanity of the Son is thus a result of the ongoing will of the Son: "He (as God) wills Himself (as man)."[45] And if you have been paying attention, then you will start to guess that we are the way we are because He is the way He is. It is almost as if we are made in *His* image.

"To be a human," "humanity," and "human nature" are thus all, for Barth, references to and descriptions of how the Son lives before the Father not only in time but in eternity as well, even before time's beginning. For, "it is not merely the eternal but the *incarnate* λόγος and therefore the man Jesus who is included in this circle" of "the Trinity."[46] So for Barth, Jesus "did not give up His eternal divinity when He concealed it to become man,"[47] but is, rather, always "both God and man."[48]

To be truly human is then not only to be truly like the birthed human Jesus, it is to be like the divine *Son* who lives the divine life in dependence,

43. *CD* III/2, 58; emphasis mine.

44. *CD* III/2, 66.

45. *CD* II/2, 117.

46. *CD* III/2, 65; emphasis mine.

47. *CD* III/2, 65.

48. *CD* III/2, 66.

gratitude, and obedience towards the Father. To be truly human is to put one's life in dependence upon God the Father and to be nourished and sustained through His Spirit. As we have seen, for Barth, a human being "is a being dependent upon God."[49] This is so because in the first instance this is how the Son of God lives before God the Father. It is Jesus the Son's "very participation in the divine which is the basis of His humanity." For Barth then, "Jesus is man in and by the very fact that He is the Son of God and that He is included in the circle of the inner life of the Godhead."[50]

Ultimately, "humanity" is a category created, defined, and upheld by the Son of God alone in His eternal self-humbling, self-subordination, and self-willed obedience in love and service towards God the Father. For Barth, all of this is learned from the *lifetime* of Jesus Christ because in that life we are shown that Jesus is the "creaturely being who as such not only exists *from* God and *in* God but absolutely *for* God instead of Himself."[51] The lifetime of Jesus is thus constitutive of what a true human life looks like *and* what the true divine life looks like.

This *existing-for-God* as the human Jesus who is, nevertheless, also the divine Son establishes that the humility of Christ's humanity is "no accident or caprice" but is "His essence."[52] For, "doing the work of God does not mean for Jesus anything alien."[53] Christ is, after all, eternally oriented toward (πρός) God. As Barth elaborates regarding the provocative nature of Christ's servanthood, this "humility in which He dwells and acts in Jesus Christ is not alien to Him, but proper to Him."[54] Barth will conclude that while "His humility is a *novum mysterium* for us in whose favour He executes it," for God the Son *ad intra* "this humility is no *novum mysterium* [i.e., a new mystery]."[55] How can this be? Let us return to the Red Hot Chili Peppers.

Red Hot Chili Peppers: *Give it Away*

0:00   0:11

49. *CD* III/2, 140.
50. *CD* III/2, 66.
51. *CD* III/2, 133; emphasis mine.
52. *CD* III/2, 220.
53. *CD* III/2, 63.
54. *CD* IV/1, 193.
55. *CD* IV/1, 193.

We return to what we earlier called the Triune Moment. This is a "moment in the circle of the inner life of God," which we have earlier described in terms of the give-it-away-ness of the triune God. Recall that this threefold "give-it-away-ing" is the ongoing manner in which God is triune. In this moment, "God stands before Himself; the Father before the Son, the Son before the Father . . . in the unity of the Holy Spirit."[56] Recall also that the tradition has affirmed the three persons of the Trinity are one in essence and substance, even while, as Augustine says, "the Father is not the Son," the "Son is not the Father," and the "Holy Spirit is neither the Father nor the Son."[57] Now we are going to zoom in on the second person, the eternal Son, and ask how it might be that this Son is both true God and true human in each triune moment.

More specifically, we can now say that in the second person as the Son, God the Son manifests His divine freedom within the Triune Moment in a way so as *not* to be self-filled by His own power and abilities but rather to empty Himself, letting the Father continually beget Him in the Spirit. In that "being begotten" the Son is found, as Augustine says, to be equal with God, in the *forma dei*, "the form of God."[58] Working from the logic of Philippians 2, and Barth argues this is the deep logic of the whole New Testament, the Son of God does not desire to be God in and of Himself by His own power and willing. Instead the Eternal Son perpetually lays down His life and gives it away in service to the Father. The Son manifests His being by humbling Himself, by making Himself not-equal to the Father, by willing Himself as not-Father, and thus reducing Himself to the *forma servi*, the form of the servant. As Augustine writes, "So the Son of God is God the Father's equal by nature, by condition his inferior. In the form of a servant which He took He is the Father's inferior; in the form of God in which He existed even before He took this other He is the Father's equal."[59] Barth will take such thinking and, rather than locate such a humbling only once in the incarnation, make it perpetually part of the uninterrupted cycle of the triune divine life.

It must be said, the goal of this subordination is not holding of the other down for oppression, but, in fact, for glorification. If there is a "lesser," a "second," a "subordinate," an "other" in God, it is so God the Father can exalt that and raise it up; so God can glorify it and give it the name above all names. So the Father, despite the perpetual humbling of the Son, is for

56. *CD* II/1, 49.

57. Augustine, *De Trinitate*, 69.

58. Augustine, *De Trinitate*, 74–75.

59. Augustine, *De Trinitate*, 74.

the Father's own part perpetually raising up the Son, exalting and glorify-ing the Son in the Spirit. Referencing *Church Dogmatic* I/1's earlier treat-ment of the "fine theologumenon of the *perichoresis*,"[60] this also means, in other words, that in the form of God, Jesus "does not seek His own glory" but humbles Himself to the form of a servant, allowing His glory to come to Him "from a very different source."[61] What is this "different source?" It is Easter's resurrection that discloses "The One who honours and glorifies Him is His Father."[62] The Son thus perpetually wills to do the will of the Father and not to do His own will in eternity and time. This perpetual will-ing is replicated and repeated in fresh ways in time, just as Jesus proclaims of Himself in John 6:38 regarding the whole of His time: "for I have come down from heaven, not to do my own will, but the will of him who sent me." Accordingly, Barth reasons on this basis:

> The giving of the Son by the Father indicates a mystery, a hidden
> movement in the *inner life* of the Godhead. But in the self-sacri-
> fice of the man Jesus for His friends *this intra-divine movement*
> is no longer hidden but revealed. For what the man Jesus does
> by this action is *to lay bare this mystery*, to actualise the human
> and therefore the visible and knowable and apprehensible aspect
> of this portion of the divine history of *this primal moment* of
> *divine volition* and *execution*.[63]

As God, the Son of God, does not choose to be God *over* the Father, relying upon the Son's own divine abilities and perfections, which He most assur-edly has as "God from God, Light from Light, true God from true God." Rather in Barth's triune logic, the Son of God perpetually volunteers to be God *under* the Father in a "self-emptying and self-humbling"[64] relation-ship upon God the Father in order to manifest the goodness, faithfulness, and reliability of the Father's continually outpouring love. Christ is thus the inverse of so many biblical narratives of sons who seek to overthrow their fathers. Contrary to an Absalom (2 Sam 15), for instance, the Son of God does not choose to establish, found, or even raise up His own life, but instead allows His life to be chosen, founded, and raised up by the Father. For Barth, this is what it means that the Son can be *human* eternally: "the humanity of Jesus and His participation in the Godhead are not irreconcil-able and antithetic, but that it is His very participation in the divine which

60. *CD* III/2, 65.

61. *CD* III/2, 65.

62. *CD* III/2, 65.

63. *CD* III/2, 66; emphasis mine.

64. *CD* IV/1, 193.

is the basis of His humanity."[65] Again, "Jesus is man in and by the very fact that He is the Son of God and that He is included in the circle of the inner life of the Godhead."[66]

Barth's logic is thus that what happens in time as revelation is a real time repetition or recapitulation of what happens in eternity as the inner triune life of God. This is, after all, what makes revelation God's *self*-revelation. For recall that Jesus is not just the truly human, He is *truly God*. And this means there is no other God apart from the one disclosed as Jesus Christ. Barth sums up this line of thought in a set of important passages in *Church Dogmatics* IV/1's aptly named paragraph §59, "The Obedience of the Son of God."[67] These passages argue that the *humility* and thus the *humanity* of Jesus is no *novum mysterium* to God but in fact exists antecedently in the humility and thus the humanity of the Son in the inner triune relations of God:

> If the humility of Christ is not simply an attitude of the man Jesus of Nazareth, if it is the attitude of this man because, according to what takes place in the atonement made in this man (according to the revelation of God in Him), there is a humility grounded in the being of God, then something else is grounded in the being of God Himself. For, according to the New Testament, it is the case that the humility of this man is an act of obedience, not a capricious choice of lowliness, suffering and dying, not an autonomous decision this way, not an accidental swing of the pendulum in this direction, but a free choice made in recognition of an appointed order, in execution of a will which imposed itself authoritatively upon Him, which was intended to be obeyed. If, then, God is in Christ, if what the man Jesus does is God's own work, this aspect of the self-emptying and self-humbling of Jesus Christ as an act of obedience cannot be alien to God. But in this case we have to see here the other and inner side of the mystery of the divine nature of Christ and therefore of the nature of the one true God—that He Himself is also able and free to render obedience.[68]

65. *CD* III/2, 66.

66. *CD* III/2, 66.

67. For an earlier corresponding treatment of the "genuine obedience" which the Son of God "renders as the Son of God" in His "active" election of Himself to be man, see *CD* II/2, 103–6, especially 105. Likewise, this obedience also takes place in time as the answer to our ethical problem. For instance, see *CD* II/2, 540: "In Him the obedience demanded of us men has already been rendered."

68. *CD* IV/1, 193.

We might also read a famous and oft-discussed passage from *Church Dogmatics* IV/1:

> We have not only not to deny but actually to affirm and understand as essential to the being of God the offensive fact that there is in God Himself an above and a below, a *prius* and a *posterius*, a superiority and a subordination. And our present concern is with what is apparently the most offensive fact of all, that there is a below, a *posterius*, a subordination, that it belongs to the inner life of God that there should take place within it obedience. We have to reckon with such an event even in the being and life of God Himself. It cannot be explained away either as an event in some higher or supreme creaturely sphere or as a mere appearance of God. Therefore we have to state firmly that, far from preventing this possibility, His divine unity consists in the fact that in Himself He is both One who is obeyed and Another who obeys.[69]

In light of this, the sermon punch line of my friend Isak is most fitting: "If God is at the bottom, what's the point of being at the top?"

III. Conclusion: Barth on Humanity and Divinity

In sum then, the ongoing *humility* of the Son of God before the Father as part of the inner triune give-it-away-ness in the unity of the Holy Spirit is, for Barth, the key that unlocks the old mystery of both "What is a human?" and "What is a god?" That *humility makes humanity* is the rule learned from Jesus of Nazareth who lives in time in correspondence and continuity with how He lives in eternity in the inner circle of the triune fellowship. This humility is eternally proper to the Son of God in His life before the Father, and this same humility is repeated and lived out in unique ways in time as Jesus. In short, for Barth, the eternal *humanity* of the Son is owing to the eternal *humility* of the Son.[70] "Because He is the Son of God, it is only as such that He is real man."[71] But this humility shows itself capable of lowliness. Indeed, not just capable, but even more it manifests its very divine power in the activity of self-humbling and self-emptying, for it is from that being in lowliness that God the Father exalts Him to the highest

---

69. *CD* IV/1, 200–201.

70. For concerns about social trinitarianism, see footnote 20 of chapter 1, page 8.

71. *CD* III/2, 70. Barth immediately sends the reader back to his earlier treatments of *anhypostasis* and *enhypostasis*. See *CD* I/2, 163–65.

place. But this means that if you want to start being truly human, you had better take up a cross and follow Him. And since the road to Golgotha is no weekend jaunt, but requires a lifetime, the answer to the question "What are we?" is revealed only as we follow Christ. And as any seasoned disciple knows, waiting and hoping for that which we do not currently have requires a good deal of patience.

Guns N' Roses: *Patience*

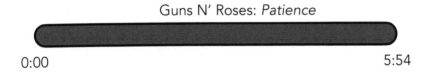

0:00   5:54

Afterword: On Nietzsche's Brilliance

> I regard Christianity as the most fatal seductive lie that has yet existed, as the great unholy lie: I draw out the after-growth and sprouting of its ideal from beneath every form of disguise, I reject every compromise position with respect to it—I force war against it.[72]

Or again,

> The Christian conception of God—God as god of the sick, God as a spider, God as spirit—is one of the most corrupt conceptions of the divine ever attained on earth.[73]

What was it that Nietzsche found so intolerable and oppressive in Christianity? In brief, I would like to suggest that it was nothing other than today's topic. In other words, Nietzsche dislikes christology and the anthropology it entails. And though I cannot make a full historical argument for it now, my own feeling is that Nietzsche and Barth are the two systematicians who have peered mostly deeply into the waters of christology. The one runs away kicking and screaming. The other dives in thinking and praising.

Why does Nietzsche have so deep a hatred for Christianity? It is not just that it is false, which Nietzsche thought it was, but that at its core Christianity glorifies the act of negating one's will. Christianity's very founder says, "Not my will." And this man Jesus is then believed to be God Himself! God is thus

---

72. Nietzsche, *Will to Power*, 117.

73. Nietzsche, *Portable*, 585.

the negation of His own will; the negation of His own will to power. Self-denial is forever elevated to the level of divinity.[74] This represents, in Nietzsche's eyes, true *evil*. "I abhor Christianity with a deadly hatred," he writes.[75] "It has waged deadly war against this higher type of man" and has "sided with all that is weak and base, with all failures; it has made an ideal of whatever *contradicts* the instinct of the strong life to preserve itself."[76]

It is important to see that Nietzsche's disgust is not based on anything other than the New Testament witness to the life of Jesus. The idea of God sacrificing himself for the sake of mankind; the idea of God redeeming the unlovable and unredeemable; the idea of God on the cross, Nietzsche admits, was a pure "stroke of genius."[77] In this he commends and respects Jesus, but only as his most sworn opponent. Thus, for Nietzsche, "Nothing is less innocent than the New Testament."[78] The Christian God as Jesus Christ on the cross must be seen as "miserable, as absurd, as harmful, not merely as an error but as a *crime against life*."[79]

Against this, Nietzsche gives us what he considers is his greatest gift to mankind: his Zarathustra, his *Übermensch*. Zarathustra is no new god, he is merely the first of the new gods. He is the example, not the leader. As he says, "This is *my* way; where is yours? . . . For *the* way—that does not exist."[80] Zarathustra comes to teach the Übermensch and to "harden" humanity and push humanity upward:

> Man needs what is most evil in him for what is best in him—
> that whatever is most evil is his best power and the hardest
> stone for the highest creator; and that man must become better
> and more evil.[81]

It is perhaps for this reason that Nietzsche latches onto the ancient god Dionysus. Dionysus, the god of wine, is the one who overcomes the self in intoxication, in revelry, in ecstasy, in madness, and in an unreflective act ontology. "I am a disciple of the philosopher Dionysus."[82] As he clarifies, "Dionysus

---

74. See, for instance, Luke 22:42 and the ethics of Romans 6.

75. Nietzsche, *Will to Power*, 364.

76. Nietzsche, *Portable*, 571.

77. Nietzsche, *Basic Writings*, 528.

78. Nietzsche, *Will to Power*, 117.

79. Nietzsche, *Portable*, 627.

80. Nietzsche, *Portable*, 307.

81. Nietzsche, *Portable*, 330–31.

82. Nietzsche, *Basic Writings*, 673.

is, as is known, also the God of Darkness."[83] Thus it is, quite literally that Nietzsche seeks to articulate a way immediately leading away from the cross. Christ on the cross is the way of weakness and negation, of dependence upon "Another." Nietzsche yearns for the maximization of solitary strength and power. Zarathustra's way is the way of the self: "At this point the real answer to the question, how one becomes what one is, can no longer be avoided . . ." Nietzsche's answer? Selfishness.[84] Selfishness, according to Nietzsche, results in our freedom for otherwise we are bound to others.

Nietzsche's anthropology is thus fundamentally—like Barth's!—consciously and systematically based on Christ. Nietzsche is not just generically anti-Christian, but deeply, purely, and brilliantly anti-*Jesus*. Here we have the antithesis distilled into its purest simplicity: *Dionysus versus the Crucified*. "Have I been understood?" Nietzsche begs of us, as he reflects back on his entire career.[85] And lest there should be any doubt, he boldly and happily proclaims, "I am, in Greek, and not only in Greek, the Antichrist."[86]

I understand. What Nietzsche represents, in many ways, is a fully coherent philosophical temper tantrum. He wants what he wants now! And he wants to be God! Ironically, if Christ elects all humanity for divine glorification and is gracious even to those by whom He is rejected, Nietzsche's time is coming. Nietzsche's greatest error, then, is not the death of God. He understands this better than the rest of us! It is that he is simply impatient for and coldhearted toward the glory Christ has destined for him. Compared with Jesus of Nazareth, the eternal divine Son, Nietzsche is impatient. And this makes Nietzsche inhuman, all too inhuman.

Nirvana: *Tourette's*

0:00   1:35

83. Nietzsche, *Basic Writings*, 768.
84. Nietzsche, *Basic Writings*, 709.
85. Nietzsche, *Basic Writings*, 791.
86. Nietzsche, *Basic Writings*, 719.

— 7 —

Justification: Testify

Rage Against the Machine: *Wake Up*

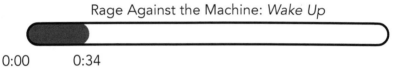

0:00   0:34

I n this chapter, we are hitting up justification by grace. Read your Calvin. Especially this week, it is radical stuff.[1] It changed the church. It changed history. It will change your life. It might even change your answers the next time you are at the grocery store. It did to me.

Listen: I was in Trader Joes one Sunday. It is 11:30 am and the store is quickly filling up. I have grabbed my goods and head to the Express Checkout. The gal at checkout asks me if I have big St. Patrick's Day plans. Slightly stunned by the pop quiz on the contents of my calendar, I mumble something about having to write a lecture. "On what?" she asks. "Oh, uh, it's on justification by grace," I respond. "Oh, what's your take on that?" she asks. "Well, uh, it's mostly a historical survey on the Reformation, John Calvin, Martin Luther, and what the Reformation was about. That kind of thing." She is not backing down, and now she looks a little interested and also slightly confused. I realize that I am talking about John Calvin like he is in the headlines. I am wondering if she's ever even heard of him? "Interesting, so what was it about, what did they say?" And now my head's racing on the theological pop quiz and whether I am going to sound totally idiotic if I say what I am thinking. I go for it. "They said that in Christ's perfect life before

---

1. Calvin, *Institutes* III.i–ii.7, ii.14–24: Calvin, *Institutes* III.iii.1–15; Calvin, *Institutes* III.xi. Tamez, *Amnesty of Grace*, 19–36.

the Father, he acquired righteousness and then gave it to us who don't have it." And then wanting to sound human I add, "And I think that is awesome shit, though I have to save that for the end." Without missing a beat, mind you she is beeping my groceries and I am putting them in the bag, she adds, "So in Corinthians there is this talk about love and perfect love and I study transpersonal psychology [I think that is what she said] and I am wondering how if love is made up of love of the self and love for others, how Jesus embodied perfect love because it seemed like He lived in more of a sacrificial way, only giving his love away to others." Now my head is spinning! I have no idea what transpersonal psych is and she is using big words like "ego." I start to question whether ten years of study is worth thirty seconds in a "15 Items or Less" checkout line.[2] I also think she has just raised an important question. I default to the material in the last chapter: "Well, it seems for Paul, in Christ's sacrificial living for others and in his giving himself away to others, and his allowing himself to be filled by the Father with the Holy Spirit, for Paul that is the purest definition of humanity." Her response throws me for a complete loop. She says, "Oh, I get it." I do not think she is being sarcastic either. Then she comes back again, "Okay, but then here is the other thing I don't get," and I am impressed, because she has put 1+1+1=3 way faster than I have. "If his love is perfect and it is given to us, then it seems we should all be home already." "Home?" I whisper, not wanting to embarrass myself before the growing line at the express check out, "you mean like *up in heaven?*" "Yeah, it seems like all this process of life should already be over." Here my mind is flooded with McTaggart (*The Unreality of Time*), "A" vs. "B" theories of time, some Einstein, and a whole bunch of Barth's treatment of the past as sin that is over (see especially *CD* III/2, 463–74, 532–40), I cannot even remember what I said at this point, but it was something like, "Well for Paul, that is right. We are over, and home is ahead of us. Time is the process of this being over. Christ is the hinge on which time turns." Now, like I said, I cannot totally remember (as I write this fifty minutes later), what I said exactly. I do remember wondering to *myself* after saying something about "Christ being the hinge on which time turns," whether what I have just said actually makes any sense at all. "Oh," she smiles back "I get it. I do. I get it." I am thinking, "YOU get it? How do you get it? I'm not even sure *I* get. I'm writing a freaking book on this and I'm not sure I get it." But she is smiling and is like "I get it. I do. I get it." She taps the screen, my receipt prints up, I grab my bag of groceries, wish her a well and happy St.

---

2. According to Wikipedia, transpersonal psychology is a school of psychology that studies the transpersonal, self-transcendent, or spiritual aspects of the human experience.

Paddy's Day and I am gone. But really, all neurons are firing to make sense of what just happened.

"What just happened" is also a fitting question concerning the matter of justification. Because in the wake of Christ's crucifixion and resurrection, the early believers, especially Paul, were consumed with the question of what the death and resurrection of God as Christ meant for our sin and our standing before the righteousness of God. They too wanted to know the full extent of what just happened.

Rage Against the Machine: *Bombtrack*

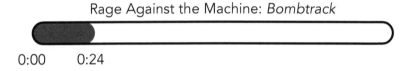

0:00   0:24

I. Justification to the Masses

Here is the course for today's treatment on justification: in the hopes that we too might "get it," I am going to start with St. Thomas Aquinas and his views on justification. Then we will turn to Calvin and finally move to Barth's attempt to improve upon Calvin. Then I want to close with a few words about Elsa Tamez's critique of justification by faith in the Latin American context and the larger (?) issues of social and structural injustice she raises.

I will put the Westminster Confession's understanding of justification on the table and then focus in on a few points that the Reformation thinkers wished to modify from their Catholic counterparts:

Chapter XI: Of Justification

I. Those whom God effectually calls, He also freely justifies; not by infusing righteousness into them, but by pardoning their sins, and by accounting and accepting their persons as righteous; not for any thing wrought in them, or done by them, but for Christ's sake alone; nor by imputing faith itself, the act of believing, or any other evangelical obedience to them, as their righteousness; but by imputing the obedience and satisfaction of Christ unto them, they receiving and resting on Him and His righteousness by faith; which faith they have not of themselves, it is the gift of God.[3]

3. Schaff, *Creeds*, 626. The remaining Westminster treatment: "II. Faith, thus

The elements from this statement that need to be fleshed out regard the notion of "infusing" and that we are accounted as righteous "not for anything wrought in us or done by us." These represent a direct rebuttal to the understanding of justification found in St. Thomas Aquinas. We may turn briefly to his *Summa Theologiae* to see why.

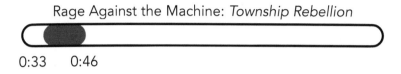

Rage Against the Machine: *Township Rebellion*

0:33   0:46

Thomas Aquinas and Justification

In the First Part of the Second Part of the *Summa*, Question 109, Article 6,[4] Thomas asks "Whether man can merit eternal life without grace?" The answer given is slightly duplicitous. Up front, the answer Thomas gives is No: "man, by his natural powers, cannot produce meritorious works proportioned to eternal life, but for this [eternal life] a higher power is needed, viz. the power of grace." How then does one merit eternal life for Thomas? Thomas's answer is that "grace" is a supernatural gift or higher power that comes from God, a gift that enables a human to know and do things they otherwise could not do. Without this superadded gift, that is,

---

receiving and resting on Christ and His righteousness, is the alone instrument of justification: yet is it not alone in the person justified, but is ever accompanied with all other saving graces, and is no dead faith, but works by love. III. Christ, by His obedience and death, did fully discharge the debt of all those that are thus justified, and did make a proper, real and full satisfaction to His Father's justice in their behalf. Yet, in as much as He was given by the Father for them; and His obedience and satisfaction accepted in their stead; and both, freely, not for any thing in them; their justification is only of free grace; that both the exact justice, and rich grace of God might be glorified in the justification of sinners. IV. God did, from all eternity, decree to justify all the elect, and Christ did, in the fullness of time, die for their sins, and rise again for their justification: nevertheless, they are not justified, until the Holy Spirit does, in due time, actually apply Christ unto them. V. God does continue to forgive the sins of those that are justified; and although they can never fall from the state of justification, yet they may, by their sins, fall under God's fatherly displeasure, and not have the light of His countenance restored unto them, until they humble themselves, confess their sins, beg pardon, and renew their faith and repentance. VI. The justification of believers under the Old Testament was, in all these respects, one and the same with the justification of believers under the New Testament."

4. Aquinas, *ST* I–II.109.5.

"Without grace, man cannot merit eternal life."[5] But the key is that *with* this super added gift of grace, that is, "once the will of man . . . be prepared with grace by God," Thomas concludes, "Man, by his will does works meritorious of eternal life."[6]

You will notice in this schema that the justification of the sinner leading to eternal life is *work* dependent. At some point, a human has to do works good enough to merit eternal life. Since the human cannot do this by her raw abilities, God needs to add something to her. This addition of grace is a kind of divine fuel that gives her the ability and power to do what she could not do before. Yet once these grace-fueled works are complete, then eternal life is merited, by virtue of the human-willed, grace-empowered, and human-completed works. Now if you ask, "How it is that we get the fuel of grace that enables us to work meritoriously?" then Thomas says that such grace is "infused." Since Thomas has a good deal to say about the process of infusion, and since the Reformers explicitly rejected it, we should briefly unpack it.

Thomas's initial example of a "superadded" form is that of water and fire.[7] Thomas notes that just as "water can heat only when heated by the fire" so too the human can only know what meritorious acts ought to be done (and how to do them) when the human intellect is "perfected by a stronger light, viz. the light of faith or of prophecy."[8] Once this happens, this "light of grace" illuminates a new path for the sinner to walk, a path that leads to justification. But not only does grace illuminate, it also, like a divine fuel, gives a "gratuitous strength superadded to natural strength."[9] This additional divine battery power enables us "to do and will supernatural good," that is, the good that is needed to merit eternal life. Now it may sound crass to talk of grace as a divine diesel, a spiritual battery, or as a super holy energy drink, but this is really how Thomas presents it. Thomas would be the first to argue that this gracious fuel is not itself *material;* it is *spiritual,* but Thomas thinks of the spiritual in terms of immaterial substances, so while grace does not exactly have mass and take up space, it is a "something," namely an immaterial divine energizing something. Incidentally, one of the main ways in which we get grace infused to us is through the Lord's Supper. Quite simply, in that act, when we consume bread and wine we take in elements that have

---

5. Aquinas, *ST* I–II.109.5.

6. Aquinas, *ST* I–II.109.5.

7. Aquinas, *ST* I–II.109.1.

8. Aquinas, *ST* I–II.109.1.

9. Aquinas, *ST* I–II.109.2.

been transubstantiated and that infuses grace into us. This empowers the human agent for supernatural action.[10]

Besides the many practical issues of church corruption surrounding the possession and distribution of sacred stuff, issues that stemmed in part from this prior theological understanding, a deeper problem the Reformers saw in this scenario was, as Thomas says, *"There is a reward for thy work"* and so "it would seem a man may merit from God."[11] On Thomas's view, our justification, that is, our movement from a state of injustice to a state of justice in the eyes of God, is then a cooperative process between us and God; one that flows from "[our] merit, inasmuch as by his [our] own will he does [we do] what he [we] ought."[12] This means that while God's grace makes justification possible, and while an illuminating faith orients our minds to what we ought be doing, *our work* is the effective component that seals the deal. Thomas's schema for our justification, that is for "our remission of sins,"[13] is something like the following. Justification is something that Christ made possible in the past (through his death for our sins) but that we and God still need to actualize in our future through our decision to turn from sin,[14] through our movement of free choice towards God[15] via grace-empowered actions that make us deserving (meritorious) of eternal life.

Now the Reformers would also argue that God gives us grace to do what we ought, but they would call this "sanctification" and they would be explicit that this process of sanctification happens *after* our total and complete justification is granted in faith; a justification that is complete in Christ and that is then applied to us, not in part but in whole. We now turn to Calvin.

Rage Against the Machine: *Know Your Enemy*

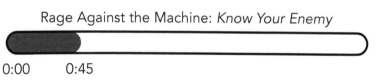

0:00   0:45

10. Aquinas, *ST* III.79.1.

11. Aquinas, *ST* I–II.114.1.

12. Aquinas, *ST* I–II.114.1.

13. Aquinas, *ST* I–II.113.1.

14. Aquinas, *ST* I–II.113.5.

15. Aquinas, *ST* I–II.113.4.

John Calvin and Justification

You may have noticed in what I have just said that the debate over justification involves two primary issues: (1) Who the active agent in our justification is and (2) what the order of our justification, adoption, and sanctification is? Questions on the ordering and coherence of the events leading to our salvation, since the seventeenth century, have been referred to as the *ordo salutis,* the order of salvation. As Bruce McCormack has noted, "by the seventeenth century, arguments over the *ordo* had become something of a favorite indoor sport."[16] And depending on what kind of churches you grew up in and go to, you may find that this sport rages on.

We need only to look once again at the Westminster Confession to see how it reforms a Catholic notion of justification:

> Those whom God effectually calls, He also freely justifies; not by infusing righteousness into them, but by pardoning their sins, and by accounting and accepting their persons as righteous; not for any thing wrought in them, or done by them, but for Christ's sake alone; nor by imputing faith itself, the act of believing, or any other evangelical obedience to them, as their righteousness; but by imputing the obedience and satisfaction of Christ unto them.[17]

In Calvin's treatment of justification, we see three elements are of paramount importance.[18]

1. Calvin's articulation results in "acquittal" and not "pardon." Here is the first big difference between Thomas and Calvin: for Thomas, we are pardoned of our sins (indeed the church was, at the time of Luther, selling "pardons," that is indulgences, from the purgatorial punishment incurred for sins in this life). For Calvin, we are acquitted of our sins. What difference does the verb make? A big one. For starters, "to pardon" means "to excuse an offense without exacting a penalty."[19] But you will see that in a pardon, the party is found "guilty" but just that they do not have to be punished. In other words, you are let off for something you did do. For instance, in college I got a $100 ticket for parking in a handicap zone. It was February in North Dakota and

---

16. McCormack, "Justified by Grace" (lecture, Princeton Theological Seminary, Princeton, NJ, Spring 2010).

17. Schaff, *Creeds*, 626.

18. The following is informed by a personal email of Bruce McCormack, March 14, 2013.

19. *Merriam-Webster's Dictionary*, s.v. "pardon."

there was so much snow covering both the parking space and the five-foot sign marking the spot that I had no idea I was parked in a handicap space. I appealed, went to court, and they let me off—I did not have to pay the $100. But of course, I had, and I admitted that I had, actually parked in a handicap space. Still they pardoned me given the snowy conditions even covered the top of the upright sign. Now "acquittal" means something entirely different. Acquittal means to be found "not guilty" and declared innocent. What Calvin and the Reformers argued, largely on the basis of Romans 5, was that we are not just pardoned of our sins: we are actually acquitted of them; we are found to never have done them in the first place! As Calvin writes, "Therefore 'to justify' means nothing else than to acquit of guilt him who was accused, as if his innocence were confirmed."[20] In other words, "since God justifies us by the intercession of Christ, he absolves us."[21] How is this so?

2. Calvin argues our acquittal is grounded in Christ's "acquired" righteousness. Acquired righteousness is the righteousness that Christ acquires before the Father through His life in time. The reason, for Calvin, that we are found "not guilty" is that Christ lives the perfect human life of obedience before the divine Father: "By his obedience, Christ truly acquired and merited grace for us with his Father."[22] Then, in His death, God substitutes Christ's righteous self for our unrighteous selves. In this substitution, through an act of God, Christ's works-earned righteousness is given to us and our sinfulness is given to Christ. He, though sinless, becomes the curse hanging on the tree (Gal 3:13), the "one great sinner" as Martin Luther put it. So it is that when God the Father looks to His Son, He sees *our* sins, and when God the Father looks to us, He sees Christ's righteousness. Thus, not only are we pardoned and forgiven, even more so we are found to be perfect and blameless in His sight, we are found to be innocent and not-guilty in the first place! God says of the human sinner, "*That one is clean, innocent, and in her is no fault.*" The application of Christ's surplus of righteousness being "applied" or "credited" to our account is the reason for our acquittal. This is the basis for what is called "alien righteousness," a righteousness that is alien to us and that really exists outside of us, but which is nonetheless declared to be our own. And so we walk out of the courtroom "not guilty." There is *no* condemnation.

20. Calvin, *Institutes*, 728.
21. Calvin, *Institutes*, 728.
22. Calvin, *Institutes*, 530.

3. So how does this work? The Reformation's mechanism was "imputa-
    tion." For Calvin and Luther, that which Christ did in time is cred-
    ited to our accounts. Instead of being dead broke, or in the red, our
    accounts are overflowing with Christ-earned-cash (metaphorically
    speaking), which is then credited to our accounts. But this means, as
    we have already said, that our righteousness is one that comes to us
    from without. It is not that God effects our justification by bringing
    about good works *in us,* as in Thomas. For Calvin, our justification is
    effected in Christ's good works in AD 1–30. We are seen to be sinless
    here and now because Jesus was seen to be sinless there and then.

As I said to the Trader Joe's clerk, this is awesome stuff. But here is the crux of
the Reformed perspective: If you ask of Calvin, "Who does this apply to?" If
you ask, "Who is seen as righteous in God's sight?" Then Calvin will respond
that this applies to the "elect," the predestined, to those who have been given
the gift of faith, to those who were chosen in advance to remain "faithful." As
you may notice in Calvin, and if you have grown up around Protestants in
general, then you will know there is a tendency to see God's justification of
you as dependent upon your decision to believe. This is a big difference over
and against Thomas, in which justification is a future potentiality secured
by our meritorious actions. In Calvin justification stands as a *present* potentiality—all you gotta do is believe. But, here is the thing, *you* really have to
accept this as true and will to believe it, accepting it as a gift to be received
in faith. In a key sense, this means that our justification is dependent upon
your accepting, believing, and being faithful. As Calvin says, "As long as
Christ remains outside of us, and we are separated from him, all that he has
suffered and done for the salvation of the human race remains useless and
of no value for us."[23] What one needs to do to make this alien righteousness
imputed to one's account is simply to have faith and believe that it is true.
Doing so makes one's justification a full and complete present actuality. But
this justification is not a present actuality until we believe: "All that [Christ]
possesses is nothing to us until we have grown into one body with him . . .
we obtain this by faith."[24] But here you should be asking yourselves a question: If believing and "having faith" in "full and fixed certainty"[25] is required
for justification to become actualized in us, how is our justification still not
dependent upon some form of human volitional activity, even if that form of
"doing" is a mental believing and not, as Thomas effectively held, a physical
working? This is where Barth kicks in.

23. Calvin, *Institutes* III.I.1, 537.
24. Calvin, *Institutes* III.I.1, 537.
25. Calvin, *Institutes* III.II.15, 560.

Rage Against the Machine: *Freedom*

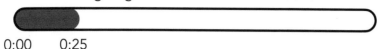

0:00   0:25

II. Karl Barth and Justification

I am going to run through a speedy survey of one of the great sections in the *Church Dogmatics*: "The Judge Judged in our Place."[26] Barth makes four points that spell out in extensive detail our justification by Christ. And since reading it is better than describing it, we will. Then we will turn to how this compares with Calvin.

1. Christ is "The Judge":[27]

    > Jesus Christ was and is "for us" in that He took our place as our Judge. We have seen that in its root and origin, sin is the arrogance in which man wants to be his own and his neighbour's judge. According to Gen. 3:5, the temptation which involves man's disobedience to God's commandment is the evil desire to know what is good and evil. He ought to leave this knowledge to God, to see his freedom in his ability to adhere to God's decisions in his own decisions. He becomes a sinner in trying to be as God: himself a judge. To be a man-in the world which is hostile to God and unreconciled with Him-is to be the pseudo-sovereign creature which finds its dignity and pride in regarding it as its highest good and most sacred duty to have knowledge of good and evil and to inform itself about it (in relation to itself and others). To be a man means in practice to want to be a judge, to want to be able and competent to pronounce ourselves free and righteous and others more or less guilty. We enjoy ourselves in this.[28]

And yet,

    > I am not the Judge. Jesus Christ is Judge. The matter is taken out of my hands. And that means liberation. A great anxiety

26. *CD* IV/1, §59.2, 211–383.
27. *CD* IV/1, 231–35.
28. *CD* IV/1, 231.

is lifted, the greatest of all. I can turn to other more important and more happy and more fruitful activities. I have space
and freedom for them in view of what has happened in Jesus
Christ. And that also means hope.[29]

2. Christ is "The Judged":[30]

That we are sinners, and what our sin is, is something we
can never know by reflection about ourselves in the light of
a standard of good and evil which we have freely chosen or
discovered. This is made impossible by the fact that with His
coming we are displaced from the office of judging. We cannot
tell ourselves that we are accused, and what the accusation is
against us. We have to be told it by that in which we fail. We
have to learn it where God Himself has told it to us by taking
so seriously the accusation against us and our corruption that
He took it upon Himself in His Son.[31]

3. Christ is "The Judgment":[32]

The decisive thing is not that He has suffered what we ought to
have suffered so that we do not have to suffer it, the destruction
to which we have fallen victim by our guilt, and therefore the
punishment which we deserve. This is true, of course. But it is
true only as it derives from the decisive thing that in the suffering and death of Jesus Christ it has come to pass that in His own
person He has made an end of us as sinners and therefore of sin
itself by going to death as the One who took our place as sinners. In His person He has delivered up us sinners and sin itself
to destruction. He has removed us sinners and sin, negated us,
cancelled us out: ourselves, our sin, and the accusation, condemnation and perdition which had overtaken us. That is what
we cannot do and are not willing to do. How can we be able
and willing to remove ourselves as those who commit sin and
therefore sin itself? That is what He could and willed to do and
actually did for us in His right and authority and power as the
Son of God when He took our place as man. The man of sin, the
first Adam, the cosmos alienated from God, the "present evil

29. *CD* IV/1, 234.
30. *CD* IV/1, 235–244.
31. *CD* IV/1, 240.
32. *CD* IV/1, 244–256.

world" (Gal. 1:4), was taken and killed and buried in and with Him on the cross.[33]

4. Christ is "The Justice of God":[34]

> The Judge, the judged, the judgment—the one Jesus Christ who is all these things and in and by Himself does all these things—is the justice or righteousness of God in the biblical sense of the term: the omnipotence of God creating order, which is "now" (νυνὶ δέ Rom. 3:21) revealed and effective as a turning from this present evil æon (Gal. 1:4) to the new one of a world reconciled with God in Him, this One. This righteousness cannot come from the world, from us. It cannot be done by us, fulfilled by us, or in any way completed or improved or maintained by us. It is the righteousness of God.[35]

With these four points, Christ as Judge, as Judged, as God's Judgment, and as God's Justice, Barth effectively turns Calvin's firehose of grace, a firehose directed at certain elect individuals, into a tidal wave that washes over the whole world. With full emphasis on a three-letter word, Barth follows Paul's emphasis in Romans 11:32 that God's merciful election is for "all." With respect to Barth's relation to Calvin, then, there are four points that can be made:[36]

1. Barth agrees that "acquittal" is "the ultimate, eschatological goal—one which is already pronounced in advance of us in the divine verdict rendered in the Resurrection."[37] Recall that on the cross, Christ became the cursed "greatest sinner"[38] who nonetheless is raised innocent. The resurrection is thus the proof of the "verdict of the Father." If Christ, the one great guilty sinner, is raised again in innocence, how much more will we be raised in innocence given that we were small sinners who have been given His righteousness?

2. With regard to Christ's acquired righteousness, as McCormack writes, "Barth is very close to Calvin here but with a slight difference. It is

33. *CD* IV/1, 253–54.

34. *CD* IV/1, 256–73.

35. *CD* IV/1, 256.

36. I owe this four-point summary of Calvin and Barth to McCormack's personal email of March 14, 2013.

37 McCormack's personal email of March 14, 2013.

38. "All the prophets well foresaw in the Spirit that Christ, by imputation, would become the greatest sinner upon the face of the earth" (Luther, *Table Talk*, 69).

God *as human* which provides the basis for acquittal."[39] So it is indeed
a human righteousness that is made ours. It is human because it is
the perfect work of the human Jesus, and His human righteousness
"corresponds" to, "conforms" to, and exegetes God's own inner divine
righteousness. The human Son thus gives a concrete and perfect outer
demonstration before the world, regarding the inner nature of triune
divine justice. That is why the act of Jesus is revelatory.

3. Barth lets go of "imputation" because he doesn't need it.[40] As we saw
   for Calvin, an "imputation" of Christ's righteousness is "something
   that takes place in the temporal life of an individual by the present-
   tense work of the Spirit." So an imputation is granted in the here and
   now. In Barth, God's *pre-temporal* election does all of the heavy-lifting
   that "imputation" once did. We are/were already in Christ when He
   did what He did. That is, when He suffers and dies in our place on
   the cross, our sin is there too. Indeed, for Barth, we are already "in
   Christ" when Christ decides, before the creation of time, to do what
   He will do.[41] As McCormack notes, Christ's righteousness "is already
   made ours in the divine verdict of the Resurrection, if not before." It
   did not need to be added to Karl, for instance, when he was confirmed
   on March 23, 1902, for it was secured for all in AD 30, when Christ is
   raised. Furthermore, for Barth, this verdict is reconfirmed by God in
   every second of our time simply by the fact that God continues to give
   this world time, time which is ever reconciled and redeemed.

4. "A final adjustment to Calvin needs to be noted. Barth too holds that
   Christ takes on our guilt. But there is more to it than that. For Barth,
   the Logos has so completely identified Himself with the sinner"[42]
   that He is the sinner. Jesus becomes the worst reprobate human in
   His death. "The difference this makes is that justification requires
   more than the taking away of guilt; it requires the destruction of the
   sinner as such—his or her death to sin and subjection to death in
   the absence of God and the descent into hell."[43] As we saw in the
   final Barth quote, we as sinners are canceled out, negated, killed, and
   over-ruled. Barth pushes this as far as he can, such that even our
   current being is not our own. *Our sinful being,* that to which we cling
   so desperately, is already gone:

39. Bruce McCormack's personal email of March 14, 2013.

40. Bruce McCormack's personal email of March 14, 2013.

41. See *CD* II/2, 123, 167, 179, 191.

42. McCormack's personal email of March 14, 2013.

43. McCormack's personal email of March 14, 2013.

> That Jesus Christ died for us does not mean, therefore, that we do not have to die, but that we have died in and with Him, that as the people we were we have been done away and destroyed, that we are no longer there and have no more future.[44]

Calvin has gestures to this, but cannot, as Barth does, give us the full systematic ticket. As Bruce McCormack says, "Calvin has none of this."[45]

Rage Against the Machine: *Killing in the Name*

0:00   0:45

III. Are Those Who Died, Justified?

Now, all too briefly, I am afraid, what might we say to Elsa Tamez? Tamez wonders whether a Reformed understanding of justification by *faith* is relevant to the radically oppressed, the destitute and poor, the unempowered, and, especially the structurally imprisoned of Latin America. She raises very important questions. Moreover, if her critique was that the Thomistic system of immaterial materialism reinforces notions of wealthy and glorious being and so actually contributes to such conditions, I think there would be good reason to accept that it can and, in many times and places, actually has. Regarding a Calvinist version of justification by faith, I also think she may have an arrow aimed at a weak spot, indeed, even a fatally weak spot. Perhaps a Calvinist understanding is overly intellectual and seeks, too shallowly, to impose or transfer a European doctrine onto a foreign and incompatible context, such that it is left "floating in ambiguity."[46] But perhaps it also does something worse. In its emphasis on faith over works, perhaps it does promote quietism and inaction in the face of social evils? If so, perhaps what the church ought to do is to seek new modes of confronting such evil empires? Perhaps the church needs newer and more radical modes of prophetic confrontation? Perhaps the church should adopt the creative methods of other cultural revolutionaries in their attempts to subvert and overthrow hegemonic discourse? Perhaps.

44. *CD* IV/1, 295.
45. McCormack's personal email of March 14, 2013.
46. Tamez, *Amnesty of Grace*, 20.

But I would like to say that it is doubtful that the church, when it divorces itself from the language and logic of Christ's sacrificial love, would ever be able to do it better than it has been done by others. This is why I am playing Rage Against the Machine. This album *is* a soundtrack for revolutionary engagement against oppressive power structures. Not wanting to "Settle for Nothing," Zach de la Rocha and company want you to "Wake Up" and "Know Your Enemy," calling for a "Township Rebellion" to yield a new egalitarian "Freedom" that "Takes the Power Back." Because theirs is fundamentally a rage against a blind and dehumanizing machine, you do this by any means you can: you do it with a "Fistful of Steel"; you do it with a "Bullet in the Head"; you do it with a "Bombtrack," even if it means "Killing in the Name" of whatever cause you think is worth more than peoples' lives. (Those are the ten track titles of their self-titled album.)

Now, perhaps something like this affords the best opportunity for radical societal, cultural, political, structural equality. Perhaps force of music, or force of art, or force of foot, fist, and fear is the greatest force we know of. Perhaps the church should set aside its nice little message of forgiveness of sins and personal peace with God and join these effective revolutionaries? As Rage asks, "Why stand on a silent platform? Fight the War. Fuck the norm. . . . Shackle their minds when they're bent on the cross. When ignorance reigns, life is lost!"[47] Is justification by faith alone a shackle that puts you under the control of the chosen whites?

Rage Against the Machine: *Killing in the Name*

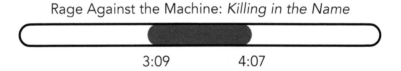

3:09   4:07

This is where I think Barth's treatment has something to offer the church and through the church *to the world*. For if Christ is judge, is judged, is judgment, and is justice; if Christ alone in His person is these things, then we are not. All our attempts at judgment, justice, and judging are riddled with sin. Indeed, they *are* sin. But if that One is alive, and if that One is present and if that One's presence is itself justice, is itself the Kingdom of God, then there is One who is more powerful than fists, feet, fear, and other foul f-words. For, if He is alive, Christ has conquered those things. And that means we do not need to do this "change or die" I-am-going-to-enforce-my

47. Morello et al., *Township Rebellion*.

justice-on-you-by-a-boot-to-the-throat. If that One is alive, then that One is actually *effective* at bringing justice, order, and life out of injustice, chaos, and death. And frankly, that is more than Rage Against the Machine can say. They've proven effective at selling albums, concerts, and making cash for their sponsors ("All of which are American dreams!"). But they have since devolved into being the "Renegades of Funk" with a twentieth-anniversary album to celebrate the fact that all this passion, rage, and hope got swallowed up by the very thing they detest: corporate American greed. Now the church can go that route. Some parts of it are trying as hard as they can. But there may be another route. The church's prophetic witness to the end of oppression, poverty, and injustice may be as simple as the public profession in thought, word, and deed that "Christ is Risen" and "Christ is Here." Certainly that takes courage, hope, and faith. If even saying it inside a friendly neighborhood grocery store makes one nervous, how about proclaiming it on the streets in the face of those who are breaking your noses, as did Martin Luther King Jr. in mid-summer 1966?:

> Bottles and bricks were thrown at us; we were often beaten. Some of the people who had been brutalized in Selma and who were present at the Capitol ceremonies in Montgomery led marches in the suburbs of Chicago amid a rain of rocks and bottles, among burning automobiles, to the thunder of jeering thousands, many of them waving Nazi flags. Swastikas bloomed in Chicago parks like misbegotten weeds. Our marches were met by a hailstorm of bricks, bottles, and firecrackers. "White power" became the racist catcall, punctuated by the vilest of obscenities—most frequently directly at Catholic priests and nuns among the marchers. I've been in many demonstrations all across the South, but I can say that I had never seen, even in Mississippi, mobs as hostile and as hate-filled as in Chicago . . . I remember walking with the Blackstone Rangers while bottles were flying from the sidelines, and I saw their noses being broken and blood flowing from their wounds; and I saw them continue and not retaliate, not one of them, with violence. I am convinced that even violent temperaments can be channeled through nonviolent discipline, if they can act constructively and express through an effective channel their very legitimate anger.[48]

So here's to King, who knew that suffering for other's well-being "is the way of Christ, it is the way of the cross."[49] Friends, in the cross, Christ's justification of all reconciles enemies and has us, in God's eyes, already home at a table

48. King, *Autobiography*, 305–6.

49. King, *Autobiography*, 103.

— 8 —

Church: Come as You Are

What is the church?

As he often does, Barth makes us rethink our most trusted answers because he makes us rethink our most basic questions. This is one reason why so many are threatened by him. Barth would have us, then, not ask, *what* (or *who*) is the church, but rather, *when* is the church? To see why this is the proper question, we must first spend some time with John Calvin on the question of election, predestination, and who is saved.

While Luther's and Calvin's Reformation theology represented a veritable revolution of thought and practice, it also had imbedded within it deep elements of continuity with Catholic thought. The five Reformation *solae* of grace alone, faith alone, Scripture alone, Christ alone, and for the glory of God alone, for instance, were in direct tension with Catholic teaching about how one was saved, the role of works in the life of the believer, the power of the ecclesial hierarchy, and the value of the biblical testimony. These are not minor issues! But deeper within these were also predicated a near-complete affirmation of Augustinian-Catholic teaching that not all were saved, that double predestination (some to heaven, some to hell) was worthy of affirmation, and that God's providential knowledge knew who these were in advance, even, of creation.

When turning to the question of the "elect," that is, those who are chosen by God, to form the church, Calvin affirms the existence of what I call a "select elect." This means that those whom God has foreknown and chosen for salvation, those whom God has elected, are a select and limited number of individuals. More importantly than simply being a discrete number (a finite population is always discrete, no matter how big), this select elect represents a subset of the general population. Not *all* are chosen for salvation.

One can see this in Calvin's *The Institutes of the Christian Religion* when he turns to his discussion of "the Holy Catholic Church."[1] Just as God is Father "for those" whom God is "pleased to gather," the church is Mother so that "they might be guided by her motherly care until they mature and at last reach the goal of faith."[2] The true church, Calvin is notable for qualifying, "refers not only to the visible church" but to "all God's elect, in whose number are also included the dead."[3] Yet, the elect are not the totality of all humans, but "a small and contemptible number" that are "hidden in a huge multitude" just as "a few grains of wheat are covered by a pile of chaff."[4] While certainly there are visible marks of faith in many individuals, "God alone" knows who the true church is, based upon their "secret election" as "his children." These, it might be added, are "his own flock" and stand distinct in God's eyes from "the ungodly" who are "wild beasts."[5] While we "are not bidden to distinguish between reprobate and elect" apart from the church's bosom, thinks Calvin, "one cannot hope for any forgiveness of sins or any salvation."[6]

While it is true that God calls His flock to the church by the merciful gift of faith apart from any merit, and so the saved have no reason to boast, the situation does leave much for the bad folks, as surely they must be, to mourn. For if the church is saved by grace, apart from merit, the damned are consigned to the lake of fire and fry regardless of what they do, as well.

Nirvana: *Lake of Fire*

0:00   2:40

The notion of a select elect has been the main thinking of the Protestant church, indeed arguably the Christian church, in one form or another since the beginning. Whether the select elect were saved because they were in the church, because of their good deeds, because of their wealth, or simply because of the inscrutable grace of God, their number

1. Calvin, *Institutes* IV.1, 1011.

2. Calvin, *Institutes* IV.1, 1012.

3. Calvin, *Institutes* IV.1, 1013.

4. Calvin, *Institutes* IV.1, 1013.

5. Calvin, *Institutes* IV.1, 1015–16.

6. Calvin, *Institutes* IV.1, 1016.

was limited and God's rationale for choosing them inaccessible. Barth will challenge both heresies.

The basis for Barth's revolution in ecclesiology is the doctrine of the Trinity. Because God has an internal and eternal κοινωνία of Otherness as Father, Son, and Holy Spirit, God can have fellowship and presence with others in time. God shares God's own self with others repeatedly, again and again, *as* time. *When* people gather for worship, *when they* call upon the Lord in humility, and *when* they turn to Scripture to see again who God is, and *when* God shows up to such ungodly church folk, according to God's covenantal promises, then fellowship with God actually happens. *Church* happens by God's grace alone.

Church is thus not a "what" or a "thing" that is qualified chiefly by the activity of humans. Church is a "when" that is characterized chiefly by the presence of God. As the community of God, called out to give witness, a gathering of people becomes the community *of God* when the triune God is present. Thus, church happens by God's grace and not by human effort. Such human effort, what Barth calls "religion," has been henceforth abolished, nullified, negated, overturned, and graciously red-lined.

True, humans do bear a responsibility to be diligent, intelligent, hopeful, and faithful in their effort to call upon the Lord. And yet, if God is there, it is because God has come again. God's presence is owing to the free choice of the One who shines further out into the darkness creating others, "alien and hostile others," to be illuminated by and united with the triune κοινωνία. In a favorite passage of mine, Barth writes:

> God's loving is concerned with a seeking and creation of fellowship without any reference to an existing aptitude or worthiness on the part of the loved. God's love is not merely not conditioned by any reciprocity of love. It is also not conditioned by any worthiness to be loved on the part of the loved, by any existing capacity for union or fellowship on his side. . . . The object of the love of God as such is another which in itself is not, or is not yet, worthy of this His pleasure. The love of God always throws a bridge over a crevasse. It is always the light shining out of darkness. In His revelation it seeks and creates fellowship where there is no fellowship and no capacity for it, where the situation concerns a being which is quite different from God, a creature and therefore alien, a sinful creature and therefore hostile. It is this alien and hostile other that God loves. Fellowship with him as such is the fellowship which He seeks and creates. This does not mean that we can call the love of God a blind love. But what He sees when He loves is that which is altogether distinct from

Himself, and as such lost in itself, and without Him abandoned
to death. That He throws a bridge out from Himself to this abandoned one, that He is light in the darkness, is the miracle of the
almighty love of God.[7]

This understanding of the church, in Barth, is reinforced by five key elements, systematically related to other elements in his theological framework,
some of which we have already encountered. These other elements are: (1)
justification has been completed in Christ; (2) sanctification is understood as
being set apart under a call unto holiness, rather than a predicate intrinsic to
believers who already have been made holy; (3) as a body of sinful, alien, and
hostile others who must rely upon the presence of God for church to happen,
the community can only witness to what God has done and promises to do.
In regards to making contact with and affecting the realm of the divine, the
church simply cannot. It is impotent to do anything; (4) this witness is gathered around a pointing to the Word of God, who is Jesus Christ; (5) since
the presence of the triune God is what determines when church happens, we
do not get to decide what a church is. Church is never a human invention,
construction, or program. Church is the presence of God in Christ. We will
now work through each of these in a bit more detail.

I. Justification.

In our last chapter on justification, we contrasted Barth's radical
developments in relation to Calvin, but also in reference to Thomas
Aquinas. What needs to be emphasized now is that, for Barth, justification
is a past-tense reality that has happened to the world in the crucifixion and
resurrection of Jesus Christ. The justification of each human person in the
eyes of God is a historical fact that has been completed. Barth's argument for
this is extensive and spans his career, from his early *Römerbrief* to the last
pages of the *Church Dogmatics*, and it is founded on a systematic exegesis
of passages throughout the New and Old Testament.[8] The summation of the
argument is Paul's statement in Romans 5:10 that "while we were enemies,
we were reconciled." Barth's conclusion is thus:

> Judgment is judgment. Death is death. End is end. In the
> fulfillment of the self-humiliation of God, in the obedience of
> the Son, Jesus Christ has suffered judgment, death and end in

---

7. *CD* II/1, 278.

8. See especially, Rom 3:21–26, Rom 4:21–26, Rom 5:6, 8, Rom 5:18, Rom 8:31–39,
9:16–18, Rom 11:32, Gal 2:15–21, Eph 2:11–22, Col 3:3, Heb 10:1–18, and 1 John 2:2.

our place, the Judge who Himself was judged, and who thereby has also judged. In His person, with him, judgment, death and end have come to us ourselves once and for all.[9]

Continuing a few pages on, Barth draws out the conclusion of the judgment and justification that has come to us, writing:

In virtue of the divine right established in the death of Jesus Christ, in virtue of the justification which has come to them in His resurrection, they are no longer what they were but they are already what they are to be. They are no longer enemies of God but His friends, His children . . . They are no longer sinners, but righteous. They are no longer lost, but saved.[10]

This fully historically realized justification leaves nothing wanting or undone. Because God has done it, it is perfect. And yet, if it is completed and perfect, we must address the church's most obvious failing: its hypocrisy and inability to be as sanctified as it says it is.

II. Sanctification

As we turn to sanctification, let us recall what have classically been seen as the three main phases of the Christian life: justification, sanctification, and glorification. Effectively, justification was often viewed as the "process" of being made righteous in God's eyes. Sanctification, was the "process" of being made more and more morally pure and holy, thus becoming more and more like Christ. Glorification was the after-death reward for having led a faithful and pure life. While we have talked about justification and discussions of glorification will be deferred for another epoch, since we are in a greater discussion of the nature of the church, we need to spend some time with sanctification. As the gathering of the justified (traditionally construed), the church has often used sanctification to give witness to the fact that it is justified, that its believers are more morally pure and upright, and that the church's superior moral character is proof of its being chosen by God. Sanctification was thus often proof and corroboration of the church's justification, and many of you may have experiences with churches that believed such. In effect, the church's superior moral character was proof that God exists, Christianity is true, and that its privileged members were chosen by God for salvation.

9. *CD* IV/1, 296.
10. *CD* IV/1, 316.

One might immediately sense how this logic has been distorted. Even in churches that advocate salvation by faith alone, the church's superior moral character was proof that they were chosen by God to have faith *because* they were to be morally superior. While a full history of the doctrine of sanctification is beyond the bounds of our current treatment,[11] one can see this view of sanctification in Calvin's general attitude of the church. As he says, "God raises his own folk upward step by step"[12] and "the church is holy, then, in the sense that it is daily advancing and is not yet perfect: it makes progress from day to day but has not yet reached its goal of holiness."[13] While some traditions do hold the possibility of becoming totally morally pure in this life, as opposed to Luther and Calvin who saw the total sanctification of the believer as an eschatological reality alone, most traditions nevertheless affirm that sanctification is the process of becoming "more and more" holy.

Barth's take on sanctification effectively nullifies this idea. For Barth, holiness is never a "more-and-more process." The church is not set aside because it is holier than thou. It is also not set apart in the first sense because it will be made holier than thou. It is set aside primarily because it has been chosen to witness to God who is the holy one. Rather than a "more and more," that is concerned with increasing attributes intrinsic to a creature, since Christ's justification of the world is already perfect and complete, we are to witness to that gracious reality "again and again." "'I will be your God' is the justification of man," says Barth. "'Ye shall be my people' is his sanctification." In this way, Barth undercuts any foundation for the church's moral superiority. This should be recognized as good news, because it means there are none who are not good enough to be loved by God. There are none who can say, "My ungodliness means Jesus doesn't want me for a sunbeam."

Nirvana: *Jesus Don't Want Me For a Sunbeam*

0:00   4:14

The theological problem lurking behind Kurt Cobain's sickness unto death is that, traditionally, sanctification was typically seen as a subset of ethics, whether or not it was openly acknowledged as such. If believers "do

---

11. Barth's history and treatment of sanctification is found in *CD* IV/2 §66.
12. Calvin, *Institutes* IV.1.5, 1019.
13. Calvin, *Institutes* IV.1.17, 1031.

the right thing," they will show they have been chosen by God. Doing the right thing typically was construed by being ethical, following the laws of God, and reliably demonstrating the fruits of the Spirit by one's own capacity. Cobain's awareness of his own inability to be holy, perfect, and blameless before God, by his own capacity, despite the suicidal outcome that came of it, is much more of a theologically appropriate attitude. We *all* are ungodly. We *all* are unworthy. We *all* are incapable of leading the perfect Christian life. Fortunately, our sanctification is not up to us. It is not ours to secure. Just as Christ is the justification of all, so too is Christ our sanctification. Thus while Barth does not collapse the two and insists, "Sanctification is not justification" and "justification is not sanctification," he also holds the two as conjoined twins. Hence there is "no justification without sanctification."[14] Or, as he says, "It is in virtue of the fact that he is justified in the presence of God by God that he is sanctified by Him."[15]

So how is one sanctified? Again Barth puts the emphasis on Christ as the pure and true human partner of God, writing,

> The sanctification of man which has taken place in this One is their sanctification. But originally and properly it is the sanctification of Him and not of them. Their sanctification is originally and properly His and not theirs. For it was in the existence of this One, in Jesus Christ, that it really came about, and is and will be, that God Himself became man, that the Son of God became also the Son of Man, in order to accomplish in His own person the conversion of man to Himself, his exaltation from the depth of his transgression and consequent misery, his liberation from his unholy being for service in the covenant, and therefore his sanctification.[16]

In other words, Christ has lived the true human life. In doing so, Jesus makes His cause our own, such that we also can live for others through Him in a way that correlates to God's intentions for life in fellowship. Importantly, however, humanity's sanctification is not for the individual's own good, or even for the good of the church. It is for the sake of the world: "In their sanctification He attests that He is the Lord of all men. In all its particularity their sanctification speaks of the universal action of God, which has as its purpose and goal the reconciliation of the world, and therefore not merely of this group of individuals in the world."[17] The

14. *CD* IV/2, 505–6.
15. *CD* IV/2, 508.
16. *CD* IV/2, 514.
17. *CD* IV/2, 518–9.

journey of sanctification is thus the life of witness, not to the righteousness of the self or of the community, but to the righteousness and grace of the triune God who gives it away. To all.

Let us then think a bit further concerning the relation between the church before the world. "How," asks Barth, "do they become witnesses of that which has come on the whole world?"[18] God, says Barth, "creates saints by giving them direction." This direction is not "merely the type one man may give to another" but is "the direction of the royal man, Jesus," who is "the eternal Logos."[19] As the only human with "divine authority," Jesus speaks "not merely in words but in acts." And "others hear him"! So "slothful, stupid, inhuman, dissipated, and careworn sinners" become "disturbed sinners"[20] when "He calls them to Himself."[21] And because the saints "are indeed at the very bottom" and "begin from the bottom upwards," all their actions, just as *all* human action, "stands in need of the forgiveness, the justification, which they cannot achieve of themselves."[22] Yet, in this "divine direction," humanity's "sinful being" is given a total freedom in the face of this total bondage.[23]

Doing the right thing, in Barth's eyes, is thus doing what Christ wills for you, and you alone, in each moment. Doing the right thing, in Barth's eyes, is allowing the Spirit to guide you into going where Christ would have you go, and in saying what Christ would have you say. Doing the right thing is never only a secularly available ethical act discernible by reason or rationality. Doing the right thing is always to give one's life away for the sake of another according to Christ's unique command for this moment. And though humans can never do this in the perfect, immediate, intuitive way in which Christ lives before the Father by the Spirit, humanity can freely and in faith do acts that correspond to the will of God in Christ and that, by grace, are accepted as the (graciously!) imperfectly perfect deed at the perfect time. Thus humanity can, again and again, moment by moment, live in correspondence with the will of God. As Barth says in *Church Dogmatics*, "all that man can and will do is to pray, to follow and to obey."[24] These are acts that take the ultimate form of "Not my will, but thine, be done."[25] And

18. *CD* IV/2, 521.
19. *CD* IV/2, 523.
20. *CD* IV/2, 524.
21. *CD* IV/2, 527.
22. *CD* IV/2, 529.
23. *CD* IV/2, 531.
24. *CD* II/2, 177.
25. *CD* II/2, 177.

when humanity lives in correspondence with God's will, again and again, humanity is gifted with a true freedom that is inaccessible by secular ethics, political liberty, free will, or even by following the precepts of any given religion (including Reformed Protestant Christianity). One gives witness to the freedom that is given by Christ. Christ's will for the believer's life is to show the world that she has been redeemed, not by her own power, effort, or intention, but by a life which gives witness to the grace of God manifested in Christ's life, death, and resurrection.

The Christian community is a community called to witness to God's holiness, Christ's justification, and the Spirit's guidance, which through God's grace, allows one to live "as a living sacrifice, holy and acceptable to God" (Rom 12:1). It is a community that responds, again and again, to Christ's call and that ever forms again (reforms) around Christ the Word. "Follow me," says Barth, "is the substance of the call in the power of which Jesus makes men saints."[26] The Christian community is a pointing community, pointing, not to its own righteousness, culture, and community, but to God's forgiveness, the Trinity's κοινωνία, and God's love of the alien and hostile other. It is a community "called out" and "set apart" not because of its own morality or holiness, but because of the God who elects to manifest the triune love through the redemption of the ungodly and immoral. Thus while Barth has much in common with Calvin at points, at its deeper levels, he runs counter to Calvin who claims, "if churches are well ordered, they will not bear the wicked in their bosom."[27] On the contrary, Barth's missional vision is much more exemplified by Bonhoeffer's *Life Together*, when it opens with, "The Christian cannot simply take for granted the privilege of living among other Christians. Jesus Christ lived in the midst of his enemies. . . . So Christians, too," demands Bonhoeffer, "belong not in the seclusion of a cloistered life but in the midst of enemies."[28] For Barth, the church's witness to Christ is thus its mission to worship *before* the world in proclamation *to* the world what God has done *for* the world. The church's mission is thus to proclaim Christ's love to the world, indeed to its own enemies. This mission is not to coerce, control, culture, or convert people so that they may become a part of the church, and thus become "like us who are justified, sanctified, and saved." The church's mission is to proclaim to those who have not heard what has been done, that they have been justified and sanctified by Christ, and that a life of true freedom is possible when one lives in correspondence with this reality. When this message is proclaimed,

26. *CD* IV/2, 533.

27. Calvin, *Institutes* IV.1.15, 1029.

28. Bonhoeffer, *Life Together*, 27.

the fellowship of believers comes alive by the presence of Christ. When this happens, captives hear they have already been freed and they may walk out of an imprisoned life. When Christ is present to the captives, the kingdom of God has drawn near and *church happens*.

When church happens, those who believe, those who used to believe, those who will someday believe, and those who cannot now believe, are elected ever and always, to come as they are and to soak up the sunbeams flowing from the One who bought the world. In Christ *all* are elected by God to be recipients of grace.

Nirvana: *Come As You Are*

0:00   4:13

— 9 —

The Lord's Supper: Hunger Strike

I n this chapter I will offer a brief proposal on the Lord's Supper. I hope this proposal opens up room for thinking about the nature of the sacraments in general while also extending more precisely into a theology of food.

First, some background on how these lights begin to flicker. As a graduate student, I once was sitting through a "discussion" on Luther's views of the Eucharist. It was not really a discussion, however, because the teaching assistant was talking most of the time. Though there were a few students nodding along in defense of Luther's high view of the Lord's Supper and in agreement that it is an important and necessary ecclesial practice, there were a few others who seemed baffled by what was being presented. There also might have been a few who were dozing off. I might have been one of those. After zoning in and out of the discussion, I blurted out, "What makes us think Christ ever wanted us to practice *sacraments* in the first place?" My intemperance surprised the room, myself included. What was this heresy I had just thrown up? Everyone knows the sacraments are the most sacred acts, unquestionably passed down from the night He was betrayed to us by faithful priests and reliable traditions! But what I was asking is this: What makes us think that Christ, on the night He was betrayed, was talking about a well-choreographed ecclesial ceremony with properly trained and officially ordained leaders, white table clothes, fancy silver (or gold!) ornamentation, industrially produced plastic cups of synthetic grape juice, with the most somber organ music Western civilization has composed droning on in the background? While Christ's institution of the Eucharist is part of a ritualized Passover lineage and tradition, what exactly did Christ institute with the Lord's Supper, and why?

I. Why a Sacrament?

Here is a bold claim. The whole matter of sacraments was largely bootstrapped by the church in the early medieval era, with much of the theological foundation of the various sacramental practices being built upon a somewhat arbitrary definition of *sacramentum*, itself a translated term based on Paul's description of the *musterion* (mystery) of marriage in Ephesians 1:9–10.[1] By the late-medieval period, most notably through Peter Lombard, the seven Catholic sacraments of baptism, Eucharist, confirmation, penance, ordination, marriage, and anointing the sick were formally adopted. The understanding of sacraments then underwent a full-scale reorganization in the Reformation era. If we think that sacraments are formally instituted means through which God, via the ecclesial community, delivers grace to its members, what justifies such a belief? Is a theology of a formal ceremony what Christ intended for the Lord's Supper?

There are a whole host of questions surrounding what it is that we think sacraments do. Do they effect the forgiveness of sins? If so, why not load up squirt guns with holy water and hose down the crowds? On the other hand, some would say, if the *act* of water baptism follows upon the efficacious baptism by the Spirit, who blows where it will, then water baptism is merely a sign, and does not *do* anything at all. Moreover, if our justification is complete in Christ "while we were yet enemies" (Rom 5), and if a sacrament is efficacious whether we believe it or not; if we have been saved by the act of Christ (on the cross), the faith of Christ (in Gethsemane), and/or the decision of Christ to play the part of sacrificial lamb (in pre-temporal election), then what role is there left for sacraments to be a means mediating grace to us? If it was *all* done there and then by Christ, and is effective whether we believe it or not, what remains to be mediated to us here and now? As Bruce McCormack notes, "Is it really surprising, in the light of these facts, that theologians like Otto Weber would prefer to abandon the concept of 'sacraments' altogether and to replace it with the more modest 'proclamation activities'?"[2] Good question. But only if you're a free thinker.

With this in mind, I want to put an offer about the table on the table.

> And he took bread, gave thanks and broke it, and gave it to them, saying, "This is my body given for you; do this in remembrance of me." (Luke 22:19)

What is His body? What is the "this" Jesus is referring to?

1. See Migliore, *Faith Seeking Understanding*, 280.

2. McCormack, "Sacraments in General" (lecture, Princeton Theological Seminary, Princeton, NJ, Spring 2010).

> In the same way, after the supper he took the cup, saying, "This cup is the new covenant in my blood, which is poured out for you." (Luke 22:20)

Which cup? The one He is holding? *Only* the one He is holding?

> "Do this in remembrance of me." (1 Cor 11:25)

What is the "this" that we are to "do" in remembrance of Him?

> "For whenever you eat this bread and drink this cup, you proclaim the Lord's death until he comes." (1 Cor 11:26)

"This bread" and "this cup": What bread? What cup? *Which bread? Which cup?* And *when* does the "whenever" apply? Does "whenever" apply only to when we are gathered in church on Sunday morning having a pastor planned, congregation approved, eleven-minute religious ritual as part of the order of worship? Or might "whenever" actually and simply mean *whenever?*

II. Barth on Jesus' Hunger Strike

What is "this"? When is "whenever"? These are the great theological questions before us today. For an entry point into a positive theological understanding of something like the Lord's Supper, lets go to my favorite place: the wilderness.

> Then Jesus was led up by the Spirit into the wilderness to be tempted by the devil. He fasted forty days and forty nights, and afterwards he was famished. The tempter came and said to him, "If you are the Son of God, command these stones to become loaves of bread." (Matt 4:1–3)

What might near-starvation in the desert have to do with sacred eucharistic practice? In commenting on this passage, Barth has the following provocative question:

> In both Evangelists the first Satanic suggestion is that after the forty days of hunger He should change the stones of the wilderness into bread in the power of His divine Sonship by His Word. What would it have meant if Jesus had yielded?

Barth's answer involves a sort of hunger strike:

> He [Jesus] would have used the power of God which He undoubtedly had like a technical instrument placed at His disposal

to save and maintain His own life. He would then have stepped out of the series of sinners in which He placed Himself in His baptism in Jordan. Of His own will He would have abandoned the role of the One who fasts and repents for sinners. He would have broken off His fasting and repentance in the fulness of divine power and with the help of God, but without consulting the will and commandment of God, because in the last resort His primary will was to live. He would have refused to give Himself unreservedly to be the one great sinner who allows that God is in the right, to set His hopes for the redemption and maintenance of His life only on the Word of God, in the establishment of which He was engaged in this self-offering. He would have refused to be willing to live only by this Word and promise of God, and therefore to continue to hunger. In so doing He would, of course, only have done what in His place and with His powers all other men would certainly have done. From the standpoint of all other men He would only have acted reasonably and rightly. "Rabbi, eat" is what His disciples later said to Him (Jn. 4:31) quite reasonably and in all innocence. But then He would not have made it His *meat* "to do the will of him that sent him, and to finish his work" (Jn. 4:34). Instead of acting for all other men and in their place. He would have left them in the lurch at the very moment when He had made their cause His own. Jesus withstood this temptation. He persisted in obedience, in penitence, in fasting. He hungered in confidence in the promise of manna with which the same God had once fed the fathers in the wilderness after He had allowed them to hunger (Deut. 8:3). He willed to live only by that which the Word of God creates, and therefore as one of the sinners who have no hope apart from God, as the Head and King of this people. His decision was, therefore, a different one from that which all other men would have taken in His place, and in that way it was the righteousness which He achieved in their stead.[3]

What is Barth saying? In sum, something like this: "Though he was really hungry, Jesus chose not to cook for himself." That is, instead of taking care of Himself, Jesus chose to rely upon the timing of the divine delivery for His takeout. But what this means is that Jesus relies upon the give-it-away-ness of God the Father. Though Jesus, as God in creaturely form, could have gone all divine microwave and zapped the stones into edibles, He chose to remain as we are, and to not do as we cannot do, though that, if we could do as He could do, we certainly would have done what He did

3. *CD* IV/1, 261–62.

not do. Jesus allows His nourishment to come from God the Father. We do not. Jesus willfully chose to live by the nourishment of the Holy Spirit. We have not. Jesus undergoes a theologically motivated hunger strike for the sake of faithfulness to God. Unless you are Gandhi's saintly mother, none of us ever would do such a thing.[4]

We need food. This is a basic fact. We need food daily. We need our daily bread. This is a troubling reality, especially if we think too much about it. For instance, Norman Wirzba opens his book *Food and Faith* with the following:

> Why did God create a world in which every living creature must eat?
>
> This is a humbling, even terrifying question, particularly for people who are intimately involved in the finding, growing, and harvesting of food. Eating is no idle or trifling activity. It is the means of life itself—but also death. For any creature to live, countless seen and unseen others must die, often by being eaten themselves. Life as we know it *depends* on death, *needs* death, which means that death is not simply the cessation of life but its precondition. Death is eating's steadfast accomplice. It is also each creature's biological end, for no matter how much or how well we eat (for the sake of life's preservation), we cannot erase our mortal condition. Why eat if eating, even vegetarian eating, implicates us in so much death? Why eat if eating is the daily reminder of our own need and mortality?[5]

But of course, once Norman has asked *that* question: "Why eat if eating is the daily reminder of our own need and mortality?"; once that question is on the table, then I think our minds ought go directly back to that more famous table on the night He was betrayed.

---

4. As Gandhi recounts in his *The Story of My Experiments with Truth* of his mother: "To keep two or three consecutive fasts was nothing to her. Living on one meal a day during Chaturmas was habit with her. Not content with that she fasted every alternated day during one Chaturmas. During another Chaturmas she vowed not to have food without seeing the sun. We children on those days would stand, staring at the sky, waiting to announce the appearance of the sun to our mother. Everyone knows that at the height of the rainy season the sun often does not condescend to show his face. And I remember days when, at his sudden appearance, we would rush and announce it to her. She would run out to see with her own eyes, but by that time the fugitive sun would be gone, thus depriving her of her meal. "That does not matter," she would say cheerfully, "God did not want me to eat today." And she would return to her round of duties. See Gandhi, *Essential*, 5–6.

5. Wirzba, *Food and Faith*, 1–2.

Food is a sign that we are "beings in dependence." Food is a sign, *no,* more than just a sign, it is *proof* that we cannot simply live by our own internal power, that we do not have eternally ever-ready batteries within us. Food is a concrete demonstration that we live off of that which is outside of us, that which is beyond us, that which is "other" than us. Food is the *death of another,* and it is in *the death of another* that we live. You are going to eat breakfast and lunch. Look at the food. Whether it is lettuce or lamb, you live, in the here and now, by *the death of another* in a there and then. This is food. This is the food industry. This is agriculture. This is life. This is death. This is food. This is not very appetizing.

III. A Cosmic Eating Disorder

Again, let us go into the wild to get a handle on the bigger theological point of food. "Where shall we buy bread for all these people to eat?" (John 6:5). Those are *Jesus'* words just before He turns into (actually before He unveils that He is already) a divine Wawa hosting a hoagie-fest out in the sandhills of Galilee. Immediately after his question comes this famous conversation:

> So they said to him, "What sign are you going to give us then, so that we may see it and believe you? What work are you performing? Our ancestors ate the manna in the wilderness; as it is written, 'He gave them bread from heaven to eat.'" Then Jesus said to them, "Very truly, I tell you, it was not Moses who gave you the bread from heaven, but it is my Father who gives you the true bread from heaven. For the bread of God is that which comes down from heaven and gives life to the world." They said to him, "Sir, give us this bread always."
>
> Jesus said to them, "I am the bread of life. Whoever comes to me will never be hungry, and whoever believes in me will never be thirsty. . . . I am the bread of life. Your ancestors ate the manna in the wilderness, and they died. This is the bread that comes down from heaven, so that one may eat of it and not die. I am the living bread that came down from heaven. Whoever eats of this bread will live forever; and the bread that I will give for the life of the world is my flesh. (John 6:30–35, 48–51)

So what am I suggesting? Well, maybe you have never noticed, but there are food stories throughout the Bible. Think of as many examples as you can.

This world has an eating disorder.[6] I do not say this trivially. Some eat too much, some eat too little. Some have too much access, some have

---

6. The sentiment is echoed by Michael Pollan with his claim that we have a "national eating disorder." See Pollan, *Omnivore's Dilemma,* 2.

too little. Some cannot eat in good conscience, some are too good at unconsciously eating. Food—how much we have, where we eat, who has it, who does not have it—is a demonstration of who is in control. It shows who has the power and privilege. But this is our fundamental mental error regarding food. And this error is not primarily an agricultural, economic, or political one. It is a *theological* error, in the fullest sense—it is an error of sin. We ought not put ourselves in charge of the storehouses:

> Therefore I tell you, do not worry about your life, what you will eat or what you will drink, or about your body, what you will wear. Is not life more than food, and the body more than clothing? Look at the birds of the air; they neither sow nor reap nor gather into barns, and yet your heavenly Father feeds them. Are you not of more value than they? (Matt 6:25–26)

If we doubt that this is true in real concrete ways, go back to the wilderness and the temptation of Christ. God shows us that this holds good for a human life, because this is how God lives out God's own human life as Jesus Christ. Jesus was hungry as a being dependent upon God and awaited the time to be fed by the Father. And so are we to be. Now Jesus was also fasting for a super long time, and I am not saying we need to do that all the time. He did not. But we too are to embody that same attitude. It is almost like we are made in His image.

IV. Whenever You Do This

Returning to the Lord's Supper, I would like to suggest—and keep in mind I might be totally wrong—that "whenever" you do "this"—that is, whenever you sit down to eat with others—you do "this" in remembrance of the fact that you live in the here and now because of the death of another in a there and then. This means that you claim the present moment, the present locale, the present company, the present activity, as that which itself stands under the gracious judgment of God in Christ crucified and raised. Food itself, then, becomes a concrete mode of demonstration, proclamation, and exemplification pointing to the fact "in him we live and move and have our being" (Acts 17:28). Even salad becomes witness. This means that we can see *food*, in the here and now, as a concrete real presence of the grace that is complete in Jesus Christ and who is Himself really present "wherever two or three gather in my name" (Matt 28:20). Food is itself witness, or at least it can be, that we do not live by McDonald's and Coca-Cola alone (or Ruth's Chris and fine Burgundies) but that His flesh "is true food" and His "blood is true drink" (John 6:55). This means that *food* itself can become a means of grace by which God demonstrates that we have been, are, and will be again taken care of. This means, "*whenever you eat this bread and drink this cup, you proclaim the Lord's death until he comes.*" So let us ask in humbleness, *give us this day our daily bread,* rather than grabbing our food by volition and force. Let us serve each other. Idealistic as this sounds, what this really means is that we ought to invite others to our tables to "taste and see that the Lord is good" (Ps 34:8). For when food is communally prepared and offered to others, we find ourselves nourished in ways that exceed the gluttony of dining alone. Those who have dined in community, whether it be at summer camps, church potlucks, familial picnics, or wedding feasts, know that this experience is richer and more rewarding, regardless of the menu, than fine cuisine consumed in segregated and selfish locations.

Life, like the Bible, is punctuated with stories about food. This is no accident. I leave you with three contemporary vignettes. In the introduction of her *The Little Paris Kitchen,* author and chef Rachel Khoo writes,

> While I was writing this book, I decided to test some of the recipes out on the public by opening up my own "underground" restaurant for just two diners, as my apartment was so small. People from all over the world (including the French) booked and came for lunch. It soon became clear that no matter what nationality they were, the thing they loved the most was the fact that it was simple home-cooked food, not Michelin-starred gastronomy. Food that any Pierre, Paul, or Jacques (Tom, Dick, or Harry!) can cook at home.[7]

This is simply to point out an obvious but deeply biblical fact, one that most restauranteurs know well: good food unites strangers and makes them friends. Hmm. It seems like that is also what Christ does.

In her book, *Take This Bread,* Sara Miles tells of her own "unexpected and terribly inconvenient Christian conversion,"[8] one brought about by a single bite:

> One early, cloudy morning when I was forty-six, I walked into a church, ate a piece of bread, took a sip of wine. A routine Sunday activity for tens of millions Americans—except that up until that moment I'd led a thoroughly secular life, at best indifferent to religion, more often appalled by its fundamentalist crusades. This was my first communion. It changed everything.[9]

7. Khoo, *Little Paris Kitchen,* 11.
8. Miles, *Take This Bread,* xii.
9. Miles, *Take This Bread,* xi.

In that moment, Sara writes, "Jesus happened to me." "And the word" she continues, "was indisputably in my body now, as if I'd swallowed a radioactive pellet that would outlive my own flesh."[10] While not traditional verbiage, such language is probably much more theologically appropriate and such experiences are the goal. Sara's own subsequent testimony to the power of food pantries and community kitchens demonstrate this goal is achievable and repeatable, by God's grace. Let her book, and work, nourish you.

Finally, in his *The Rural Life*, Verlyn Klinkenborg notes that Goethe contends, "Everything is leaf."[11] While this may indeed succinctly describe the ecology of food chains, perhaps we can think even deeper into the metaphysical unity that holds all things together. May we all come to see "Every leaf is Christ," so that decadence is humbled, the powerless are raised up, babies *play* in the fields, the slaves are freed, the choking stops, and none go hungry.

Temple of the Dog: *Hunger Strike*

0:00   4:06

10. Miles, *Take This Bread*, 58–59.
11. Klinkenborg, *Rural Life*, 153.

— 10 —

Ethics + Prayer: Personal Jesus

I. Lost

Have you ever been lost? On a highway? On a trail? Perhaps en route to Mordor? Or maybe just while just checking your mail?

As most people will tell you, when you are lost, the thing you need is a good set of directions. Directions will tell you where you are and how to get to where you are going. But let us think about this a little bit, because I will be honest, I have often felt very lost in this little town of Princeton, even when I know how to get everywhere I am going, and yes, very often while just walking to the mailboxes to check for mail.

Perhaps it would be good to take a step back. Here I have a set of directions from Seattle to the summit of Mt. Rainier. These directions are true and they are accurate. I have employed them and can attest to them, as many others can as well. Granted, they are not the easiest to follow and require some skills and equipment. But they are, nonetheless, true and right and they would be good things to follow if you were in their starting point and if you wanted to go to their ending point.

But suppose you are lost here and now; here in New Jersey, now in seminary. These directions up Mt. Rainier are probably of little use to you. First of all, because you may not be in Seattle. Second of all, because it is doubtful you want to trek up a big mound of rock and snow anyway. How would doing that there get you unlost here? You get what I am saying: if you are not in point A and if you do not want to go to point B, they are utterly useless to you, however right, accurate, and true they are.

This, it seems to me, is the problem with ethics. Historically, the goal in ethics is to find a set of directions or rules that can tell us what we need to know when confronted with a particular issue. But if we do not have that issue in front of us, what good are they? What if we are not trying to get up

Rainier? Likewise, given that somebody else's directions are often likely to get me even more lost, how useful are an "objective set of directions"? What if I do not want to travel like they are traveling? Now do not get me wrong, I am not interested in moral relativism and neither was Barth. But even Mt. Rainier has many of routes to the top. Supposing you want to climb it, which route should you choose? And suppose you pick one, how free are you to vary from its prescribed course?

What would really be useful is a personalized ethical guide that deals with *us*—*us* in our daily lives, *us* as we try to navigate the mountains and molehills that we seem to face, and that we often face alone, *us* as we figure out what to do, where to go, how to be. What we need is a something akin to a personal Global Positioning System. Now if only we had one of these for all our ethical dilemmas. Actually, scratch that. If only we had one of these for *our lives*. Well then, you just couldn't get lost.

Your life is a journey. You have come from someplace and you are going someplace. And now here you are. But just because you know where you came from (and certainty on that might be more elusive than we assume), just because you think you know where you want to go (and I would be wary of being overly certain on that too), and just because you know that you are sitting here and can find your way back to your room, to the coffee shop, or the brewery, is it still not possible that you are lost? Maybe you do not feel like it, though maybe you do, but certainly it is possible that we are lost and do not know where to go. Given the infinite array of options to the above questions, and given the infinite array of the way people answer them, how could we not be lost? I mean look around you. Listen around you. Who knows why they are here? Who knows why you are here? Do they? Do you? Are you sure about that? What we need, what I need, and what you need is a GPS navigator, maybe a universal one for all of humanity, but certainly a particular one just for me and you. One that can tell you and me where I am and where I should go next. Wouldn't this be great? Wouldn't this be *good*?

Depeche Mode: *Personal Jesus*

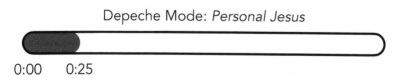

0:00   0:25

Now if *that* sounded good to you, a personal GPS, a personal Jesus who hears *your* prayers, who cares for *you*, who is there for *you*, and who will save *you* from being lost, then let us flash back to Dietrich Bonhoeffer, the

forging of his ethics during Nazi Germany, and a small but significant encouragement he received from Karl Barth.

   Like a Nelson Mandela or a Martin Luther King Jr., Bonhoeffer has become something of a Protestant saint. I want to spend less time summarizing
his overall story, and more time investigating the foundation, one encouraged
by Barth, that leads Bonhoeffer to live the kind of life he did and to think the
way he thought. I also hope this foundation will guide us as we live our lives
in this our modern and intelligent world. "This foundation" says Bonhoeffer,
"is the living, dying, and rising of the Lord Jesus Christ."[1]

Depeche Mode: *Personal Jesus*

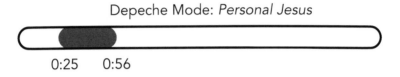

0:25   0:56

II. Bonhoeffer's Strange Foundation

First some biography. Bonhoeffer was born, with his twin sister, Sabine, in
1906. The family had eight children and it must be said that the two World
Wars were brutal on their family. Only one son, Karl, the oldest, died a
natural death (1957). Walter was killed in WWI, and Klaus and Dietrich
were both hanged by the Nazi's in relation to conspiracies to kill Hitler. And
though the four daughters all survived, Ursula and Christine's husbands
were executed by the Nazis, also for their roles in the conspiracy.

   With an aristocratic, intellectual, and musical family, Dietrich excelled
at academics, entered graduate theological education at age seventeen, and
completed a still impressive dissertation, *Sanctorum Communio*, by age
twenty-one. After traveling and studying in Barcelona, Mexico, Cuba, and
New York, he returned to Germany and became involved in the intellectual, ecclesial, and political resistance to Hitler amidst the rise of National
Socialism. Bonhoeffer was critical of National Socialism from the start,
giving a long radio address against Hitler, whom he calls a fool who has
believed his own idolatrous self-image, just two days after Adolf is installed
as Chancellor in 1933. As the Nazi party sought to co-opt the church, and,
sadly, it must be said, as the German church sought to align itself with
Hitler's racial, cultural, and nationalist agenda, Bonhoeffer, as part of the

---

1. Bonhoeffer, *Ethics*, 147.

opposing Confessing Church, became the director of a resistance seminary at Finkenwalde. It is during this time that he writes *Life Together*. Because such seminaries denied that Hitler was the head of the church, they were eventually closed. Bonhoeffer contacts German Resistance (this is 1938) and travels to America in 1939 for a safe and sufficient academic post, but decides he cannot stay away from his country. He returns to Germany on the last civilian ship to sail the Atlantic for Germany. As things spiral downwards in Germany, Bonhoeffer is forbidden from publishing and public speaking. Then, without clear reason he is arrested and imprisoned in Tegel Prison in Berlin on April 5, 1943. Unbeknownst to the Nazis, while they are suspicious of Bonhoeffer's international travel and suspect him of spying—which in fact he seems to have been doing—they do not know that he, along with others, have been plotting assassination attempts on Hitler's life. When the final attempt on Hitler's life fails—the July 20, 1944 Klaus von Stauffenberg "Valkyrie" plot—the imprisoned Bonhoeffer knows that their political resistance has failed, that he will likely die in prison, and that his life is nearly over. When documents are found incriminating Dietrich, he is transferred to the Flossenberg Concentration camp and hanged on April 3, 1945. For those of you who know your history, within that next *month*, Hitler will commit suicide (April 30), Berlin will fall (May 2) and Germany will surrender (May 7). May 8 is Victory in Europe Day. Bonhoeffer almost made it. He missed it by one month. And yet, it almost seems a forgone conclusion that, given his personality and commitments, he simply cannot have survived the Third Reich.

So what is it about Bonhoeffer's life that we might find useful and worthy of emulation? I want to pick up a thread from a letter Bonhoeffer wrote to his friend Paul Lehmann when he first met Karl Barth. In an August 23, 1931 letter, Bonhoeffer writes:

> The time in Bonn was marvelous not only from the theological point of view but also or perhaps even more by the fact that I learned to know Barth personally. He really is a theologian at home as well as in the classroom. His whole thinking swings around one point, and whosoever is willing to keep his eyes straight on this point is considered by Barth a good theologian no matter however he tries to formulate his ideas and views. I do not have to tell you that this point is the cross and the resurrection of Christ, truly a strange thing for a modern and intelligent man to concentrate his thoughts and his whole life to. But when you see Barth you know at once—even if [you]

come entirely from outside—that there is something worthwhile to risk one's life for.[2]

As you can see from this letter, Barth made a "marvelous" impact on Bonhoeffer, and ultimately I think Bonhoeffer lives out, somewhat like a parable, much of Barth's thinking. Since Bonhoeffer's extensive relationship with Barth is not the primary topic for this essay, I will only say that I think on the whole Bonhoeffer and Barth are in vast agreement, even if they occasionally argue about the footnotes.

What Bonhoeffer found in Barth was encouragement to risk his life for a strange foundation: "This foundation is the living, dying, and rising of the Lord Jesus Christ."[3] Bonhoeffer's commitment to this foundation is evident throughout his career as we can see through three essays from three different periods. Through these different periods of Bonhoeffer's life, we can align, counter-intuitively, Christ's rising with our living, Christ's dying with our rising, and Christ's living with our dying.

We can start with his early "Basic Questions of a Christian Ethic" to see how the younger Bonhoeffer, who had only read Barth at this point (he had yet to meet him personally), thinks we should determine our actions based upon the cross of Christ.

Depeche Mode: *Personal Jesus*

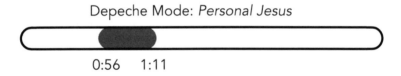

0:56   1:11

Christ's Rising: Our Living

As a 1929 lecture delivered in Barcelona to his German congregation, "Basic Questions of a Christian Ethic" includes not only bold and heady claims but ones that will seem to haunt his later years. Let us investigate.

Bonhoeffer's starting point in the lecture is the disclaimer that "we do not intend to embark on the essentially hopeless attempt to present universally valid Christian norms and commandments as applicable to

2. Bonhoeffer, *Ecumenical, Academic, and Pastoral Work*, 42. I have held the handwritten original of this letter, part of the Princeton Theological Seminary Special Collections.

3. Bonhoeffer, *Ethics*, 147.

contemporary ethical questions."[4] Bonhoeffer is wary, indeed downright antagonistic toward "universally valid Christian norms" because, he thinks, such norms have been struck down in the coming of Christ. "[W]hereas ethics speaks of the path from human beings to God, about the encounter between holy God and the holy human being," Bonhoeffer insists, "the Christian message speaks of grace."[5] Grace, says Bonhoeffer, is "the exclusive path from God to human beings from within God's own compassionate love toward the unholy, the sinful."[6] It is grace—specifically, God's grace—that comes to us in Christ that Bonhoeffer sees as bringing about the "dismissal of principles" or "of fundamental rules."[7] Why so? Because in Christ we have been set free from laws, from rules, from codes, from external impersonal norms of behavior that are binding regardless of who or where the human is underneath them. Rather than *law*, we have only Christ. Citing passages such as Galatians 5:1, Bonhoeffer is insistent: "For freedom Christ has set us free. Stand firm, therefore, and do not submit again to a yoke of slavery."[8] Since "Christ is the bringer of freedom,"[9] he writes, we stand not under a law or before a set of rules, but instead face to face with the living God who has confronted us and continues to confront us in the living person of Jesus Christ. This means we are beholden to a living, willing, deciding, individual rather than to impersonal codes or norms. And this individual is Jesus. Ethics, then, is no longer an eternally static set of navigational directions such as "Always go right after a stop sign," but is rather a person-to-person navigational guidance. What should you do today? Well it depends on where Christ has placed you today and where Christ would like to take you later today. So Bonhoeffer writes:

> Never however can yesterday decisively influence my moral actions today. I must rather always establish anew my immediate relationship with God's will. I will do something again today not because it seems the right thing to do yesterday, but because today, too, God's will has pointed me in that direction.[10]

Bonhoeffer seeks to jettison "traditional morals" such as those found in the laws of the Ten Commandments or the rules of the secular maxims of the

4. Bonhoeffer, *Reader*, 74.

5. Bonhoeffer, *Reader*, 77.

6. Bonhoeffer, *Reader*, 77.

7. Bonhoeffer, *Reader*, 80.

8. Bonhoeffer, *Reader*, 81.

9. Bonhoeffer, *Reader*, 81.

10. Bonhoeffer, *Reader*, 81.

Enlightenment (Kant: "I am never to act otherwise than so that I could also will that my maxim should become a universal law";[11] or Mill: "Nothing is a good to human beings but in so far as it is either pleasurable, or a means of attaining pleasure or averting pain"[12]). Indeed, if we talk of various theories of ethics such as utilitarian (like Mill), deontological (like Kant), virtue (like Aristotle), divine command (like Aquinas), or egoism (like Nietzsche), Bonhoeffer will reject them all. For all such ethical theories are founded in some sort of generic law, code, rule, quality, or individual will that needs to be maximized, actualized, and applied to all. For Bonhoeffer, all such approaches have been overturned *in* grace, *by* grace, and *through* grace in the coming and guiding of Jesus Christ. Hence for Bonhoeffer, traditional ethics is sin. Ethics is sin because it essentially puts the human in charge of her life rather than the living Christ who has been raised from the dead. Barth argues this as well:

> If special ethics becomes casuistry, this means that the moralist wishes to set himself on God's throne, to distinguish good and evil, and always to judge things as the one or the other, not only in relation to others but also to himself. He makes himself lord, king and judge at the place where only God can be this. He does so by claiming that in a *summa* [compendium] of ethical statements compiled by him and his like from the Bible, natural law, and tradition, he can know the command of God, see through and past it, and thus master and handle it, i.e., apply it to himself and others, so that armed with this instrument he may speak as law. He also does it by arrogating to himself the competence so to know human action—his own or that of others—that it seems to him possible and permissible to see its basis in this or that concrete particular form, and relying on his mastery of this instrument to adjudge its character, whether it is good or evil before God.[13]

Barth and Bonhoeffer thus put us all in the position of the disciples who had simply to follow Christ wherever He went. The disciples did not have the 27 *Life Rules of Jesus Followers*, an ability to decipher the Jesus code, or even any knowledge of the larger game plan. They were so clueless. They only had Christ. They could only follow Christ. They either had to go where Jesus went, or cease to be His disciples. Echoing the Kierkegaard of *Fear and Trembling*, Bonhoeffer seeks to make us disciples too, preaching in 1929:

11. Kant, *Fundamental Principles*, 160.

12. Mill, *Utilitarianism*, 276.

13. *CD* III/4, 10.

Traditional morals—even if propagated for Christians—or public opinion can never provide the standards for the action of Christians.

Christians act according to how God's will seems to direct them, without looking sideways at others, that is, without considering what is usually called morals. No one but Christians and God, however, can know whether they are indeed acting rightly or wrongly. Ethical decisions lead us into the most profound solitude, the solitude in which a person stands before the living God. Here no one can help us, no one can bear part of the responsibility; here God imposes a burden on us that we must bear alone. Only in the realization that we have been addressed by God, that God is making a claim on us, does our self awaken. Only through God's call do I become this "self" isolated from all other people, called to account by God, confronted, alone, by eternity. And precisely because I am face-to-face with God in this solitude, I alone can know what is right or wrong for me personally.

There are no acts that are bad in and of themselves; even murder can be sanctified. There is only faithfulness to or deviation from God's will.[14]

Now Bonhoeffer knows that "only faithfulness to or deviation from God's will" is, in fact, the hardest thing. He is, however, confident that like members of a symphony, though we are not all playing the same music, we can be guided and directed by the conductor who guides our unique role and produces something beautiful from our interacting contributions. And like a timpani player who must await her cue from Christ the conductor, we too must play at the best time and in the most beautiful way, even when our timpani might be broken or the wrong instrument altogether:

From day to day and from hour to hour, however, we are confronted by utterly new situations in which we are supposed to make decisions and in which we repeatedly have the surprising and terrifying experience that God's will as a matter of fact does not reveal itself to us as clearly as we might have hoped. Because God's will seems to contradict itself, because two of God's orders seem to conflict, we find ourselves in a position of having to choose not between good and evil, but between evil and evil. It is here that we encounter the real, most difficult problems of ethics.[15]

14. Bonhoeffer, *Reader*, 81.
15. Bonhoeffer, *Reader*, 83.

Encountering the real, most difficult problems in ethics is, however, when we finally and fully must reach out and "trust in the LORD with all your heart and lean not on your own understanding" (Prov 3:5–6).

In "Basic Questions of a Christian Ethic," Bonhoeffer has argued that there are no rules, no ultimate rights or wrongs, that we have total freedom before Christ, that we ought to allow ourselves to be guided by Christ, that this will frequently leave us in a position of having to choose between two or more "not good" options, but that ultimately we stand in freedom and "responsibility before God."[16] Moreover, he is confident that "such an ethic will never fail us"[17] and that it is only "God's grace which releases us from the crisis of our age."[18] The reason why God's grace releases us and why such an ethic will never fail is because Christ has risen from the dead. Christ is not bound by death, time, place, or power, and promises to guide us from wherever we are. This ethic cannot fail us because of the *living* foundation upon which it is built. "This foundation," says Bonhoeffer, "is the living, dying, and rising of the Lord Jesus Christ."[19]

Depeche Mode: *Personal Jesus*

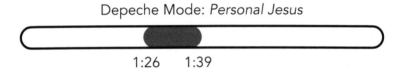

1:26   1:39

Christ's Dying: Our Rising

Since Bonhoeffer knew something about the crisis of the age, we now turn to how we ought to view the world around us as we follow Christ's navigation through it.

In a later essay from the mid-1930s, "Ultimate and Penultimate Things," Bonhoeffer seeks to have us anchor our lives on the one thing in this world that is certain: "the justification of the sinner by grace alone."[20] A rather

---

16. Bonhoeffer, *Reader*, 87.
17. Bonhoeffer, *Reader*, 87.
18. Bonhoeffer, *Reader*, 90.
19. Bonhoeffer, *Reader*, 614.
20. Bonhoeffer, *Reader*, 615.

strange certainty! Yet, in this we again see Bonhoeffer's ethical foundation "is the living, dying, and rising of the Lord Jesus Christ."[21] He writes,

> The dark tunnel of human life, which was barred within and without and was disappearing ever more deeply into an abyss from which there is no exit, is powerfully torn open; the word of God bursts in. In this saving light, people recognize God and their neighbors for the first time. The labyrinth of their previous lives collapses. They become free for God and for one another.[22]

Bonhoeffer believes that when we understand that the world is justified by Christ on the cross, our whole perspective on how things are, indeed, even *what* things are will change. God's grace will then become the certain foundation that gives context to the whole world. The justification of the sinner by grace is the compass by which we navigate through the world's fog. Instead of seeing everyone and everything, including ourselves, "as it is," we will see such things as something for which Christ died, something which Christ has redeemed, and something which someday will have been completely purified, sanctified, transformed, redeemed, and raised again. For Bonhoeffer this means our perspective will shift because whatever we thought was the ultimate truth about someone or some element in the world is only penultimate and is replaced by the ultimate truth that is grounded in God's claim on us in Christ. So he seems to write autobiographically, if somewhat cryptically:

> He never knew before what life is. He did not understand himself. He could only try to understand himself and to justify his life by his own potentialities or his own works. So he justified himself before himself and before a God of his own imagination. The possibilities and works of the living God had to seem inaccessible to him, and a life rooted in those possibilities and works is inconceivable. Life on another foundation, drawing on another strength and another help, remained alien to him. He found his life when he was justified by Christ in Christ's own way.[23]

Looking to Christ's justification of us grants a secure foundation for our lives, one that is not inside us, but one that exists securely and independently in the eternal living of Christ. Again, Bonhoeffer concludes,

> Faith means to base life on a foundation outside of myself, on an eternal and holy foundation, on Christ.

21. Bonhoeffer, *Reader,* 614.

22. Bonhoeffer, *Reader,* 614.

23. Bonhoeffer, *Reader,* 615.

Faith means to be torn out of the imprisonment in one's own ego.

Faith alone is certainty; everything outside of faith is subject to doubt.[24]

The justification of the sinner is the ultimate truth that can be spoken about the temporal finite world: "There is no word of God that goes beyond God's grace."[25] But as the justification of a passing, finite, temporal, limited, flawed world is the ultimate truth, we must not be tempted to incorrectly value the things of this world, what Bonhoeffer calls the penultimate. Here we could easily fall to one of two extremes: the "Radical," which is content to see the world burn because of its inability to live up to its ultimate destination, and "Compromise," which is so skeptical of God's solution that it seeks to deal only with the world in short-sighted and worldly means. These two extreme alternatives, like gutters alongside a bowling alley, must be equally avoided, for "Christ does not make compromises" but neither is He "the radical" according to a worldly conception. Bonhoeffer juxtaposes the two views accordingly:

Radicalism hates time. Compromise hates eternity.

Radicalism hates patience. Compromise hates decision.

Radicalism hates wisdom. Compromise hates simplicity.

Radicalism hates measure. Compromise hates the immeasurable.

Radicalism hates the real. Compromise hates the word.[26]

Where does this leave us? With his earlier 1929 essay discussed above, Bonhoeffer put ethical human life in a place where it cannot know where to go. Humanity is lost, traditional ethics is of no help, and we will remain lost until we seek the guidance of Christ to navigate us, as Bunyan says, "through the wilderness of this world."[27] Navigationally, our only way forward, our only way to the good, our only way out is to follow Christ. Christ is our truth, Christ is our light, Christ is our guide. And for this reason Bonhoeffer sees the fundamental question of human behavior not as "What is the good and right thing to do?" but rather, as he writes to his friend Eberhard Bethge from Tegel Prison: "Who is Christ actually for us today?"[28]

---

24. Bonhoeffer, *Reader*, 615.

25. Bonhoeffer, *Reader*, 616.

26. Bonhoeffer, *Reader*, 621.

27. Bunyan, *Pilgrim's Progress*, 17.

28. Bonhoeffer, *Letters and Papers*, 362.

From his work "Ultimate and Penultimate Things," we see Bonhoeffer wanting to put all things in relation to their ultimate end in Christ. In effect, this tells us our ultimate destination, navigationally speaking, and should also clarify why Christ navigates us to any particular penultimate destination. Anyone or anything we encounter has to be understood not in relation to itself (i.e., as "good in itself" or as "bad in itself"), to its past, or to any other things in this world. The essence of anybody or anything is not ultimately in itself. This mandates that if we are to properly define, understand, perceive, and hear truthfully, we must define, understand, perceive, and hear penultimate things as those things which are elected, upheld, and loved by God in grace, things for which God has sacrificed, and things which through Christ may be dramatically transformed from their current state. Certainly, the Christian is to know that all things will someday pass away. This can be some comfort in some times. But Bonhoeffer takes solace in more than a "this too shall pass," for he thinks that in Christ's death, all dying is forever altered, indeed that all things that will die need to be wholly revaluated in light of the cross. For instance, "only from the perspective of the ultimate can we recognize what a human being is, and therefore, how being human is based on and determined by being justified."[29] Not only will things pass, they will be made new. Christ's dying thus redefines all that is. Bonhoeffer elaborates,

> Christ comes to his creation that, despite the fall, remains his creation. Christ comes not to devils but to human beings, certainly to sinful, lost, and damned humans, but still to human beings. Because Christ comes to them, because Christ redeems them from sin and from the power of the evil, sinful human beings are still human, the fallen creation remains creation. From a Christian perspective the fallen world becomes understandable as the world preserved and maintained by God for the coming of Christ. . . . But where human beings become things, commodities, or machines,—where orders are arbitrarily destroyed and the distinction is no longer made between "good" and "evil"—a special hindrance is placed in the way of receiving Christ that goes beyond the world's general sinfulness and forlornness.[30]

And so, contrary to traditional ethics, which always placed temporal goods as good in relation to other temporal goods, "The human and the good should not be made into self-sufficient values, but they may and should be claimed

29. Bonhoeffer, *Reader*, 623.
30. Bonhoeffer, *Reader*, 627.

for Jesus Christ."[31] In "Ultimate and Penultimate Things," we see again how Bonhoeffer risks all ethical behavior on the foundation of the cross. Truly a strange thing for those who have always looked everywhere else to define what is good! But only on this foundation can the home of the good be built. Only on this foundation does a new world arise. "This foundation," says Bonhoeffer, "is the living, dying, and rising of the Lord Jesus Christ."[32]

Depeche Mode: *Personal Jesus*

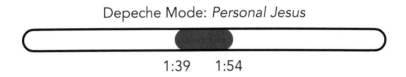

1:39   1:54

Christ's Living: Our Dying

On July 21, 1944, the day after the final failed attempt on Hitler's life, Bonhoeffer wrote to his friend Eberhard Bethge. Bonhoeffer already knew the attempt was unsuccessful since it had been all over the news, was the subject of radio broadcasts, and was much talked about by the prison staff. Hitler claimed that his survival was due to providence and was proof that he was God's chosen Führer. Amidst this, Bonhoeffer writes: "In the last few years I have come to know and understand more and more the profound this-worldliness of Christianity. The Christian is not a *homo religiosus*, but simply a man, in the same way Jesus was a human being—in contrast, perhaps to John the Baptist."[33] He continues,

> Later on I discovered, and am still discovering to this day, that one only learns to have faith by living in the full this-worldliness of life. If one has completely renounced making something of oneself—whether it be a saint or a converted sinner or a church leader (a so-called priestly figure!), a just or an unjust person, a sick or a healthy person—then one throws oneself completely into the arms of God, and this is what I call this-worldliness: living fully in the midst of life's tasks, questions, successes and failures, experiences, and perplexities—then

31. Bonhoeffer, *Reader*, 630.

32. Bonhoeffer, *Reader*, 614.

33. Bonhoeffer, *Letters and Papers*, 485.

one takes seriously no longer one's own suffering but rather the suffering of God in the world.

He concludes this thought:

> I am grateful that I have been allowed this insight, and I know that it is only on the path that I have finally taken that I was able to learn this. So I am thinking gratefully and with peace of mind about past as well as present things.[34]

Yes, Jesus was perplexed. Yes, Jesus was troubled. Yes, Jesus wept. Yes, Jesus was angry. Yes, Jesus was frustrated by a sick world. Yes, Jesus was anxious. Yes, Jesus was abandoned. Yes, Jesus was arrested. Yes, Jesus too had to live by faith. And yes, this meant letting God the Father sort out how He was to be who and what He was. But for Bonhoeffer, this means that Christ's faithful living in this world, amidst all of its uncertainties, remains a living that can guide our dying, even within our uncertainties. For we will die with only God truly knowing who we really were.

> Who am I? They mock me, these lonely questions of mine.

> Whoever I am, Thou knowest, O God, I am thine![35]

Depeche Mode: *Personal Jesus*

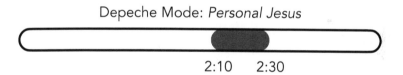

2:10   2:30

III. Bonhoeffer's Personal Jesus

Bonhoeffer is in many ways an idealistic figure who shows no compromises. He writes his book *[The Cost of] Discipleship* partially, as he says, because he "I thought I could acquire faith by trying to live a holy life, or something like it."[36] But Bonhoeffer's idealism is compelling because (1) it is intellectually rich, and (2) it is born from a dark period where so many ethical ideals were perverted toward horrific ends. More importantly, his

---

34. Bonhoeffer, *Letters and Papers*, 486.

35. Bonhoeffer, *Letters and Papers*, 460.

36. Bonhoeffer, *Letters and Papers*, 486.

"idealism," if we call it that, is in the end a *faith* that is committed to following Christ even to and through suffering.

Bonhoeffer, I maintain, is uncompromising, but this is all grounded in a strategic, realistic outlook on the world. Bonhoeffer is not naive. He is not unlived. He is not primarily a man committed to principles. Bonhoeffer's uncompromising commitment to speak truth, to live truth, and to live it deeply, purely, and communally means that his uncompromising vision is flexible, encompasses others, and the contributions and detours they may bring. This is because, for Bonhoeffer, the truth is who Christ is and what Christ has done for a sinful world. All truths that we profess need to give witness to that ultimate Truth.

Bonhoeffer's faith is grounded not in abstract ideals, complex theories, or even lofty medieval conceptions of theology. His faith is again and again directed at Jesus and in following Jesus through the labyrinth of this world. Bonhoeffer does not deny this world is convoluted, confusing, dark, and difficult. But he is convinced God dwells with us in the darkness, knows the way forward, and guides us with a navigational light that can be seen, felt, and heard.

In a world of cheaply bought compromises that offer few lasting gains, Bonhoeffer is aware that the Christian life can be lived without either a blindly radical "eyes only on eternity" or a "sell it all for a few more drinks on the deck while the Titanic is sinking" mentality. While being a middle ground, this is itself not a compromise, because it takes self-criticism seriously, is willing to endure pain, and so does not seek primarily one's own protection. It also, uncompromisingly, leaves no aspect of our lives untouched.

In realizing that there is no perfect action, that all actions done by us are tainted with sin, Bonhoeffer nevertheless trusts that God's grace guides us to the right action in the right time. When we trust that even if we play crudely, God will redeem, sanctify, and employ our deeds, Bonhoeffer gives us hope that a beautiful symphony of witness may emerge, even if "the answers" are never fully given.

Ultimately, I think what stands as Bonhoeffer's greatest contribution is that just about every aspect of his political and theological life, certainly every aspect of his life that we think is worth remembering, is witness to his divine foundation: "This foundation is the living, dying, and rising of the Lord Jesus Christ."[37]

Who stands fast? Only the one who does a truly strange thing for a modern and intelligent person to do. Only the one, among a world of many others, who like Bonhoeffer or Barth upholds a policy of truth and risks

---

37. Bonhoeffer, *Reader*, 614.

one's life for Christ's crucifixion and resurrection. Only the one who, well, Depeche Mode says it best. . .

Depeche Mode: *Personal Jesus*

2:52   3:46

— 11 —

Time: Today

I was camping with friends after my senior year of high school. On the ground next to the fire circle in my sleeping bag, I awoke to the distortion of Smashing Pumpkins. My Toyota station wagon was backed up just a few feet away with the trunk open. Since I had cleverly rigged a way for the doors to stay open with the stereo on and not drain the battery, the album, *Siamese Dream*, had been on repeat all night long. This song was playing:

Smashing Pumpkins: *Today*

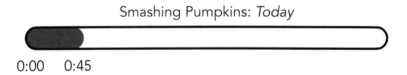

0:00   0:45

"How?" I wondered in a groggy state of mind, "How could they be so convinced that today was the greatest day, when it was still so early in the morning?" Admittedly I was not fully awake and it did not occur to me that perhaps the song had been written at the end of the day. Still, I was struck by their attitude. What would it be like, could it even be possible, to say with confidence early on any given day, that this day, this today, is the greatest day that ever was? It seemed they knew.

While it is not necessarily the prevalent attitude, it is an attitude that we see often enough in motivating and optimistic works of art and inspiration. "Today," the message goes, "is your day. Reach out, believe, and make the choices that allow you to be who you want to be. With boldness and courage, live your dream. And then take lots of pictures and post them all over the internet to prove that you are the greatest, freest, most enviable human around." Okay, so maybe it is the prevalent attitude in the todays of the social media era.

It is an attitude that, if partially embodied by many, is articulated maximally by one: the grand mustached arch-atheist, Friedrich Nietzsche. Consider this aphorism, from his manifesto for life in the wake of the death of God:

> The greatest stress: How, if some day or night a demon were to sneak after you into your loneliest loneliness and say to you, "This life as you now live it and have lived it, you will have to live once more and innumerable times more; and there will be nothing new in it, but every pain and every joy and every thought and sigh and everything immeasurably small or great in your life must return to you—all in the same succession and sequence—even this spider and this moonlight between the trees, and even this moment and I myself. The eternal hourglass of existence is turned over and over, and you with it, a dust grain of dust." Would you not throw yourself down and gnash your teeth and curse the demon who spoke thus? Or did you once experience a tremendous moment when you would have answered him: "You are a god, and never have I heard anything more godly!" If this thought were to gain possession of you, it would change you, as you are, or perhaps crush you. The question in each and every thing, "Do you want this once more and innumerable times more?" would weigh upon your actions as the greatest stress. Or how well disposed would you have to become to yourself and to life to *crave nothing more fervently* than this ultimate eternal confirmation and seal?[1]

Nietzsche is too fascinating to say too little about, but he is also too rich to say much about now. In my opinion, he is the most consistent atheist, and atheists who have yet to encounter him have not thoroughly faced up to what they actually should believe. The same is true for Christians! I have learned more Christian theology from what Nietzsche rejects than from what most professing Christian theologians affirm. What Nietzsche asks of us in this aphorism is to envision our lives on infinite repeat. While this may seem like a simple thought experiment, it is worth saying that Nietzsche understood this to be reality. In a universe with finite matter, finite energy, and infinite time, Nietzsche held the eternal return as an actual cosmological principal, not just a motivating ethical hypothetical. Thus he asks us to confront our whole lives, not just our best vacations or our cutest selfie, and to ask ourselves whether we have the strength, courage, and will to live all our

---

1. Nietzsche, *Portable*, 101–2.

moments over and over again. If we can own our lives, thinks Nietzsche, if we can will our whole life over and over again, if we can see, as he says in one of his most tweeted lines, that "what does not kill me makes me stronger";[2] if we can have the power to will this for eternity and in eternal repetition, then we can become the god of the universe who says of this cosmos, "Let it be." As Nietzsche says in his most famous aphorism: "God is dead! God remains dead! And we have killed him! . . . Shall we not ourselves have to become Gods, merely to seem worthy of it?"[3]

I bring in Nietzsche because one way in which we might say that any and every "today" is the greatest day is to rise to the status of Übermensch and to view our time, our life, and indeed, this moment, as the center of the universe toward which all time flows. Indeed, this is what Nietzsche asks of us in *The Gay Science, Beyond Good and Evil, Thus Spake Zarathustra*, and *Twilight of the Idols*. In *The Antichrist*, he begs us to orient the world's timeline around *him*.[4]

What an ego! But truth be told, that is pretty much how I lived and acted my senior year of high school and first year of college.

Is there another way? And what is it, again, that we are even trying to figure out?

I propose that at the heart of the matter of whether today is the greatest is a set of questions that revolve around: "What is time, history, my life, and the meaning of the universe?" Just a few basic queries to go with our morning coffee. And yet, if you are like me, you find yourself asking these just about every afternoon between 3:30 and 6.

Smashing Pumpkins: *Today*

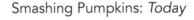

0:46 0:58

2. Nietzsche, *Portable*, 467.

3. Nietzsche, *Gay Science*, 181.

4. So Nietzsche concludes *Antichrist*: "This eternal accusation against Christianity I shall write upon all walls, wherever walls are to be found—I have letters that even the blind will be able to see. . . . I call Christianity the one great curse, the one great intrinsic depravity, the one great instinct of revenge, for which no means are venomous enough, or secret, subterranean and *small* enough,—I call it the one immortal blemish upon the human race. . . . And mankind reckons time from the *dies nefastus* when this fatality befell—from the first day of Christianity!—Why not rather from its last?— From today?—The transvaluation of all values!" Nietzsche, *Portable*, 656.

I. A Brief History of Time

We start with the simple question: What is time?

Actually, maybe this question is not so simple. In his famous treatment of God and time in *The Confessions*, Augustine admits, "What is time? I know what it is if no one asks me what it is; but if I want to explain it to someone who has asked me, I find that I do not know."[5] The multi-year survey of the subject I undertook in graduate school showed me that, nearly two-thousand years later, time is a problem in which we are still lost. Confirming my own experiences, philosopher Anthony Kenny writes, "Nineteenth- and twentieth-century treatments of these matters have added very little to the work of earlier philosophers and theologians."[6] If true, this means it is among the great philosophical questions. For as Ludwig Wittgenstein notes, "A philosophical problem has the form: 'I don't know my way about.'"[7]

So it is that time remains an *aporia* for philosophers and physicists. Consider just a few of the questions open for resolution:[8]

- Is time real? Is its reality an external something? Or only an internal perception?

- Does time exist when nothing is changing?

- Why does time have a sense of flow?

- Is time's arrow, its flow, directed at anything?

- How can time, as a sequence of beginnings, itself have a beginning, as described by classical Big Bang Theory?

- Are the future and the past real? Where are they?

- Do all different times exist "at once," as in a so-called "block"?

- Where is the future coming from?

- What is the relationship between time and those who perceive it? Why are we all now?

- Is God timeless or temporal? Does God's knowledge change? Does God know what time it is?

- Can we move multi-dimensionally through time, as we do through space?

---

5. Augustine, *Confessions* XI.14, 262.

6. Kenny, *God of the Philosophers*, 8.

7. Wittgenstein, *Philosophical Investigations*, 42e.

8. See for instance *Internet Enclyopedia of Philosophy*, s.v. "Time."

- Why doesn't everything happen at once?

Time remains an equally perplexing problem for theologians, or at least for those who have not read (or understood) Karl Barth. Theological doctrines and debates such as those over election, divine foreknowledge, free will, God's nature, the whence and why of creation, the efficacy of prayer, and the meaning of theological language all reference conceptions of time and God's relationship to it. But do we have a good understanding of God's relationship to time?

Consider some of the theological questions open for clarification:

- What is the distinction between time and eternity?

- Is time a category that pertains to divine being? Does God get older?

- How is God related to temporal events? Does God experience them as we do? Does Got get surprised?

- If God is timeless, does this mean God does not exist in time?

- If God is temporal, does this limit God's being/knowledge/power?

- Does the passage of time affect divine knowledge? Does God forget?

- Are scientific and philosophical explanations of time, such as a theory of relativity, relevant in gaining knowledge of God's relationship to time?

- Is eternity, "the whole, simultaneous, perfect possession of limitless life"?[9] How would we know?

- Does God's knowledge of the future impose necessity upon that future?

- What does divine revelation and the affirmation that "the Word became flesh" mean for how God exists in eternity?

Given the manifold conundrums and confusions one can be dizzied by, physicist and philosopher of time Paul Davies openly confesses, "We are far from having a good grasp of the concept of time."[10]

One strategy for gaining new ground on these problems has been Ludwig Wittgenstein's call for a new, non-metaphysical language of time and space. Wittgenstein wrote, "[A]s long as we continue to talk of a river of time, of an expanse of space, etc., etc., people will keep stumbling over the same puzzling difficulties and find themselves staring at something which

---

9. Boethius, *Consolation*, 168.

10. Davies, *About Time*, 9.

no explanation seems capable of clearing up."[11] It is my contention that Karl Barth effectively answers this call, preemptively as it were, by developing a non-metaphysical language through which we can talk about time, eternity, and their intersection. This language is grounded, not in being, movement, or predicates of nature or reason *per se*, but rather in the particular life-time and life-history of Jesus. Not only does this way of thinking and speaking establish that time is real in my eyes (a genuine problem in its own right), it also establishes the epistemological route by which we understand what our time, and all time, is really about. The result is, quite simply, a view of time like we have never seen before. By way of a quick tour of time according to Barth, rather than exegete particular sections, we will break down some of his commonly used vocabulary and nomenclature.

II. Turn Towards Barth, Head Straight for Jesus Christ

How do we know our time is real? Without committing too heavily to what might be an overly literal interpretation of Genesis 1, most Christians would probably take comfort in our knowledge of the reality of time because of God's creation of it. Whether we view the "days" as sun-ups to sun-downs, epochs, eras, or something else, most would likely say that God's rhythm of creation over six periods shows that time is real. Barth disagrees!

Lost time: According to Barth, we do not live in time. We do not have time. We do not understand time. Our time is a lie. Our time is a false myth. The histories we write are not true histories. The clocks and calendars we watch subsist only as "highly questionable" pseudo-realities.[12] We live in lost time. This time is a confusion. Our pasts haunt us in the present. Our present perpetually and immediately evaporates into the dark abyss of the past. Our future is an uncertain cause of anxiety, full of danger, terror, and death. We are lost in time. We grasp at distraction. We cling to icons of stability. We build storehouses of security. We write narratives of longevity. We scrape with desperation at the overhanging cliff of ticks and tocks in a futile attempt to make something in our lives permanent. We fail. We fall. We do not understand our lives. We do not understand history. We do not know where the world is going. We do not know where we are going. Our time is lost. We are lost in sin. Ours is sinful time. Ours is fake time. Ours is fallen time. The grass withers and the flower fades. The mist burns off.

11. Wittgenstein, *Culture and Value*, 15e.
12. *CD* I/2, 59.

The mountains crumble. We are over. Our time is past. Our time is gone. Sinful time is lost time.

Barth's diatribe against the arrogance with which we think we have time and the meanings we construct off our idolatrous projections is decapitating. We stand over an abyss. We have no anchor. We have no foundation. As a madman says, "Do we not dash on unceasingly? Backwards, sideways, forwards, in all directions? Is there still an above and below? Do we not stray, as through infinite nothingness?"[13] The Christian might counter that God is real and God created time, but Barth's contention is that "created time" is not what we have. That time fell. That time is lost. Thus, as he says in his *Epistle to the Romans*, our false time is the experience of "KRISIS," "THE NIGHT," and "the road of negation."[14]

Created time: This is the time of Genesis 1 and 2. This is characterized, not in a flat-footed uncritical literalist way as seven twenty-four hour days, but as the relation of God to the created reality in a face-to-face manner. True, this time had some sort of metric and rhythm, but those were not what defined its essence. It was God's presence to the world, God's making and taking time for the world, God's being visibly present to the world, that gave the world its present. Whether we argue this time is history, pre-history, myth, legend, or saga (Barth effectively argues it is all of these), created time, while not the *telos* of time itself, is the good basis for God's guiding and parental presence to the world. This time, this "time of creation," is gone. After Eden, we wander through lost time.

Real time: Real time is not a clock. Real time is not a Zen-moment. Real time is not the best time you had with your girlfriend/boyfriend/wife/husband/family/sports car. Real time is Jesus Christ. Jesus Christ is the "fullness of time." No, Jesus Christ is not your alarm clock. Jesus Christ is God-present, the point of time, and the one through whom and for which time is created. Just as the throne room is not the king, or just as the invitation is not the party itself, while being less so than even the one who is having the birthday, our times, created and lost, are not the full and true version of God's presence to a "wholly distinct" reality of an O/other. Jesus, however, *is* the full and true version of God present to a "wholly distinct" O/other. Hence, Jesus is Real Time. That Jesus Christ is real time is the "secret of time," and His true time stands as a perpetually contemporary, alternative, judgmental "third time" to the not-really-real created-times and lost-times above. Jesus Christ's real time on earth is thus "the time of God" and is "mastered time." As "the time of revelation," Christ is the

---

13. Nietzsche, *Gay Science*, 181.

14. See for instance Barth, *Epistle to the Romans*, 17, 42, 87.

unique manifestation of the God who weaves history. In this sense, Christ is "non-historical," though He cannot be known except in and through His life-history as attested in the Scriptures. Christ, as the revelation of God to the world, as the one who manufactures real history, is not then ultimately a product of all the natural and historical forces that operate on the rest of us. The Christ event is not simply one among all the other normal events happening around us. True, God's presence to the world as Christ-in-time takes place on the plane of dirt, clocks, and history books, but as the actor is the one who says, "Very truly, I tell you, before Abraham was, I am" (John 8:58), this actor is not bound and limited by all the forces binding the rest of the world of dirt, clocks, and historical narratives. This actor in history is, in fact, the true author *of* history. The resurrection, the event of all events, and the *telos* of time itself, while happening in the world of time, is not caused in a deterministic way by the events preceding it. Christ is not resuscitated from the dead by another preceding event from within the plane of dirt, clocks, and history books. Judas betraying Jesus did not cause the resurrection to happen. Christ is raised from the dead by God the Father through the power of the Holy Spirit. This act happens *from* eternity *to* the world of time, "as a tangent touches a circle."[15] It is an act that transcends the abilities of dirt, clocks, and history. It is an event that transcends the capacity of Judas, Pilate, John, or Peter, and which graciously redeems them all. Revelation and resurrection are both miracle. So Barth will say, as we cited earlier, "Revelation is not a predicate of history, but history is a predicate of revelation."[16] This means God's time as Christ is the really real time that secures this world's dirt, clocks, and history as "real-enough for God to redeem." Finally, as the one who is, was, and will be, as the true author of history and the true God-present, as the Alpha and the Omega, Jesus Christ is the "Lord of Time." No, this doesn't mean He can time travel. He does not need to.

God's time: This is eternity, the true, unfractured, wholly united, ever-flowing stream of the triune κοινωνία. In the perpetual and perpetuating love for Another, the triune God, as we detailed in chapter 2, lives God's own life in the pre-temporality, supra-temporality, and post-temporality of the glorious eternity. This, "the simultaneity and coinherence of past, present, and future," is, as Barth says, God's "own dimension."[17] And yet, this dimension is not selfishly hoarded in heavenly kingdoms, it is shared with this reality distinct from God, over and over again, as time. Eternity is not

---

15. Barth, *Epistle to the Romans*, 30.

16. *CD* I/2, 58.

17. *CD* III/2, 526.

overly difficult to comprehend. It is God "once and again and a third-time" as Father, Son, and Holy Spirit forever and ever.[18]

Given time: "Given time" is the time of our humanity. *Church Dogmatics* III/2's extensive treatment of both Christ as the Lord of Time, and of humanity as the recipient of God's gift of time, graciously restores the security of our temporal dimensionality. Humanity can have time for life. Humanity *may* have time. Humanity may live in the time it needs to flourish within the gift of our "allotted time." Reconciled and healed as "lost time" is in Christ, our past is rendered a forgiven, passed-over state to which we can never return. Graciously granted through the presence of Christ, our present presents itself as a genuine opportunity to receive real time from Christ. Destined and oriented towards the universal Lordship of Christ, the future offers a hopeful arrival that is bound toward redemption with others and with the triune God from whom all goodness and beauty flows. This will be glorious. Death, under this light, is understood as a gracious "it is enough" granted by grace to creatures who could never climb high enough, purify deeply enough, or work long enough to become the kingdom of their own ability. The end of our lives means we do not have to forever climb a stairway to heaven, the top of which we would never even gain. The essential truth that pertains to all things, regardless of when we might find them in time, is that Christ's election for glorification stands before all worldly beginnings, just as Christ's invitation for sanctification stands present to all moments, just as Christ's redemption stands after all endings. Christ alone is the Alpha and the Omega, the beginning and end, from whom all blessings flow and whose own "time of revelation" to our world's time secures our temporal lives as real, elected, and redeemed by the God who negates our lost sinfulness and who grants us a seat of honor at the eternal royal feast. Indeed, the world's time keeps ticking, so to speak, even though time's end was fully accomplished in the resurrection. It does so precisely so more and more distant and strange creatures can be brought in to enjoy the feast again and again for longer and longer.

III. Christ Is Time

While Barth's treatment of time and eternity is dispersed throughout each volume of the *Church Dogmatics*, and has barely been summarized above, its summit is a short section deep in III/2. It is this section to which all earlier treatments ascend and from its vantage point all subsequent sections flow. It is both pinnacle and foundation. And more so than a triple trouble

18. *CD* II/1, 615.

tongue twister, it is a delightfully mind-blowing two pages. Speaking of the first Easter and the resurrection of Jesus, here goes Barth:

> We have called this time of His at the heart of other times the time of God: eternal time; the time which God has assumed for us, and thus granted to us, the men of all times; the time of His covenant; or, as the Bible sees it, the great Sabbath; the year of salvation; fulfilled time. We must now try to assess the material implications of all this for our understanding of this particular time.
>
> Our previous deliberations should have made it clear that in the first instance the time of Jesus is also a time like all other times; that it occurred once and once for all; that it had beginning, duration and end; that it was contemporary for some, future for others, and for others again, e.g., for us, past. Only a docetic attitude to Jesus can deny that His being in time also means what being in time means for us all. Our recognition of His true humanity depends on our acceptance of this proposition. Even the recognition of His true deity, implying as it does the identity between His time and God's, does not rule out this simple meaning of His being in time. On the contrary, it includes it. Of course there is much more to see and say, but it would all be pointless if we ignored or minimized this simple truth.
>
> It is as well to realize how closely the relevant New Testament formulae support this view. This is the case with the formula which constantly recurs in different forms in the Apocalypse (Rev. 1:4, Rev. 1:8, Rev. 1:17, Rev. 4:8, Rev. 21:6, Rev. 22:13), in clear reminiscence of Is. 41:4, Is. 44:6, Is. 48:12: I am he that was, and is, and is to come, the beginning and the ending, the first and the last, the Alpha and Omega. Of course these formulae are much too solemn to be taken simply as a description of the being of a man in its temporal limits and in its beginning, duration and end in time, and therefore as a being contemporary, future or past to that of others. The formula says much more than this. But it does include this, as a primary truth within its wider implications. The same holds good of Heb. 13:8: "Jesus Christ the same yesterday, and today, and for ever." This again means more than that the man Jesus lived in a movement from yesterday through to-day to to-morrow. Yet we miss the deeper implications if we overlook the primary and simple meaning of the words.
>
> The three dimensions which play a part in any conception of time are equally important for an understanding of the time of Jesus as the time of God. But there is a further point to be

noticed. The time of Jesus is not only a time like all others; it is also different from them. For all other times are confined to the three dimensions. They begin, they endure, and they come to an end. According to the standpoint of the observer, they are future, contemporary or past.

1. Every other time begins, and therefore from the standpoint of an earlier time it is a future time. This means that it does not yet exist at this earlier time.

2. Every other time has duration, and therefore from the standpoint of the same time it is present. This means that its contemporaneity is limited to its duration, and to that of the contemporary observer.

3. Every other time comes to an end, and therefore from the standpoint of a later time it is already past. This means that it no longer exists at this time.

But these limitations of all other times—the times of all other living creatures—do not apply to the time of the man Jesus.

1. To be sure, the life of the man Jesus has a beginning, and His time was once future. Yet this does not mean that it did not then exist.

2. The life of Jesus has duration, and therefore it was once contemporary. Yet this does not mean that it was present only in its duration, and from the standpoint of contemporaries.

3. The life of Jesus comes to an end and therefore it became past. Yet this does not mean that it then ceased to be.

The removal of the limitations of its yesterday, to-day and to-morrow, of its once, now and then, is the distinctive feature of the time of the man Jesus. For as such, according to its manifestation in Easter-time, it is also the time of God; eternal time; the time of the covenant; the great Sabbath; the year of salvation; fulfilled time. What is for all other times, the times of all other living creatures, an absolute barrier, is for Him in His time a gateway. We shall now try to formulate positively what we have so far stated only in the form of delimitation.

1. The life of Jesus begins, and therefore it was once future. But the man Jesus already was even before He was. Hence the time before His time, the time when this was still future, because it hastened forward to His future, was also His time, the time of His being.

2. The life of Jesus has duration, and therefore it was once present. But for all its singularity this present reaches back to His past when His time was still future, and forward to His future when His time will be past. The man Jesus is as He was and will be. Even the time of His present, just because it is the time of His present, is also the time before and after His time, and is thus His time, the time of His being.

3. The life of Jesus comes to an end, and therefore there was a moment when His time became past. But its end is such that it is always present and still future. The man Jesus was as He is and will be. Even the time after His time, the time in which His time is already past time, because it is the time of His past, the time which derives from Him, is the time of His renewed presence, the time of His new coming, and therefore again His time.

This means, however, that from the standpoint of the three dimensions of every conception of time, His time is not only the time of a man, but the time of God, eternal time. Thus, as the title of this sub-section suggests, He not only is in time and has time like other men, but He is also Lord of time.[19]

When I first read passage, I was studying at an indoor rock climbing gym near Princeton. I gasped, wrote marginal notes with cuss words, nearly rent my garments, and promptly climbed the hardest problem I was working on. Wow. My brain still fireworks whenever I read it.

Beastie Boys: *So What'cha Want*

1:38   2:16

My mind aside, Barth sees this as the only proper inference from a rigorous exegesis of a host of biblical passages, including Exodus 3:14, Hebrews 13:8, Revelation 1:8, 1:17, and 22:13 and more. "There is such a wealth of exegetical material available," he writes, "we must confine ourselves to a few concrete manifestations."[20] And he then spends forty pages, most of it fine print, working through Jesus' present, past, and future to show: "Since

19. *CD* III/2, 462–64.
20. *CD* III/2, 468.

my present includes the past and the future it is both the first and last of all other times. All times have their source and end in my time. . . . I was, and I am to come, as surely as I am and live."[21] So it is that in God's time as Christ, which never ends and so is eternal, all times find their true birth and real goal. If you are into hallucinogens, and even if you are not, I encourage you to get lost, er, I mean found, in these pages. It's a trip.

Returning to the classical metaphysical questions concerning the nature of time presented above, we can see why regardless of one's philosophical preferences, the physicist, the philosopher, and even most preachers for that matter won't understand the nature of time. It is because ultimately Christ is time. And until one encounters Jesus Christ, one will not and cannot reason, hypothesize, test, chronologize, or historicize one's self into the true understanding of the meaning and nature of time. Time flows from its creation to the event of the resurrection. And time flows from Christ's resurrection back out to all creation. All other times and places are upheld by Christ and indeed God's revelation as Christ to time is the foundation for a true consciousness of time and history. The revelation of God's grace as Christ is thus the umbrella under which the rest of the world's time and places finds shelter. And yet, when Christ is encountered, when one's life is given over to Him as Lord, when one repents of trying to be the *Übermensch* at the center of all history, when one sets aside one's own master-plan and simply follows the Rabbi down uncharted roads, then one begins to understand that *this* life, *our* lives, *her* life, and indeed *my* today is a gift of the crucified and resurrected Lord of Time, who is Jesus of Nazareth. As Proverbs 20:24 says, "All our steps are ordered by the Lord, how then can we understand our own ways?" This means each *now* is a gift woven by the triune God into a cosmic garment in which all threads give witness to the redeeming providence and unrelenting love of Jesus Christ.

In the face of this wondrous tapestry, metaphysical deliberations fall away and worship, gratitude, and awe can be our only proper response. For each era, each day, each moment, is offered to show us grace. Christ is time. And this means, well you guessed it, that today *is* the greatest day:

Smashing Pumpkins: *Today*

0:00   Apocalyptic Arrival of the Eschaton

21. *CD* III/2, 465.

— 12 —

Conclusion: Christ in
~~Pop Culture~~ the World

John Calvin wrote in book 2 of the *Institutes*:

> Therefore, in reading profane [secular] authors, the admirable
> light of truth displayed in them should remind us, that the hu-
> man mind, however much fallen and perverted from its original
> integrity, is still adorned and invested with admirable gifts from
> its Creator. If we reflect that the Spirit of God is the only foun-
> tain of truth, we will be careful, as we would avoid offering insult
> to him, not to reject or condemn truth wherever it appears. In
> despising the gifts, we insult the Giver.[1]

The music I listened to in high school did something to me. It awoke
an intense lust for life, an urge to be wild, a need to grind against something, and, I believe, a desire to find resolution to the knots and tangles
presented with one-of-a-kind creativity, style, and sometimes, flat out ab-
surdity. This is to say that I *listened* to the music I listened to. Yes, the beats
and rhythms hooked me. But so did the bare souls who were so honest
about their appetites for destruction.

Mostly through negative examples, these artists forced me to think
about what it means to be human, if there is meaning in the world, and how
to find ways to live life to the fullest. But even beyond such philosophically
friendly life lessons, were there not at times things distinctly *Christian* about
the voices emerging out of the cultural chaos? Despite my attempts to shed
Christianity, did not something *holy* speak to me through such lyrics? Even
more than offering memorable heuristics, perhaps pop culture can offer
deep, profound, and true, if occasional, glimpses into the real and lasting
truths of the Christian faith.

1. Calvin, *Institutes* 2.2.15.

But there is a flip-side. Pop culture is not divine. Those familiar with any element of it know there is much that is not worth talking about. Even if, as John Calvin says, "the admirable light of truth" is present in authors who in a secular sense are "profane," there is much that is simply "fallen and perverted" and "profane" in a truly vulgar and soul-warping sense. This raises two important questions. The first is: Should we look to the "profane" world of pop culture for truth? The second is essentially Pilate's question to Jesus, "What is truth anyway?" (John 18:38).

The German theologian Dietrich Bonhoeffer offers tested insight into the later question. Coming from a context in which the church was actively trying to read divine truths off of the flux and flow of contemporary culture, Bonhoeffer argued we need to look elsewhere. In an essay, "Christ, Reality, and Good," Bonhoeffer argues that "ultimate reality is no other than the self-announcing, self-witnessing, self-revealing God in Jesus Christ."[2] Taking John 14:6 ("I am the way, the truth, and the life") seriously, Bonhoeffer argues that whenever we set out to seek the real, the good, the true, or the beautiful, ultimately we will be led (by the Holy Spirit?) to Christ. Jesus Christ, the self-expressed Word of God, not only discloses, but *is* the ultimate truth of God. Thankfully for us, this meant for Bonhoeffer that the German political culture of the 1930s was *not* the gospel. Only the ultimately redemptive reality of Christ is the will of God.

Surprisingly, Bonhoeffer's radical exclusivity necessitates that we answer the first question, "Should we look for truth in pop culture?" with a "Yes." If, as Bonhoeffer says elsewhere, "the ultimate has become real" in "Jesus Christ crucified,"[3] then we *must* look into the world of pop culture, and beyond, for truth. Yet the truths we must look for are not the edicts proclaimed by the royalty of pop and their lesser subjects. From them come many proclamations about fame, glory, wealth, sex, and self-worth that must, ultimately, be seen as false. On the contrary, the truth we must look for is the "self-announcing, self-witnessing, self-revealing God of Jesus Christ" who has redeemed the fallen world. If there is truth in pop culture, or elsewhere, it is only when the lyrics, scenes, messages, and events serve as a witnessing parable to the ultimate reality of Christ's redemption of the world through the cross. Bonhoeffer's friend and mentor Karl Barth called such instances "secular parables."[4] And like Christ's parables of the Bible (which were also simple secular stories), we see them and understand them as *true* only when we see them through the lens of the life, work, love, and faith of the crucified

2. Bonhoeffer, *Ethics*, 49.

3. Bonhoeffer, *Ethics*, 158.

4. *CD* IV/3.1, §69.2, 115.

and risen Christ. Parables are not, then, a natural theology. For they remain meaningless, random, arbitrary, and, at best, hypothetical, until Christ takes them and uses them as a mode of self-revelation.

Christ comes into the world and so is also present in pop culture. The proclivity of the risen, and often incognito, Jesus Christ to go *everywhere* means that encounters with Christ can be had *anywhere*. Indeed, as the bringer of ultimate reality, Christ can be disclosed, witnessed to, and spoken of whenever, wherever, and by whomever. This might be entirely unintentional or accidental, for God always works with subjects beyond their natural capacities. Such is grace. Yet, those who look and listen in faith may only conclude that, as Calvin says, the Spirit of God is pouring forth the truth which we can now clarify *is* Christ. Think, for instance, of Lady Gaga's admission of being a "Fame hooker, prostitute wench," and admitting that while "Jesus is my virtue, Judas is the demon I cling to."[5] Should we not all, at times, confess likewise? Could pop culture offer a more honest confession of sin? In the Bible, God repeatedly uses fallen, "bent" (to use C. S. Lewis's term from *Perelandra* for the perversion of sin), and profane people to give direct and indirect witness to the ultimate reality of Christ's loving redemption. What other kind of people are there? Think of Judas, Pharaoh, Peter, Rahab, Moses, Mary, and Paul. Cannot God do the same with today's people, some of whom are musicians?

Lady Gaga: *Judas*

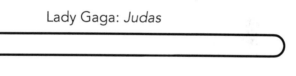

0:00   0:25

How then, will we distinguish between the "light of truth" and what Bonhoeffer called the "dark tunnels of human life"?[6] With biblical literacy, theological maturity, and an adventurous personal faith in the ongoing work of Jesus Christ, we must look upon the whole world with sensitive eyes (and ears) of faith. Whether we look to the purities of the natural wilderness, the profane world of pop culture, or to the struggling slums of Nairobi (and we should *probably* look there first), we are looking for the living, loving, redeeming God who is known to us as Jesus. This is effectively a "Where's Waldo?"

5. Lady Gaga, "Judas."
6. Bonhoeffer, *Ethics*, 158.

puzzle except that we go forth in hope looking for the Christ. And we must ask the Holy Spirit to guide us to where this ranger king is.

And if we find the Kingdom of God (who is Jesus) under the bridge with Los Angeles's broken addicts, bringing peace to the angry and violent neighborhoods of those who proclaim the world is "Blackened," being humble with the arrogant and privileged knuckleheads of juvenile rappers, or there on the brutal highways alongside those stricken with angst and forlornness, may we know it and see it as a merciful act of the Holy Spirit who discloses the stranger walking (and perhaps rocking) among us, as Jesus Christ.

Lady Gaga: *Million Reasons*

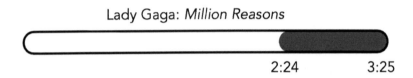

2:24   3:25

— Appendix —

The Trinity and Election Debate: An Analytic Proposal

In the following chapter, I am going to take a stab at solving the puzzle of the relation between Trinity and election, which has rent Barth studies into a house divided.

The debate over what takes priority in Barth's theology, God's nature as triune, or God's election of the world in Jesus Christ is well documented[1] and has been chiefly carried out by the two greatest proponents of Barth's theology in the English-speaking world, both of whom taught for many years at Princeton Theological Seminary. Both were on my dissertation committee. For those not familiar with the debate, the sides are roughly as follows:[2]

Trinity: Trinity takes logical priority in Barth's theology and there is a triune God above and behind the decision for election. This protects God's being from being necessarily dependent upon the world but potentially opens the door for an "unknown" God behind Jesus who is not disclosed to us and threatens to make election a contingent or arbitrary decision of the triune God. That is, in some alternative world there might be a triune God who does not elect humanity's salvation.

Election: Election takes logical priority in Barth's theology and God becomes triune to carry out Jesus Christ's decision to redeem the world. This means the God we see in Christ is the only God there is or ever could be, but potentially threatens to make God's being dependent upon the world. If Christ's humanity is the constitutive element of the triune being of God, and

---

1. See especially, McCormack, "Grace and Being"; Dempsey, *Trinity and Election.*

2. Readers are again referred to Dempsey's *Trinity and Election* for the complex history of this debate. The problem with the following construal is that it overlooks the many nuances and historical developments within the history of the debate. These are what I term the "philosophical" construals of the respective positions.

humanity is a worldly entity, this would seem to make God's being reliant upon the world in order for God to be God, even as it affirms that knowledge of Jesus Christ is knowledge of the only God there ever could be.

The debate over "Trinity versus election" began as a disagreement, morphed into a feud, became a battle, and now sadly has entrenched itself into a standing feature of Barth studies. It has long been my desire to see a solution to the matter, rather than a victory by one of the parties, even as I regard both sides to have their finger on an important element of Barth's radical dialectical theology. Moreover, it is my opinion that there is an actual solution to the dilemma, one that dissolves the opposing views. I am further convinced that this solution is no new corrective, but is in fact analytic to the text and theology of the *Church Dogmatics*. It is my contention that the chief proponents have effectively been arguing half of Barth's own dialectics against each other. Indeed, sometimes the *verso* has been used against the *recto*.[3]

My own feeling is that, as I say below in thesis 6, (1) Trinity is analytic to election, and (2) election is analytic to Trinity. Once we understand how Barth defines these terms, neither has logical priority over the other. Indeed, they are analytic to each other.

"Trinity is analytic to election" means that Christ's decision to be human (in a *homoousious* manner, not as an organic carbon-based being), as we saw in chapter 6, is an eternal decision to be "Other" than the Father and to put His divine life in dependence upon the Father by the Spirit. Hence, the triune persons are a perpetual result of the self-differentiation that happens between the Son and the Father in election. Conversely, "Election is analytic to Trinity" means that since there is an eternal will in God to love Others in freedom (chapter 1), and since this is the eternal nature of the triune God, this will is repeatedly continued in the decision to elect other others (*ad extra/ex nihilo/*in time). Hence the election of the human other, of which Jesus Christ is the archetype, is a result of the triune self-determination to be the God who loves Others in freedom. These analytic relationships and determinations are graciously extended *ad extra* in a way wholly continuous with how God is *ad intra*.

---

3. For instance, quotes on p. 168 of *CD* II/2 (a *verso* page) are used by McCormack to defend the logical priority of election, while quotes on p. 169 of *CD* II/2 (a *recto* page) are used by George Hunsinger to defend the logical priority of Trinity. See Mc-Cormack, "Grace and Being," 107; Hunsinger, "Election and Trinity" 103. Indeed, despite its length, the *CD* is a finite product and there are passages that both authors cite in favor of their view. See for instance when both use a lengthy quote on *CD* II/2, 77. See McCormack's "Seek God Where He May be Found," 276, n. 41; Hunsinger, "Election and Trinity," 102.

In many ways then, my proposed "analytic proposal" (which I take to be Barth's solution to this dilemma; a solution to a problem I believe he was well aware he was offering) is more or less a result of adding chapters 1 and 2 on triunity and eternity with chapter 6 on christology and humanity. Theses 1 through 4, then, should be taken as largely non-controversial, basically summarizing what Barth says in a way that recapitulates their treatment in earlier chapters of this work. Theses 5 and 6 will be read as being more contentious, though I think they are accurate, and thesis 7 seeks to defend against possible objections that the "analytic proposal" is speculative or the result of an imported foreign element, say from, perhaps, the school of analytic philosophy.

———

Thesis 1: For Barth, God's living has a temporality both *ad intra* (*in se*, in eternity) and *ad extra* (*pro nobis*, in time).

Objection: This makes God a god of process, development, and historical actualization. Barth wanted no part of such things. Any attribution of time, history, growth, or development to God is incompatible with the God of the *Church Dogmatics*. Many passages could be cited in favor of Barth's objection to Hegelian process theology.

Response: Despite the surface plausibility of the objection, Barth does indeed argue throughout volumes I, II, and III that God's triune living is not a "uniform grey sea"[4] but is comprised of an ongoing willing, affirming, and confirming[5] of God's own triunity as Father, Son, and Holy Spirit. Eternity is the life of this triune κοινωνία: "A correct understanding of the positive side of the concept of eternity, free from all false considerations, is gained only when we are clear that we are speaking about the eternity of the triune God."[6] For Barth, this means that God's eternal being is an act, and hence has historicity, even in God's-self. Barth elaborates God's historical eternality in II/1 §31.3 and in III/2 §47.1 with the language of pre-temporality, supra-temporality, and post-temporality.[7] In brief, these look like the following:

> 1. God's eternality is pre-temporal (*vorzeitlich*): God is be-
> fore time and time itself is of His making. Before time and
> any "reality that is distinct from God" there is the only the

4. *CD* II/1, 640.
5. *CD* II/2, 155, 183.
6. *CD* II/1, 615.
7. *CD* II/1, 619.

One triune God whose "existence precedes ours and that of all things."[8]

2. God's eternality is supra-temporal (*überzeitlich*):[9] God is not limited by time and so resides above it and "embraces time on all sides."[10] But more importantly, God is *with* time and enters *into* it. God walks in it and alongside of it. Barth admits *mitzeitlichkeit* or *inzeitlichkiet* could better express this theme.

3. God's eternality is post-temporal (*nachzeitlich*):[11] Time as we know it will end but God's life will continue: "Just as God is before and over time, so He is after time, after all time and each time."[12]

In the language of pre-temporality, supra-temporality, and post-temporality, we see the entire never-ending and unified history of the triune God. Moreover, Barth argues explicitly that there is a clear and sustained directional orientation uniting these three aspects of eternity. Barth argues that the forward orientation of our time and history "pre-exists" and has its "prototype" in eternity:

> What distinguishes eternity from time is the fact that there is in Him no opposition or competition or conflict, but peace between origin, movement and goal, between present, past and future, between "not yet," "now" and "no more," between rest and movement, potentiality and actuality, whither and whence, here and there, this and that. In Him all these things are *simul*, held together by the omnipotence of His knowing and willing, a totality without gap or rift, free from the threat of death under which time, our time, stands. *It is not the case, then, that in eternity all these distinctions do not exist.*[13]

This tripartite, genuine, pre-, supra-, post-temporal concept of a unified temporal eternity can be seen as implicit in the following:

8. *CD* II/1, 621.

9. *CD* II/1, 623.

10. *CD* II/1, 623.

11. *CD* II/1, 629.

12. *CD* II/1, 629.

13. *CD* II/1, 612; emphasis mine.

> The eternal will of God which is before time is the same as the eternal will of God which is above time, and which reveals itself as such and operates as such in time.[14]

God's dynamic, though unified, historicity is also implicit throughout Barth's preferential description of "an activist" understanding of God's living.[15]

Thesis 2: The source of eternity's "perfect"[16] temporality is the ongoing triune loving of each Other.

Objections: Too many to be named.

Response: Without being either Arian, a social Trinitarian, or modalistic,[17] Barth explicitly argues in the triune God we have, "Gott einmal und noch einmal und noch einmal."[18] In this way, God is "one time" as the Father, "and again one time" as the begotten Son, and then posited again "again one time" as the Holy Spirit. But this "once and again and a third time"[19] is a threefold possession in *simul* both as a temporal/chronological statement and an ontological one. Barth's point is this: God is *repeatedly* this same triune God over and over again: "The name of Father, Son and Spirit means that God is the one God in threefold repetition."[20] Barth's understanding of the threefold repetition as Father, Son, and Holy Spirit generates an "uninterrupted cycle";[21] a God who is God in *this* way:

> The name of Father, Son and Spirit means that God is the one God in threefold repetition, and this in such a way that the repetition itself is grounded in His Godhead, so that it implies no alteration in His Godhead, and yet in such a way also that He is the one God *only in this repetition,* so that His one Godhead

14. *CD* II/2, 156.

15. *CD* II/2 184–88.

16. Barth refers to the triune temporality as "perfect," "genuine," (*CD* II/1, 617) "authentic," and "supremely temporal" (*CD* II/1, 614).

17. *CD* I/1, 382ff.

18. *KD* II/1, 693. "God is once and again and a third time" (*CD* II.1, 615).

19. *CD* 693 II.1, 615. "Gott einmal und noch einmal und noch einmal" (*KD* 1/1).

20. *CD* I/1, 350. Cf., *CD* IV/1, 205.

21. *CD* I/1, 370.

stands or falls with the fact that He is God in this repetition, but for that very reason He is the one God in each repetition.[22]

This repetition (*Wiederholung*) is freely upheld as a "*repititio aeternitatis in aeternitate*."[23] No one, no thing, no law, no rule, no necessity forces God to be triune. God chooses to freely manifest God's one common will in the triune three modes of being. In this way, Barth argues God's being has an ongoing temporality *because* it has an ongoing triunity.

Addendum: God's willing of Himself in the perpetual and ongoing Triune Moment is a free and faithful upholding of His own promise to do so and not "a mechanistic exposition of the divine will."[24]

Question: What exactly is the "one common will" being repeated as the three modes of being?

In a reflection on the implications of God's inherently gracious way of triune being, Barth writes, "God already negates in Himself, from eternity, in His absolute simplicity, all loneliness, self-containment, or self-isolation."[25] God wills, from eternity, in eternity, and to eternity, to love and be with "Others" in and as the triune forms. We see the manifestation of this ontological self-differentiation and self-determination of God's loving for the divine "Other" explicitly described, for instance, towards the end of *Church Dogmatics* I/1:

> Also and precisely in Himself, from eternity, in His absolute simplicity, God is orientated to the Other, does not will to be without the Other, will have Himself only as He has Himself with the Other and indeed in the Other.[26]

The correctly translated and capitalized "Other" (*Andern*), as well as Barth's marking this "gerade in sich selbst" denotes Barth is speaking of God's *primären Gegenständlichkeit*; the immanent Trinity; God in Himself; God *ad intra*. This means God continually and perpetually wills to

---

22. *CD* I/1, 350; emphasis mine.

23. *CD* I/1, 353. "Repetition of eternity in eternity." As a concept inspired by Anselm, Barth uses this *repetitio aeternitatis in aeternitate* formulae throughout *CD* I/1 §9, see also pp. 350, 366, 394. Barth reaffirms it in *CD* IV/1, 205: "For the basis and development and explanation of the doctrine of the Trinity in its own context and in all its details, and for an understanding of its exegetical and historical implications, we must refer back to *CD* I/1 § 8-12."

24. *CD* II/2, 189.

25. *CD* I/1, 483.

26. *KD* I/1, 507; *CD* I/1, 483.

live in the threefold willing, affirming, and confirming of what I call the Triune Moment.

The use of "Other" as a referent for the three divine modes of being is reaffirmed in II/2 and in IV/1 in the following:

> Primarily and originally and properly it is not the cosmos or man which is the other, the counterpart of God, that which co-exists with God. Primarily and originally and properly God is all this in Himself . . . God is both One and also Another, His own counterpart, co-existent with Himself.[27]

Corollary 2.1: God's *actus purus et singularis*, that is "the pure and singular act in which God has God's being" can be expressed as the equivalent of "I am always willing to love an Other in freedom."

———

Thesis 3: Despite there being an *ad intra* and an *ad extra* in God, there is no metaphysical gap or epistemological moat between God's *ad intra* and God's *ad extra*.

Objection: Barth denies a God *ad intra,* as he says, "There is no such thing as Godhead in itself. Godhead is always the Godhead of the Father, the Son and the Holy Spirit. But the Father is the Father of Jesus Christ and the Holy Spirit is the Spirit of the Father and the Spirit of Jesus Christ."[28] Since Jesus Christ is God *pro nobis,* there is no God *ad intra* apart from/ or before the *ad extra.*

Response: What Barth does not do is deny the existence of a God *ad intra.* What Barth does do is argue that the God *ad intra* is known fully, completely, purely, and totally in God's revelation *ad extra* as Jesus Christ. That this inner life of God was continually trumpeted as ineffable, mysterious, dark, and hidden by the earlier theologians, and that the *ad intra* was not seen as revealed in Jesus Christ is, for Barth, "one of the great puzzles of history."[29] Nevertheless in Barth there is still a Godhead "in Himself." This allows Barth to say:

> We must not allow God to be submerged in His relationship to the universe or think of Him as tied in Himself to the Universe.[30]

27. *CD* IV/1, 201.
28. *CD* II/1, 115.
29. *CD* II/1, 147.
30. *CD* II/2, 155.

And,

> God does not, therefore, become the living God when He works
> or decides to work *ad extra* in His being *ad extra* He is, of course,
> the living God in a different way—but His being and activity *ad
> extra* is merely an overflowing of His inward activity and being,
> of the inward vitality which He has in Himself.[31]

This raises the question: How is the *ad intra/ad extra* distinction overcome? What dissolves the metaphysical gap, dissipates the unknown
decretum absolutum and abolishes the *Deus nudus absconditus*?[32] Barth
lays out his answer throughout the whole of the *Church Dogmatics* but
especially in *Church Dogmatics* II/2's "The Eternal Will of God in the Election of Jesus Christ," and *Church Dogmatics* IV/1's "The Way of the Son of
God into the Far Country."

———

Thesis 4: Barth's claim that Jesus Christ is "the electing God" and "the
elected Man"[33] dissolves "the mystification of an unknown God and unknown man"[34] while also upholding the "inward activity and being" of the
triune God.

Objection: Jesus Christ's being both the subject and object of election
means the creaturely man Jesus is a necessary eternal component of the
Trinity such that God's own triune life is oriented around this Man's
earthly life history, either by way of anticipation or recollection. Therefore,
God cannot not create the world, as creation is entailed as a necessary
component of Jesus' electing life. *Ergo*, there is no pre-temporal choosing-
to-create in the divine life.

Response: The election of Jesus Christ to be the elected human in our time
is a *repetition* of, and in full correspondence with, the Son of God's intra-
Trinitarian decision to not be equal to God the Father. Recalling Theses 2,

---

31. *CD* II/2, 175.

32. "We could think of a *decretum absolutum* as a lifeless and timeless rule for temporal life," says Barth (*CD* II/2, 187; see also: 68–76, 100, 103–07, 113–15, 134–45, 140,
158–61, 167, 181, 187, 192, 222, and 333). The *Deus nudus absconditus*, another bogy-
man Barth wants to argue against, is an unidentifiable hidden or naked God, whose
character and purposes are impenetrable to faith, reason, or any kind of rationality. See
for instance, *CD* II/2, 111: "The electing God of Calvin is a *Deus nudus absconditus*."

33. *CD* II/2, 45.

34. *CD* II/2, 147.

the triune Persons live in perpetual and ongoing *willing, affirming, confirming of each Other*. One way to say this is that they will not to be each Other, but rather are self-determined in their self-differentiation to give their own lives to each Other. For Barth, this happens *perichoretically*. The NT way to speak of this relationship deals primarily with inheritance and obedience: the Father wills to give His kingdom to the Son; the Son wills not to "consider equality with the Father something to be grasped" (Phil 2:6) and so "humbles himself," making Himself "O/other" than the Father. The Father's and the Son's common Spirit—which is the Holy Spirit—to "love One Another" unifies them across their self-distinctions and self-differentiations.

So Barth writes of the Father-Son relationship:

> God Himself becomes Another in the person of His Son. The existence of the world is not needed in order that there should be otherness for Him. Before all worlds, in His Son He has otherness in Himself from eternity to eternity.[35]

The primary way in which the Son wills, affirms, and confirms Himself as "Other" to the Father is by saying, "Not my will, but thy will be done." This perpetual, active, eternal willing not-to-be the Father renders the Son in an ongoing state of self-willed dependence, gratitude, and obedience upon the Father. This is what makes the Son of God a Human, indeed *the* Human, *even within the triune life of God* ad intra *and apart from any creation.* "In this divinely free volition and election, in this sovereign decision . . . God is *human*."[36] This pre-temporal Human Son of God *ad intra* is no shadowy mysterious character or generic impersonal individual. The Son of God is known by us in His self-repetition in history as the man Jesus Christ. "[God] has the freedom in all His *opus ad extra* to remain the One who He is."[37] But this also means that creation is not necessary for God to be oriented to a human. Already within the triune life, there is a divinely willed human (*the* Human) who is the Son of God.

Corollary 3.1: The identity, actions, and essence of Jesus Christ in time (i.e., the lifetime of the A.D. 1–30 man Jesus) are a consistent set of unique historical repetitions that reveal to us how the Son of God has always lived faithfully before the Father. "He Himself [is] the Lamb slain from the foundation of the world. There is, then, no background, no *decretum absolutum*,

---

35. *CD* II/1, 317.

36. Barth, *Humanity of God*, 51.

37. *CD* II/1, 316.

no mystery of the divine good pleasure, in which predestination might just as well be man's rejection."[38]

Corollary 3.2: Humanity is primarily found in Jesus Christ and secondarily in us, in His gracious upholding of lives we lay down. "To be a human" means fundamentally that we put our lives in dependence, relationship, and gratitude towards the Father, in the same way Jesus did. The height of human action is to say, "Not my will." (cf., Barth's anthropology of III/2 and the ethics of II/2). This is what the *analogia relationis* refers to when, for instance, Barth writes, "There is an *analogia relationis*. The correspondence and similarity of the two relationships consists in the fact that the freedom in which God posits Himself as the Father, is posited by Himself as the Son and confirms Himself as the Holy Ghost, is the same freedom as that in which He is the Creator of man, in which man may be His creature, and in which the Creator-creature relationship is established by the Creator."[39]

———

Thesis 5: Barth's concept of "election" in *Church Dogmatics* II/2 has multiple referents. Election primarily refers to an inner moment in which there is an internal self-differentiation in which God determines God's own being. Election secondarily refers to an outer moment in which God shares the triune κοινωνία with others *ex nihilo*.

Objection: Election is only oriented *ad extra* and refers to created humanity's "gain" of "election, salvation and life" and God's "loss" into "reprobation, perdition and death."[40]

Response: Election can and does refer to created humanity's "gain" of "election, salvation and life" and God's "loss" into "reprobation, perdition and death." Yet election also refers into the inner life of God apart from any "reality distinct from Himself." There is an active sense in which the Son of God wills to be "Another" to the Father and in which He humbles Himself as the means of self-differentiation from the Father. The Son carries out this willing in the *forma Dei*.[41] Yet, there is an additional active willing to "hold fast" to the form into which He humbles Himself, that of the human *forma*

38. *CD* II/2, 167.
39. *CD* III/2, 220.
40. *CD* II/2, 162–63.
41. *CD* IV/1, 188.

servi.[42] The incarnation[43] is yet another repetition within the history of the Son of God's eternal choosing (i.e., "electing") to be "other than the Father." In support of Thesis 4, this re-establishes that there is an eternal *forma servi* in the inner Trinitarian relationship. The Son perpetually humbles Himself from His as-begotten-equal-to-the-Father status into the *forma servi.* The Son did this even in pre-temporal eternity as His "personal"[44] manifestation of the God's one will to love the Other according to the *actus purus et singularis* in which God has God's three modes of being.

The Son of God's self-determination to self-differentiate Himself according to the *actus purus et singularis* means there is an *eternal* human Son of God in the inner triune life even apart from creation. Yet, in that God is in God's triune nature eternally oriented towards a discrete *homoousious* Human Other (the Son of God) and given that God is in self-repetition toward this Human Other, in the creation *ex nihilo* the triune relationship is self-consistent in its free orientation toward additional human others *ad extra/ex nihilo.* This is the meaning of "In that He (as God) wills Himself (as man), He also wills them."[45] Double predestination can thus also refer to God's decision to repeat the Trinitarian relationship that is proper to Himself as He is *homoousious* with the "reality that is distinct from Himself." Just as the Son of God whom we know as Jesus Christ is the inner cause and object of this self-determination, "Man is the outward cause and object this overflowing of the divine glory."[46]

Corollary 5.1: The descent of the Son of God into time, creation, flesh, death, and hell is not an inner requirement for the Son's self-humbling life before the Father, for even in the inner Trinitarian relationship there is sufficient "otherness" in God's self. The descent of the Son of God into time, creation, flesh, death, and hell is the ultimate ontic extreme which manifests (ontically and noetically) the faith of the Son in the Father to be other than the Father. It is carried out so we might have, and *know* that we have, absolute reconciliation with God.

Corollary 5.2: Without denying other truths about hell, hell is additionally the radical extreme of "otherness" from God and is the *telos* of where God pursues creatures whom He loves, i.e., "Those whom He will find and have for Himself He pursues to the remotest corner where their backs are to the

---

42. *CD* IV/1, 188.

43. In which death is analytic; see *CD* IV/1, 165.

44. *CD* II/2, 159; IV/1, 205.

45. *CD* II/2, 117.

46. *CD* II/2, 169.

wall and they can no longer escape Him."[47] God's love for the other takes the Son of God as Jesus Christ to Hell in pursuit of the "most-other," those *ex nihilo* beings who hate God.

———

Thesis 6: Election is analytic to Trinity. Trinity is analytic to Election.

Objection: Logically, if not also temporally, one of these must come first.

Response: Barth's concept of Triunity entails that election is analytic to Trinity. Given what we have said, "election" can mean:

1. the Son of God's eternal decision to self-differentiate from the Father and be *homoousios* in the *forma servi* as the divine Human Other *ad intra*, and

2. God's continuation of this choosing of the *ex nihilo* human-other as an outward repetition of God's own inner willing, affirming, and confirming.

Election *ad intra* is analytic to Trinity because in the Second Person of the Trinity's self-differentiating from the First Person of the Trinity, the "Son of God" perpetually wills Himself as the true Human. The Son of God puts Himself in a dependent, serving, grateful, obedient relationship to the Father and in so doing elects to be Himself in the inner Trinitarian relationship as the Human Other *homoousios*. This is not social Trinitarian because according to the one act of God in which God has being, i.e., the *actus purus et singularis*, it is one will manifested in three modes of being.

Likewise, Barth's concept of election entails that Trinity is analytic to election, because in self-differentiating Himself as the Human Other *homousious*, God self-differentiates God's very being into the triune three modes of being as the self-differentiating Father and Son and their uniting Holy Spirit. There is no ontological or logical priority to either Trinity or election *ad intra*. They are analytic to each Other (pun intended). There is ontological and logical priority of God *ad intra* over God *ad extra* because God extends to others *ex nihilo* the relationship God repeatedly has in the triune κοινωνία. Thus God *ad intra* is no dark unknown, no inaccessible mystery, no incomprehensible light. God's inner Trinitarian being *ad intra* is fully manifested *ad extra* in the *Lebenszeit* of Jesus Christ: "[I]n the eternal predestination of God we have to do *on both sides* with only one name

47. *CD* III/2, 609.

and one person, the same name and the same person, Jesus Christ."[48] The continuity of identity across time and eternity allows Barth to fully uphold that Jesus Christ *is* the Son of God.

———

Thesis 7: This is known only via Easter, or it is not known at all. In other words, noetic priority goes to God *ad extra*. There is no knowledge of God's *ad intra* apart from Easter.

Objection: Such things can be intuited apart from revelation by natural philosophy or even derived from an analysis of the incarnation in itself.

Response: Nein. The ontic reality of God's ongoing triune relationship *ad intra* as Father, Son, and Holy Spirit is manifested ontically and noetically in the historical three-day (at least) Easter event.[49] It is here that we see fully that the Son lives, not by His own will, but by the will of the Father, i.e., He lives "in the Holy Spirit," i.e., He lives in perpetual affirmation of His self-negating, "Not my will, but thine." But Easter also is the manifestation ontically and noetically that God does not will to remain isolated in God's own inner Trinitarian completeness, but that "in God's love for Another," God wills to be the God who "is also *Himself* outwards in relation to another"[50] thus extending this inner Trinitarian relationship to another, and another, and another. God's ongoing inclusion of others *ex nihilo* (also known as, election *ad extra*) is "the secret which is hidden in world-history" (II/2, 185). Indeed, it is the secret for which there is world history. Indeed it is the reason clocks keep ticking.

"Jesus Christ is the Son of God" means that in God's outward movement there is a perfect correspondence, revelation and manifestation of how God has always been *ad intra*. Easter is no fluke or anomaly in the triune life. On the contrary it is a unique historical repetition of how the triune God always lives. Easter is the noetic doorway into the eternal ontic reality of God. It is where we see that there is a triune God who is "self-posited"[51] as a Son who lays down His life in His not wanting to be equal to the Father

48. *CD* II/2, 146.

49. I say "three-day-at-least" because when does Easter really begin? At the crucifixion? At the Last Supper? At "Christmas"? And when does Easter really end? At the resurrection? After forty days in the ascension? If the Easter events are analytic to the life of Jesus Christ, who is the Son of God, then as He lives (eternally) it seems to me that Easter is an extending ongoing eternal reality.

50. *CD* II/1, 532.

51. *CD* IV/1, 209.

(i.e., a Son who is truly Human); a Father who gives His life and kingdom to the Son; and their Holy Spirit who is their "mutual affirmation and love."[52]

Conclusion: In this proposal, I have suggested Trinity and election are not in tension or rivalry to one another, but are rather analytic to each other. By this I mean that God's election to be "for" a Human is analytic to a full and proper understanding of the Trinity. Likewise, I have suggested that Barth's understanding of Trinity is analytic to the Son of God's election to be self-differentiated from the Father. I have sought to ground this argument in the knowledge of God given at Easter, a knowledge that reveals that, "Jesus Christ is the Son of God." By this I understand Barth to be telling us that the *ad intra* of God has been graciously poured out *ad extra*. Our cups (and clocks!) overflow. The essence of the triune love, it would seem, is to give it away, give it away, give it away now. And that reminds me of a song I used to love . . .

52. *CD* IV/1, 209.

Bibliography

Agamben, Giorgio. "The Time That Is Left." *Epoche* 7.1 (Fall 2002) 1–14.

Albert, David Z. *Time and Chance*. Cambridge: Harvard University Press, 2000.

Anselm. *The Major Works*. Edited by Brian Davies. Oxford: Oxford University Press, 2008.

Aquinas, Thomas. *Basic Writings of Saint Thomas Aquinas*. 2 vols. Edited by Anton C. Pegis. New York: Random House, 1945.

———. *Summa Theologiae: Vol. 2, Existence and Nature of God (Ia. 2-11)*. Blackfriars Edition. Edited by Timothy McDermott. London: Blackfriars, 1963.

Aristotle. *The Complete Works of Aristotle, Vol. I*. Edited by Jonathan Barnes. Princeton: Princeton University Press, 1984.

Augustine. *Confessions*. Translated by Henry Chadwick. Oxford: Oxford University Press, 1991.

———. *Confessions*. Translated by Rex Warner. New York: Mentor, 1963.

———. *Earlier Writings*. Translated by John H. S. Burleigh. Philadelphia: Westminster, 1953.

———. *Later Works*. Translated by John Burnaby. Philadelphia: Westminster, 1955.

———. *On Genesis*. Translated by Edmund Hill. Hyde Park, NY: New City, 2002.

———. *The City of God*. Translated by Marcus Dods. New York: Modern Library, 1993.

———. *The Trinity (De Trinitate)*. Translated by Edmund Hill. Hyde Park, NY: New City, 1991.

Barbour, Ian G. *Religion in an Age of Science: The Gifford Lectures 1989–1991, Vol. I*. San Francisco: Harper, 1990.

Barbour, Julian. *The End of Time: The Next Revolution in Physics*. Oxford: Oxford University Press, 2000.

Barrett, Helen M. *Boethius: Some Aspects of His Times and Work*. Cambridge: Cambridge University Press, 1940.

Barth, Karl, and Emil Brunner. *Natural Theology: Comprising "Nature and Grace" by Professor Dr. Emil Brunner and the Reply "No!" by Dr. Karl Barth*. Translated by Peter Fraenkel. Eugene, OR: Wipf & Stock, 2002.

Barth, Karl. *Church Dogmatics*. 4 vols. Edited by Geoffery Bromiley and Thomas F. Torrance. Edinburgh: T & T Clark, 1956–69, 1975.

———. *Karl Barth-Rudolph Bultmann: Letters 1922–1966*. Edited by Bernd Jaspert. Translated by Geoffery Bromiley. Grand Rapids: Eerdmans, 1981.

———. *The Göttingen Dogmatics: Instruction in the Christian Religion, Vol. I.* Translated by Geoffery Bromiley. Grand Rapids: Eerdmans, 1991.

———. *The Word of God and the Word of Man.* Translated by Douglas Horton. Gloucester, MA: Peter Smith, 1978.

———. "Fate and Idea in Theology." In *The Way of Theology in Karl Barth.* Edited by H. Martin Rumscheidt. Eugene, OR: Pickwick, 1986.

———. *Anselm: Fides Quaerens Intellectum.* Translated by Ian W. Robertson. London: SCM, 1960.

———. *Deliverance to the Captives.* Translations by various authors. Eugene, OR: Wipf & Stock, 1978.

———. *Die kirchliche Dogmatik.* 4 vols. München: Chr. Kaiser, 1932.

———. *Evangelical Theology: An Introduction.* Translated by Grover Foley. New York: Holt, Rinehart and Winston, 1963.

———. *Karl Barth and Radical Politics.* Translated and Edited by George Hunsinger. Philadelphia: Westminster, 1976.

———. *Letters 1961–1968.* Edited by Jürgen Fangmeier and Hinrich Stoevesandt. Translated by Geoffery Bromiley. Grand Rapids: Eerdmans, 1981.

———. *Protestant Theology in the Nineteenth Century: Its Background and History.* Translated by Brian Cozens and John Bowden. Grand Rapids: Eerdmans, 2002.

———. *Revolutionary Theology in the Making: Barth-Thurneyson Correspondence, 1914–1925.* Translated by James D. Smart. Richmond: John Knox, 1964.

———. *The Early Preaching of Karl Barth: Fourteen Sermons with Commentary by William H. Willimon.* Translations by John E. Wilson. Louisville: Westminster John Knox, 2009.

———. *The Epistle to the Romans (Sixth Edition).* Translated by Edwyn Hoskyns. Oxford: Oxford University Press, 1968.

———. *The Humanity of God.* Translated by Thomas Weiser and John Newton Thomas. Louisville: Westminster John Knox, 1960.

Beilby, James K., and Paul R. Eddy. *Divine Foreknowledge: Four Views.* Downers Grove, IL: InterVarsity, 2001.

Beilby, James K. *For Faith and Clarity: Philosophical Contributions to Christian Theology.* Grand Rapids: Baker Academic, 2006.

Black, Max. "The 'Direction' of Time." *Analysis* 19.3 (January 1959) 54–63.

Bobik, Joseph. *Aquinas On Being and Essence: A Translation and Interpretation.* Notre Dame: University of Notre Dame Press, 1965.

Boethius. *The Consolation of Philosophy.* Translated by David R. Slavitt. Cambridge: Harvard University Press, 2008.

———. *The Theological Tractates.* Translated by H. F. Stewart and S. J. Tester. Cambridge: Harvard University Press, 1973.

Bonhoeffer, Dietrich. *The Bonhoeffer Reader.* Edited by Clifford Green and Michael DeJonge. Minneapolis: Fortress, 2013.

———. *Ecumenical, Academic, and Pastoral Work: 1931–1932: Dietrich Bonhoeffer Works, Vol. 11.* Minneapolis: Fortress, 2012.

———. *Ethics: Dietrich Bonhoeffer Works, Vol. 6.* Edited by Clifford Green. Minneapolis: Fortress, 2005.

———. *Letters and Papers from Prison: Dietrich Bonhoeffer Works, English Vol. 8.* Edited by John de Gruchy. Minneapolis: Augsburg Fortress, 2009.

————. *Life Together: Dietrich Bonhoeffer Works, English Vol. 5*. Translated by Gerhard Ludwig Müller and A. Schönherr. Minneapolis: Fortress, 1996.

Boyd, Gregory A. *God of the Possible: A Biblical Introduction to the Open View of God*. Grand Rapids: Baker, 2000.

Bunyan, John. *The Pilgrim's Progress*. New York: Signet Classic, 1981.

Burnett, Richard E. *Karl Barth's Theological Exegesis: The Hermeneutical Principles of the* Römerbrief *Period*. Grand Rapids: Eerdmans, 2004.

Busch, Eberhard. *The Great Passion: An Introduction to Karl Barth's Theology*. Translated by Geoffery W. Bromiley. Grand Rapids: Eerdmans, 2004.

————. *Karl Barth: His Life from Letters and Autobiographical Texts*. Translated by John Bowden. Grand Rapids: Eerdmans, 1994.

Calvin, John. *Institutes of the Christian Religion*. Edited by John T. McNeill. Translated by Ford Lewis Battles. Philadelphia: Westminster, 1960.

Camus, Albert. *Christian Metaphysics and Neoplatonism*. Translated by Ronald D. Srigley. Columbia: University of Missouri Press, 2007.

————. *The Myth of Sisyphus and Other Essays*. Translated by Justin O'Brien. New York: Vintage, 1983.

Chellas, Brian F. *Modal Logic: An Introduction*. Cambridge: Cambridge University Press, 1980.

Clark, Gordon H. "Plotinus on the Eternity of the World." *The Philosophical Review* 58.2 (March 1949) 130–140.

Cone, James H. *A Black Theology of Liberation (Fortieth Anniversary Edition)*. Maryknoll, NY: Orbis, 2012.

Craig, William Lane. *Theism, Atheism and Big Bang Cosmology*. Oxford: Clarendon, 1995.

————. *Time and Eternity: Exploring God's Relationship to Time*. Wheaton, IL: Crossway, 2001.

Crisp, Oliver D., and Michael C. Rea. *Analytic Theology: New Essays in the Philosophy of Theology*. Oxford: Oxford University Press, 2009.

Cullman, Oscar. *Christ and Time: The Primitive Christian Conception of Time and History*. Translated by Floyd V. Filson. Philadelphia: Westminster, 1950.

Curtis, Jason M. "Trinity and Time: An Investigation into God's Being and His Relationship with the Created Order, with Special Reference to Karl Barth and Robert W. Jenson." PhD dissertation, University of Edinburgh, 2007.

Davies, Paul. *About Time: Einstein's Unfinished Revolution*. New York: Simon & Schuster, 1995.

————. *God and the New Physics*. London: J. M. Dent & Sons, 1983.

————. *The Goldilocks Enigma: Why Is the Universe Just Right for Life?* London: Penguin, 2006.

————. *The Mind of God: The Scientific Basis for a Rational World*. New York: Simon & Schuster, 1992.

Day, Dorothy. *The Long Loneliness: The Autobiography of the Legendary Catholic Social Activist*. New York: HarperOne, 1997.

de Duve, Christian. *Vital Dust: Life as Cosmic Imperative*. New York: Basic, 1995.

Dempsey, Michael T, ed. *Trinity and Election in Contemporary Theology*. Grand Rapids: Eerdmans, 2011.

DeWeese, Garrett J. *God and the Nature of Time*. Aldershot: Ashgate, 2004.

Disalle, Robert. *Understanding Space-Time: The Philosophical Developments of Physics from Newton to Einstein.* Cambridge: Cambridge University Press, 2006.

Dr. Dre. "Nuthin but a G'Thang." *The Chronic.* Death Row Records, compact disc. 1992.

Drury, John L. "The Resurrected God: Karl Barth's Trinitarian Theology of Easter." PhD dissertation, Princeton Theological Seminary, 2011.

Dyson, Freemon J. *Infinite In All Directions: The Gifford Lectures.* New York: Harper & Row, 1988.

"Echkhart: The Man." *The Eckhart Society.* https://www.eckhartsociety.org/eckhart/eckhart-man.

Eckhart, Meister. *Meister Eckhart: The Essential Sermons, Commentaries, Treatises, and Defense.* Translated by Edmund Colledge and Bernard McGinn. New York: Paulist, 1981.

Eckhart, Meister. *Meister Eckhart: Teacher and Preacher.* Edited by Bernard McGinn. New York: Paulist, 1986.

Edwards, Mark James *The Divine Moment: Eternity, Time, and Triune Temporality in Karl Barth's* Church Dogmatics. PhD dissertation, Princeton Theological Seminary, 2013.

Eire, Carlos. *A Very Brief History of Eternity.* Princeton: Princeton University Press, 2010.

Eliade, Mircea. *Myth and Reality.* Translated by Willard Trask. New York: Harper Torch, 1975.

———. *The Myth of the Eternal Return.* Translated by Willard Trask. Princeton: Princeton University Press, 2005.

Emery, Giles. *The Trinity: An Introduction to Catholic Doctrine on the Triune God.* Translated by Matthew Levering. Washington, DC: Catholic University Press, 2011.

Evans, Gareth. "The Causal Theory of Names." *Proceedings of the Aristotelian Society* 47 (1973) 187–225.

Fitzgerald, Paul. "Stump and Kretzmann on Eternity." *The Journal of Philosophy* 82.5 (May 1995) 260–269.

Flett, John G. *The Witness of God: The Trinity, Missio Dei, Karl Barth, and the Nature of the Christian Community.* Grand Rapids: Eerdmans, 2010.

Flew, Antony, and Alasdair MacIntyre. *New Essays in Philosophical Theology.* London: SCM, 1955.

Franke, John R. *Barth for Armchair Theologians.* Louisville: Westminster John Knox, 2006.

Frankfurt, Harry G. *On Bullshit.* Princeton: Princeton University Press, 2005.

———. *The Importance of What We Care About: Philosophical Essays.* Cambridge: Cambridge University Press, 1988.

Frege, Gottlob. *Begriffsschrift.* In *The Frege Reader.* Edited by Michael Beaney. Oxford: Blackwell, 1997.

———. *On Concept and Object.* In *The Frege Reader.* Edited by Michael Beaney. Oxford: Blackwell, 1997.

———. *Sinn und Bedeutung.* In *The Frege Reader.* Edited by Michael Beaney. Oxford: Blackwell, 1997.

Gadamer, Hans-Georg. *Truth and Method.* Translated by Joel Weinsheimer and Donald G. Marshall. London: Continuum, 2004.

Gale, Richard M. *The Language of Time.* New York: Humanities, 1968.

Gandhi, Mahatma. *The Essential Gandhi.* Edited by Louis Fischer. New York: Vintage, 2002.

Ganssle, Gregory. *God and Time: Four Views.* Downers Grove, IL: InterVarsity, 2001.

Gibson, Margaret. *Boethius: His Life, Thought and Influence.* Oxford: Blackwell, 1981.

Giles, Kevin. "Barth and Subordinationism." *Scottish Journal of Theology* 64.3 (2011) 327–46.

Gilkey, Langdon. *Religion and the Scientific Future: Reflections on Myth, Science, and Theology.* New York: Harper & Row, 1970.

Gilson, Ettienne. *God and Philosophy.* 2nd ed. New Haven: Yale University Press, 2002.

Goldman, David P. "Sacred Music, Sacred Time." *First Things: A Monthly Journal of Religion and Public Life* 197 (2009) 31–36.

Greene, Brian. *The Fabric of the Cosmos.* New York: Alfred A. Knopf, 2005.

Gribbin, John. *The Birth of Time: How Astronomers Measured the Age of the Universe.* New Haven: Yale University Press, 1999.

Griswold, Daniel. *Perichoretic Eternality: God's Relationship to Time in Karl Barth's Church Dogmatics.* PhD dissertation, Southern Methodist University, 2010.

Gunton, Colin E. *Act and Being: Towards a Theology of the Divine Attributes.* London: SCM, 2002.

———. *The Cambridge Companion to Christian Doctrine.* Cambridge: Cambridge University Press, 1997.

Hasker, William. *God, Time, and Knowledge.* Ithaca, NY: Cornell University Press, 1989.

Hawking, Stephen, and Kip Thorne. *The Future of Spacetime.* New York: W. W. Norton, 2003.

Hawking, Stephen, and Roger Penrose. *The Nature of Space and Time.* Princeton: Princeton University Press, 1996.

Hawking, Stephen. *A Brief History of Time: From the Big Bang to Black Holes.* New York: Bantam, 1990.

———. *The Universe in a Nutshell.* New York: Bantam, 2001.

Hector, Kevin W. *Theology without Metaphysics: God, Language, and the Spirit of Recognition.* Cambridge: Cambridge University Press, 2011.

———. "Immutability, Necessity and Triunity: Towards a Resolution of the Trinity and Election Controversy." *Scottish Journal of Theology* 65.1 (2012) 64–81.

Heller, Michael, and W. Hugh Woodin. *Infinity: New Research Frontiers.* Cambridge: Cambridge University Press, 2011.

Heller, Michael. "Where Physics Meets Metaphysics." In *On Space and Time,* edited by Shahn Majid, 238–77. Cambridge: Cambridge University Press, 2008.

Helm, Paul. *Eternal God: A Study of God without Time.* Oxford: Clarendon, 1988.

Heraclitus. *Fragments.* Translated by Brooks Haxton. New York: Viking, 2001.

Holmes, Christopher R. J. *Revisiting the Doctrine of the Divine Attributes: In Dialogue with Karl Barth, Eberhard Jüngel, and Wolf Krötke.* New York: Peter Lang, 2007.

Honderich, Ted. *The Oxford Companion to Philosophy.* 2nd ed. Oxford: Oxford University Press, 2005.

Horovitz, Adams, Adam Nathaniel Yauch, and Michael Louis Diamond. "So What'cha Want." *Check Your Head.* Universal Music Publishing Group. 1992.

Hume, David. *Dialogues Concerning Natural Religion and The Natural History of Religion.* Edited by J. C. A. Gaskin. Oxford: Oxford University Press, 1993.

Hunsinger, George. *How to Read Karl Barth: The Shape of His Theology.* Oxford: Oxford University Press, 1991.

———. "Barth on the Form of Theological Statements." Unpublished paper, Princeton Theological Seminary, 2010.

———. *Disruptive Grace: Studies in the Theology of Karl Barth.* Grand Rapids: Eerdmans, 2000.

———. "Election and Trinity: Twenty-Five Theses on the Theology of Karl Barth." In *Trinity and Election in Contemporary Theology,* edited by Michael T. Dempsey, 91–114. Grand Rapids: Eerdmans, 2011.

———. *The Eucharist and Ecumenism: Let Us Keep the Feast.* Cambridge: Cambridge University Press, 2008.

———. *For the Sake of the World: Karl Barth and the Future of Ecclesial Theology.* Grand Rapids: Eerdmans, 2004.

———. "Jesus as the Lord of Time According to Karl Barth." Unpublished paper, Princeton Theological Seminary.

———. "Karl Barth's Doctrine of the Trinity, Some Protestant Doctrines After Barth." In *The Oxford Handbook of the Trinity,* edited by Mathew Levering and Emery Giles, 294–313. Oxford: Oxford University Press, 2011.

———. "On the Immanent Trinity in Barth." Unpublished paper, Princeton Theological Seminary, 2007.

———. "The Same Only Different: Karl Barth's Interpretation of Hebrews 13:8." Unpublished paper, Princeton Theological Seminary.

———. *Thy Word Is Truth: Barth on Scripture.* Grand Rapids: Eerdmans, 2012.

Izmirlieva, Valentina. *All the Names of the Lord: Lists, Mysticism, and Magic.* Chicago: University of Chicago Press, 2008.

Jackson, Frank. "Reference and Description Revisited." In *Philosophical Perspectives, Vol. 12: Language, Mind, and Ontology,* edited by James E. Tomberlin, 201–18. Cambridge: Blackwell, 1998.

———. "Why We Need A-intensions." *Philosophical Studies* 118.1–2 (March 2004) 257–77.

Jastrow, Robert. *God and the Astronomers.* New York: W. W. Norton, 1978.

Jenson, Robert W. "Once More the *Logos asarkos.*" *International Journal of Systematic Theology* 13.2 (April 2011) 130–133.

———. *God After God: The God of the Past and the God of the Future As Seen in the Work of Karl Barth.* Minneapolis: Fortress, 2010.

———. *Systematic Theology, Vol. 1: The Triune God.* Oxford: Oxford University Press, 1997.

Johnson, Adam J. *God's Being in Reconciliation: The Theological Basis of the Unity and Diversity of the Atonement in the Theology of Karl Barth.* London: T & T Clark, 2012.

Johnson, Keith L. *Karl Barth and the Analogia Entis.* London: T & T Clark, 2010.

———. "A Reappraisal of Karl Barth's Theological Development and His Dialogue with Catholicism." *International Journal of Systematic Theology* 14.1 (January 2012) 3–25.

Jüngel, Eberhard. *God as the Mystery of the World: On the Foundation of the Theology of the Crucified One in the Dispute between Theism and Atheism.* Translated by Darrell L. Guder. Grand Rapids: Eerdmans, 1983.

———. *God's Being Is in Becoming: The Trinitarian Being of God in the Theology of Karl Barth, a Paraphrase.* Translated by John Webster. Grand Rapids: Eerdmans, 2001.

Kant, Immanuel. *Critique of Pure Reason*. Translated by Paul Guyer and Allen W. Wood. Cambridge: Cambridge University Press, 1998.

———. *Fundamental Principles in the Metaphysic of Morals* in *Basic Writings of Kant*. Edited by Thomas Abbot. New York: Modern Library, 2001.

Kaufman, Eleanor. "The Saturday of Messianic Time." *South Atlantic Quarterly* 107.1 (Winter 2008) 36–54.

Kennedy, Darren M. *A Personalist Doctrine of Providence: Karl Barth's Church Dogmatics III/3 in Conversation with Philosophical Theology*. PhD dissertation, University of Edinburgh, 2007.

Kenny, Anthony. *The God of the Philosophers*. Oxford: Clarendon, 1979.

Kerr, Nathan R. *Christ, History and Apocalyptic: The Politics of Christian Mission*. Eugene, OR: Cascade, 2008.

Khamara, E. J. "Eternity and Omniscience." *The Philosophical Quarterly* 24.96 (July 1974) 204–19.

Khoo, Rachel. *The Little Paris Kitchen: 120 Simple but Classic French Recipes*. San Francisco: Chronicle, 2012.

Kiedis, Anthony, and Larry Sloman. *Scar Tissue*. New York: Hachette, 2004.

Kierkegaard, Soren. *Concluding Unscientific Postscript to the "Philosophical Fragments."* In *A Kierkegaard Anthology*. Edited by Robert Bretall. Princeton: Princeton University Press, 1973.

Kiley, John F. *Einstein and Aquinas: A Rapprochement*. Leiden: Martinus Nijohff, 1969.

Kim, Eunsoo. *Time, Eternity, and the Trinity: A Trinitarian Analogical Understanding of Time and Eternity*. Eugene, OR: Pickwick, 2010.

Kim, Sung-Sup. *Deus Providebit: Barth's Critical Engagement with Calvin and Schleiermacher on the Providence of God*. PhD dissertation, Princeton Theological Seminary, 2012.

Klinkenborg, Verlyn. *The Rural Life*. Boston, MA: Little, Brown, and Company, 2003.

Kneale, Martha. "Eternity and Sempiternity." *Proceedings of the Aristotelian Society*, New Series 69 (1968–69) 223–38.

Kneale, W. "Time and Eternity in Theology." *Proceedings of the Aristotelian Society* 61 (1960–1961) 87–108.

Kojiro, Masami. *God's Eternal Election in the Theology of Karl Barth*. PhD dissertation, University of Aberdeen, 1996.

King, Martin Luther. *The Autobiography of Martin Luther King, Jr.* Edited by Clayborne Carson. New York: Grand Central, 1998.

Kripke, Saul. *Naming and Necessity*. Cambridge: Harvard University Press, 1972.

Kuhn, Thomas S. *The Structure of Scientific Revolutions*. Chicago: Phoenix, 1962.

Lady Gaga. "Judas." *Born This Way*. Interscope Records. 2011.

Langdon, Adrian. *God the Eternal Contemporary: Trinity, Eternity, and Time in Karl Barth*. Eugene, OR: Wipf & Stock, 2012.

Larson, Duane H. *The Temporality of the Trinity: A Christian Theological Concept of Time and Eternity in View of Contemporary Physical Theory*. PhD dissertation, Graduate Theological Union, 1993.

Le Poidevin, Robin. *Questions of Time and Tense*. Oxford: Clarendon, 1998.

Leftow, Brian. "A Timeless God Incarnate." In *The Incarnation: An Interdisciplinary Symposium on the Incarnation of the Son of God*, edited by Stephen T. Davis and Gerald O'Collins, SJ, 273–302. Oxford: Oxford University Press, 2002.

———. "Anti-Social Trinitarianism." In *The Trinity: An Interdisciplinary Symposium on the Trinity*, edited by Stephen Davis, Daniel Kendall, and Gerald O'Collins, 203–250. Oxford: Oxford University Press, 1999.

———. *Time and Eternity*. Ithaca, NY: Cornell University Press, 1991.

———. "Why Didn't God Create the World Sooner?" *Religious Studies* 27.2 (June 1991) 157–172.

———. "Why Perfect Being Theology." *International Journal for Philosophy of Religion* 69 (2011) 103–118.

Leith, John H. *Basic Christian Doctrine*. Louisville: Westminster John Knox, 1993.

Lewis, David, *Attitudes De Dicto and De Re. Philosophical Review* 88 (1979) 513–543.

———. *On the Plurality of the Worlds*. Malden, MA: Blackwell, 1986.

Lindbeck, George A. *The Nature of Doctrine: Religion and Theology in a Postliberal Age*. Philadelphia: Westeminster, 1984.

Lockyer, Herbert. *All the Divine Names and Titles in the Bible*. Grand Rapids: Zondervan, 1975.

Luther, Martin. *Table Talk*. Translated by William Hazlet. Grand Rapids: Christian Classics Ethereal Library, 2004.

Lycan, William G., and Jesse Prinz. *Mind and Cognition: An Anthology*. 3rd ed. Malden, MA: Blackwell, 2008.

Malcom, Norman. *Wittgenstein: A Religious Point of View*. Edited by Peter Winch. Ithaca, NY: Cornell University Press, 1993.

McCormack, Bruce L. *Engaging the Doctrine of God: Contemporary Protestant Perspectives*. Grand Rapids: Baker, 2008.

———. "God *Is* His Decision: The Jüngel-Gollwitzer 'Debate' Revisited." In *Theology as Conversation: The Significance of Dialogue in Historical and Contemporary Theology: A Festschrift for Daniel L. Migliore*, edited by Bruce L. McCormack and Kimlyn J. Bender, 48–66. Grand Rapids: Eerdmans, 2009.

———. "Grace and Being." In *The Cambridge Companion to Karl Barth*, edited by John Webster, 92–110. Cambridge: Cambridge University Press, 2000.

———. *Justification in Perspective: Historical Developments and Contemporary Challenges*. Grand Rapids: Baker, 2006.

———. *Karl Barth's Critically Realistic Dialectical Theology: Its Genesis and Development 1909–1936*. Oxford: Clarendon, 1995.

———. *Orthodox and Modern: Studies in the Theology of Karl Barth*. Grand Rapids: Baker Academic, 2008.

———. "Processions and Missions: A Point of Convergence between Thomas Aquinas and Karl Barth." Paper presented at Thomas Aquinas and Karl Barth: An Unofficial Protestant-Catholic Dialogue, Princeton, NJ, June 20, 2011.

———. "The Being of Holy Scripture is in Becoming: Karl Barth in Conversation with American Evangelical Criticism." *The Princeton Theological Review* 9.1 (March 2003) 4–15.

———. *The Doctrine of the Trinity after Barth* in *Trinitarian Theology after Barth*. Edited by Myk Habets and Phillip Tolliday. Eugene, OR: Pickwick, 2011.

McCormack, Bruce L., and Clifford B. Anderson. *Karl Barth and American Evangelicalism*. Grand Rapids: Eerdmans, 2011.

McCormack, Bruce L., Günter Thomas, Rinse H. Reeling Brouwer. *Dogmatics After Barth: Facing Challenges in Church, Society and the Academy*. Leipzig: CreateSpace, 2012.

McGinn, Bernard. *The Mystical Thought of Meister Eckhart: The Man From Whom God Hid Nothing*. New York: Herder and Herder, 2001.

McGrath, Alister E. *Christian Theology: An Introduction.* 4th ed. Oxford: Blackwell, 2007.

McInerny, Ralph. "Introduction." In *Thomas Aquinas: Selected Writings*, ix–xxxiv. London: Penguin, 1998.

McKenny, Gerald. *The Analogy of Grace: Karl Barth's Moral Theology.* Oxford: Oxford University Press, 2010.

McLure, Robert. *The Philosophy of Time: Time before Times.* London: Routledge, 2005.

McTaggart, J. Ellis. "The Relation of Time and Eternity." *Mind* 18.71 (July 1909) 343–62.

———. "The Unreality of Time." *Mind* 17.68 (October 1908) 457–74.

———. *The Nature of Existence.* 2 vols. Cambridge: Cambridge University Press, 1927.

Migliore, Daniel L. *Faith Seeking Understanding: An Introduction to Christian Theology.* 2nd ed. Grand Rapids: Eerdmans, 2004.

Miles, Sara. *Take This Bread: A Spiritual Memoir of a Twenty-First-Century Christian.* New York: Ballantine, 2008.

Mill, John Stuart. *Utilitarianism.* In *Basic Writings of John Stuart Mill.* Edited by Dale Miller. New York: Modern Library, 2002.

Miller, Alexander. *Philosophy of Language.* 2nd ed. Montreal: McGill-Queen's University Press, 2007.

Molnar, Paul D. *Divine Freedom and The Doctrine of the Immanent Trinity: In Dialogue with Karl Barth and Contemporary Theology.* London: T & T Clark, 2002.

Moltmann, Jürgen. *The Trinity and the Kingdom.* Translated by Margaret Kohl. San Francisco: Harper & Row, 1981.

Monod, Jacques. *Chance and Necessity: An Essay on the Natural Philosophy of Modern Biology.* Translated by Austryn Wainhouse. New York: Vintage, 1972.

Moore, G. E. *Some Main Problems of Philosophy.* New York: Collier, 1962.

———. "Russell's 'Theory of Descriptions.'" In *Philosophical Papers*, 151–65. New York: Collier, 1962.

Morello, Tom, Brad Wik, Tim Commerford, and Zack de la Rocha. *Township Rebellion.* Epic Records, 1992.

Mueller, David L. *Karl Barth.* Waco: Word, 1972.

Neder, Adam. *Participation in Christ: An Entry into Karl Barth's Church Dogmatics.* Louisville: Westminster John Knox, 2009.

Nielson, Kai, and D. Z. Phillips. *Wittgensteinein Fideism.* London: SCM, 2006.

———. "Wittgenstein and Wittgensteinians on Religion." In *Wittgenstein and Philosophy of Religion*, edited by Robert Arrington and Mark Addis, 137–66. London: Routledge, 2001.

———. "Wittgensteinein Fideism." *Philosophy: The Journal of the Royal Institute of Philosophy* 42.161 (July 1967) 191–209.

Nietzsche, Friedrich. *Basic Writings of Nietzsche.* Translated and edited by Walter Kaufman. New York: Modern Library, 2000.

———. *The Gay Science.* Translated by Walter Kaufmann. New York: Vintage, 1974.

———. *The Portable Nietzsche.* Translated and edited by Walter Kaufman. London: Penguin, 1982.

———. *The Will to Power.* Translated by Walter Kaufmann and R. J. Hollingdale. New York: Vintage, 1968.

Nimmo, Paul T. *Being in Action: The Theological Shape of Barth's Ethical Vision.* London: T & T Clark, 2007.

Oblau, Gotthard. *Gotteszeit und Menschenzeit: Eschatologie in der Kirchlichen Dogmatik von Karl Barth.* Düssledorf: Neukirchener Verlag, 1988.

Oh, Peter S. *Karl Barth's Trinitarian Theology: A Study in Karl Barth's Analogical Use of the Trinitarian Relation.* London: T & T Clark, 2006.

Parke-Taylor, G. H. *Yahweh: The Divine Name in the Bible.* Ontario: Wilfrid Laurier University Press, 1975.

Pike, Nelson. *God and Timelessness.* New York: Schocken, 1970.

Plantinga, Alvin. *God and Other Minds: A Study of the Rational Justification of Belief in God.* Ithaca, NY: Cornell University Press, 1967.

Plato. *Plato: Collected Dialogues.* Edited by Edith Hamilton and Huntington Cairns. Princeton: Princeton University Press, 2005.

Plotinus. *The Enneads.* Translated by Stephen MacKenna. London: Penguin, 1991.

Pollan, Michael. *The Omnivore's Dilemma: A Natural History of Four Meals.* New York: Penguin, 2006.

Price, Huw. *Time's Arrow and Archimedes' Point: New Directions for the Physics of Time.* Oxford: Oxford University Press, 1996.

Price, Robert B. *Letters of the Divine Word: The Perfections of God in Karl Barth's Church Dogmatics.* London: T & T Clark, 2011.

Prior, A. N. "Thank Goodness That's Over." *Philosophy* 34.128 (January 1959) 12–17.

———. "Time after Time." *Mind* 67.266 (April 1958) 244–46.

Putnam, Hilary. "The Meaning of 'Meaning'." In *Mind, Language and Reality,* 215–71. Cambridge: Cambridge University Press, 2008.

Quinn, Phillip. "Untitled Review of Brian Leftow's *Time and Eternity.*" *The Philosophical Quarterly* 46.182 (January 1996) 131–33.

Reichenbach, Hans. *The Philosophy of Space and Time.* Translated by Maria Reichenbach. New York: Dover, 1958.

Richards, Jay Wesley. *The Untamed God: A Philosophical Exploration of Divine Perfection, Simplicity, and Immutability.* Downers Grove, IL: InterVarsity, 2003.

Roberts, Richard H. "Karl Barth's Doctrine of Time: Its Nature and Implications." In *Karl Barth: Studies of his Theological Method,* edited by S. W. Sykes, 88–146. Oxford: Clarendon, 1979.

Ruether, Rosemary Radford. *Sexism and God-Talk: Toward a Feminist Theology.* Boston: Beacon, 1983.

Russell, Bertrand. *The Philosophy of Logical Atomism.* Chicago: Open Court, 1985.

Sansbury, Timothy N. *Divine Temporal Transcendence: A Defense of the Traditional Theological Position in Science, Philosophy, and Theology.* PhD dissertation, Princeton Theological Seminary, 2006.

Schaff, Philip. *The Creeds of Christendom, Vol. II: The Greek and Latin Creeds.* Grand Rapids: Baker, 1998.

Schleiermacher, Friedrich. *The Christian Faith.* Translated and edited by H. R. Mackintosh and J. S. Stewart. Philadelphia: Fortress, 1976.

Selinger, Suzanne. *Charlotte von Kirschbaum and Karl Barth.* University Park, PA: Pennsylvania State University, 1998.

Soames, Scott. *Reference and Description: The Case against Two-Dimensionalism.* Princeton: Princeton University Press, 2005.

Searle, John R. *Mind: A Brief Introduction.* Oxford: Oxford University Press, 2004.

Seow, C. L. *A Grammar for Biblical Hebrew.* Rev. ed. Nashville: Abingdon, 1995.

Silk, Joseph. *The Infinite Cosmos: Questions from the Frontiers of Cosmology.* Oxford: Simon & Schuster, 1992.

Stanley, Timothy. *Protestant Metaphysics after Karl Barth and Martin Heidegger.* Eugene, OR: Cascade, 2010.

Stout, Jeffrey. *The Flight from Authority: Religion, Morality, and the Quest for Autonomy.* South Bend, IN: University of Notre Dame Press, 1987.

Strawson, P. F. "On Referring." *Mind* 59.235 (July 1950) 320–344.

Stump, Eleonore. *Aquinas.* London: Routledge, 2003.

Stump, Eleonore, and Brian Davies. *The Oxford Handbook of Aquinas.* Oxford: Oxford University Press, 2012.

Stump, Eleonore, and Norman Kretzmann. "Eternity." *The Journal of Philosophy* 78.8 (August 1981) 429–58.

———. *The Cambridge Translations of Medieval Philosophical Texts: Vol. 1, Logic and the Philosophy of Language.* Cambridge: Cambridge University Press, 1988.

Swinburne, Richard. *The Coherence of Theism.* Rev. ed. Oxford: Clarendon, 1993.

Tamez, Elsa. *The Amnesty of Grace: Justification by Faith from a Latin American Perspective.* Translated by Sharon Ringe. Nashville: Abingdon, 1993.

"The Theological Declaration of Barmen." In *The Church's Confessions Under Hitler,* by Arthur C. Cochrane, 237–42. Philadelphia: Westminster, 1962.

Tillich, Paul. *Systematic Theology.* 2 vols. Chicago: University of Chicago Press, 1951, 1957.

Tolkien, J. R. R. *The Silmarillion.* New York: Ballantine, 1977.

Torrance, Thomas F. *Space, Time and Resurrection.* Grand Rapids: Eerdmans, 1976.

———. *Theological Science.* Oxford: Oxford University Press, 1969.

van Driel, Edwin Chr. "Karl Barth on the Eternal Existence of Jesus Christ." *Scottish Journal of Theology* 60.1 (2007) 45–61.

von Balthasar, Hans Urs. *The Theology of Karl Barth: Exposition and Interpretation.* Translated by Edward T. Oakes, SJ. San Francisco: Ignatius, 1992.

von Leyden, W. "Time, Number, and Eternity in Plato and Aristotle." *The Philosophical Quarterly* 14.54 (January 1964) 35–52.

Vonnegut, Kurt. *Cat's Cradle.* New York: Random House, 2010.

Webster, John. *Cambridge Companion to Karl Barth.* Cambridge: Cambridge University Press, 2006.

Weil, Simone. *Gravity and Grace.* Translated by Emma Crawford and Mario von Der Ruhr. New York: Routledge, 1999.

White, Thomas Joseph. *The Analogy of Being: Invention of the Antichrist or the Wisdom of God?* Grand Rapids: Eerdmans, 2011.

Whittaker, John. "The 'Eternity' of the Platonic Forms." *Phronesis* 13.2 (1968) 131–44.

Wilson, E. O. "The Riddle of the Human Species." *New York Times,* February 24, 2013 http://opinionator.blogs.nytimes.com/2013/02/24/the-riddle-of-the-human-species/.

Wirzba, Norman. *Food and Faith: A Theology of Eating.* Cambridge: Cambridge University Press, 2011.

Wittgenstein, Ludwig. *On Certainty.* Edited by G. E. M. Anscombe. New York: Harper Torchbooks, 1969.

———. *Philosophical Investigations.* Translated by G. E. M. Anscombe. Oxford: Blackwell, 2001.

———. *Tractatus Logico-Philosophicus.* Translated by C. K. Ogden. New York: Barnes & Noble, 2002.

———. *Culture and Value.* Translated by Peter Winch. Chicago: University of Chicago Press, 1980.

Index

Note: the terms *Barth, eternal/ity, Jesus, God, grace,* and *time* appear on most every page.

As they should, given that the Gospel according to Karl Barth is that God graciously gives away eternity as the time of Jesus Christ.